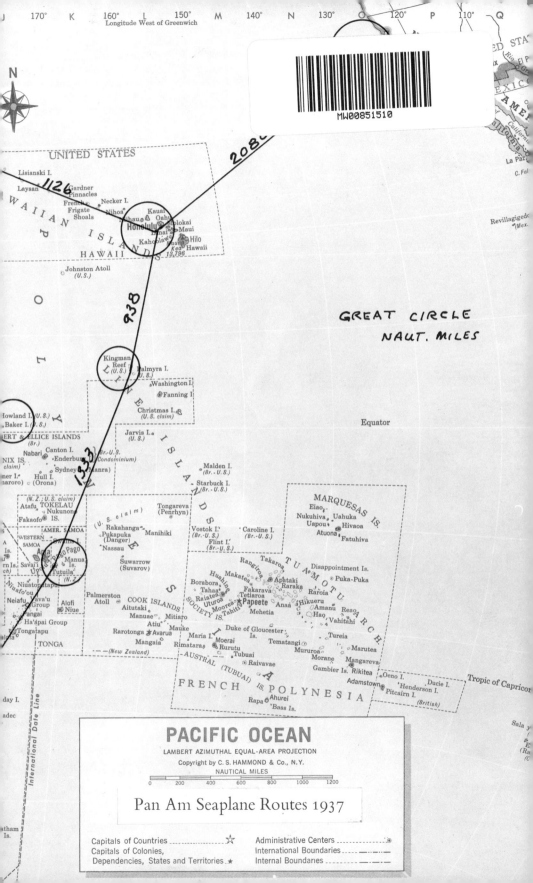

PACIFIC OCEAN

LAMBERT AZIMUTHAL EQUAL-AREA PROJECTION

Copyright by C. S. Hammond & Co., N.Y.

NAUTICAL MILES

0   200   400   600   800   1000   1200

Pan Am Seaplane Routes 1937

Capitals of Countries ....☆   Administrative Centers ....⊙
Capitals of Colonies,   International Boundaries .... ____ . ____
Dependencies, States and Territories ..★   Internal Boundaries ...._____

FLYING THE OCEANS

A Pilot's Story of Pan Am

FLYING THE OCEANS

A Pilot's Story of Pan Am

1935–1955

BY HORACE BROCK

THIRD EDITION

JASON ARONSON, INC.

NEW YORK · LONDON

*To those who shared with the author the
trials and achievements of Pan Am.*

Third Edition
Copyright © 1978 by Horace Brock
10 9 8 7 6 5 4 3 2 1

Library of Congress Cataloging in Publication Data

Brock, Horace.
Flying the oceans.

Bibliography: p. 315
Includes index.
1. Pan American World Airways, inc.—History.
I. Title.
HE9803.P36B75   1983   387.7′065′73   83-2720
ISBN 0-87668-632-3

Autobiography is the most absurd of literary forms for reasons that are reasonably evident. Anyone who writes a book should be able to write. He should also have something interesting or useful to write about. He should also be able to see his subject with some clarity and deal with it with reasonable honesty and detachment. The rarest accident apart, the autobiographer is, in the nature of things, deprived of all these requisites.

J. K. GALBRAITH

That which I have seen myself and have gone through, with the help of God, I will describe quite simply as a fair witness, without twisting events one way or another. I am now an old man and, as luck would have it, I have gained nothing of value to leave to my children and descendants but this true story and they will presently find out what a wonderful story it is.

BERNAL DIAZ DE CASTILLO
The Discovery and Conquest of Mexico

Contents

Foreword to the Third Edition

A NUMBER of books have been written about Pan American World Airways. For the most part, they have been the products of historians who remained "omniscient" and who thus purported to be objective. Captain Horace Brock, however, has given us this rare, inside, subjective story, based on many years of flying in Pan Am cockpits during the company's most colorful days, when its famous Clippers opened the air routes across the world's great oceans.

For the Pan Am crews, there was more to carrying the U.S. flag than wearing a naval-type uniform, dining ocean liner–style and cruising among the world's glamour spots. There were inoculations to be taken every six months; there was refueling to be managed, wrestling with five-gallon cans in the middle of dangerous currents; and there were maddening difficulties with radio communications and a dearth of radio navigation aids. There were times when the weather was far worse than forecast, food on board turned bad, and an entire crew might be laid low with dysentery at a far-off stop. And no pilot could avoid the threat of logs that, floating hidden beneath the surface of the water, could easily wreck his plane. Language barriers could just as easily wreck turnaround schedules, while omnipresent adverse winds constantly made launching, taxiing and docking the most hazardous phases of any trip.

Captain Brock colorfully details his entire life in aviation, including his early days as a cadet in the Army Air Corps, as well as, much later, his experience as part of Pan Am's management. At the heart of *Flying the Oceans* is what he tells of the tribulations of being a young co-pilot flying the Caribbean in flying boats, his transition to captain and—best of all—his wonderful yarns about fellow pilots, newly told stories that surely will become classics among airmen.

Through him, you will meet such characters as Captain Fatt, the chief pilot whose powers to intimidate resided largely in his voice; Captain Ed Musick, a former rum runner who became legendary as a pioneer of the Pacific routes; Captain Leo Terletzky, the Russian whose personal gremlin was instrument flying; Captain Steve Bancroft, whose unique way of avoiding customs checks should be left for the reader to discover in these pages; and many others.

Captain Brock's account is entertaining as well as informative for those who can value the special experiences and perspectives (and opinions) of a pilot blessed with excellent recall of events and personalities in and out of aviation.

CARROLL V. GLINES
Editor, *Air Line Pilot*

Preface to the Third Edition

IT is not necessary to be an aeronautical expert to come quickly to the conclusion that the men who flew for Pan American in the early days of aviation were in all truth a very special breed. These men paid due attention to what was required of them by a most demanding routine. All too often, the survival of a plane and its crew depended on sheer, raw courage.

One of the true pioneers, Captain Horace Brock soon found in his career with Pan Am how indispensable it was to learn to live a life built around discipline, stamina and skill. He tells of pilots who voluntarily quit flying due to the terrific physical strain imposed on them. They were, he says, always over water, with "one engine out". An engine failure meant ditching in rough, shark-infested seas—with no hope of rescue.

During World War II, the demands of Pan American's flying routine included shipping desperately needed weapons, which quickly found their place on the battlefields. Few people realize that at the time that Pan Am was operating in North Africa, it was actually involved in Great Britain's campaign against Rommel. Anything affecting the crucial battles for Egypt was of the highest priority.

Captain Brock illustrates this with a story of one Pan Am DC-3 that ran out of fuel in a storm and crash landed near Fort Lamy, in the middle of the Sahara Desert. The next day, two Americans were flown in with money and tools. One hundred hired natives cleared a runway in one day. A second DC-3 followed, landed and picked up the precious cargo of anti-tank shell fuses. That shipment reached Cairo only 36 hours after the first DC-3 went down. In all, 15 tons of fuses were delivered to the British Eighth Army in the operation of which this emergency was an unscheduled part.

The shells fitted with the fuses stopped Rommel's Afrika Korps in the second battle of El Alamein. Hermann Goering, it was said, couldn't believe that British shells *flown from America* had stopped the German tanks. "Nothing but latrine rumors", Goering told Rommel. "Americans only make razor blades and refrigerators". Rommel, in response, asked if his army could be issued similar razor blades.

From hard experience, Captain Brock understood the complexities of flying planes, especially large sea and land transports. He understood the rôle they could play in a world war, and in this book he well describes Pan Am's work in getting shipments to General Montgomery in North Africa or to Chiang Kai-shek and General Stilwell in China. The author of *Flying the Oceans* knew how modern technology could be used to help the fighting man to go where duty calls and passengers to cross the seas in peacetime.

I hope this book will inform and educate those who still "fly the oceans", and inspire them as I have been.

HENRY CABOT LODGE
Beverly, Massachusetts

CHAPTER I

—◇—

Army Air Corps Training Center at Randolph Field and Kelly Field, Texas; and Langley Field, Virginia

OCTOBER 1933 – OCTOBER 1935

"A" STAGE

ON the morning of October 8, 1933 I arrived by train at San Antonio, Texas and took a taxi to the Army Air Corps Training Center at Randolph Field, just a few miles outside the city. The base was brand new, and as a member of the third class to enter, I expected to be there eight months: four months in primary training, called A Stage, four in basic, called B Stage; and then go to Kelly Field for four months of advanced training. Kelly was the famous flying school for American aces in the First World War and Lindbergh trained there.

It was the very bottom of the depression. Franklin Delano Roosevelt was President, the banks had been closed, 3.2% beer was legal but Prohibition was soon to be repealed. Officially, unemployment was 25% but, of the young starting out in life at my age, it was nearly 100%. One of my college roommates had been looking for a job for four years and now his mother made his clothes. Another had given up and gone out west to write poetry. The Army Flying School was deluged with applicants.

I got my first taste of flying as a boy in Lebanon, Pennsylvania. An Army plane landed on a field outside of town as part of a Victory Bond rally in 1918, and the Army lieutenant who was to speak and the sergeant who was the pilot came to lunch with my family. At a lucky interlude I, who was 10 years old at the time,

1

and my sister, a year younger, prevailed on the sergeant to take us up for a ride, unbeknownst, of course, to our parents. It was so thrilling for us both that we were scolded but not punished and from then on, my heart was set on flying. But there was little I could do about it through two boarding schools, Fay School in Southborough, Massachusetts and St. Paul's at Concord, New Hampshire.

When I got to Yale, I promptly formed the Yale Flying Club with two friends (so as to get a group discount) to learn flying at the Curtiss Wright School at Stratford, Connecticut. Since cars were then banned at Yale except for Seniors, we three would proceed on our motorcycles twice a week to the Stratford Airport for flying lessons. Two thirds of the Club soon dropped out when the lessons became too expensive, but I persisted. I got my private flying license at Roosevelt Field, Mineola, Long Island on March 31, 1930. During my three years at the Harvard Law School, I joined the Harvard Flying Club,[1] which generous alumni had endowed with a Commandaire biplane and, later, a De Havilland Gypsy Moth, a Waco and a Bird. I flew them all and, by the time I got to Randolph, I had a total of 64 hours.

My father died while I was in college, and it was my mother's hope that I would practice law in Pennsylvania. To do so I had to have six months' work as a law clerk before I took the state exams for admission to the Bar. Consequently, I spent every Christmas, Easter and summer vacation while at law school as a clerk with the firm of Montgomery and McCracken in Philadelphia. For this, of course, I received no salary as it was considered a privilege to work in that office. But indeed, I felt I was doing a good deal of work for the partners at no salary. One day I entered the sanctum of my cousin Billy Montgomery, who had founded the firm with Owen Roberts, then on the Supreme Court, and said I had decided to join the Air Corps and learn to fly. I was promptly offered a salary, $450.00 a month, and, when this was declined, I was offered a partnership even though I was not yet admitted to the Pennsylvania Bar. But I had had enough of the law.

Next I proceeded to the Army recruiting station in the "band box" district of North Philadelphia (the worst slum area) and enlisted, requesting an appointment to the Air Corps Training Center at Randolph Field, San Antonio, Texas. The War Department promptly sent me an appointment to report on January 1, 1934, which I returned, saying I wished to be appointed to the October 1, 1933 class. I was given that appointment and I accepted.

My class consisted of 150 men. There were 75 of us civilians out of 2,500 who had applied, and another 75 student officers just graduated from West Point, commissioned as 2nd lieutenants who had chosen the Air Corps. My class also had a few Annapolis graduates not taken into the Navy because of insufficient Congressional appropriations although they were graduated ensigns. Normally all Annapolis graduates choosing to be pilots and passing the physicals went to Pensacola, Florida, where the Navy had its flying school. So our class had half student officers, commissioned graduates of West Point and half ex-civilians called flying cadets including the Annapolis graduates.

I paid off my taxi at the main entrance gate. The field was one mile square with the Administration Building right in the center. It was a half-mile walk to Headquarters and it was hot, but I had no bag, having brought only a toothbrush as I expected to get all my clothes as Army issue uniforms.

Halfway to the building I met a ramrod-straight young man in a blue uniform whom I took to be a flying cadet, and so he was. "Where are you going, Mister?", he shouted at me. "I'm checking in". "Tack a Sir on it, Mister". "O.K., Sir". "Take off, Mister", and I started to run. Thank God no bag. I should move on a run for the next month now.

At headquarters I was assigned to "A" Company by height—it looks better in drill to have men about the same size together. The taller "A" Company were called "hi-pockets" and the shorter "B" Company "sand blowers". Each Company had its own barracks and would, in time, have its own cadet officers. Student officers lived apart. We cadets had our own mess and mixed with the student officers only on the flying line. The upper class cadets provided for our discipline and made the inspections.

On reporting in I was told where to find my bunk and where to draw a uniform and underclothes. On the run, I proceeded to the quartermaster's office where I drew blue trousers, white socks, black low shoes, underclothes, handkerchiefs, uniform shirts and a cap. I also got a name tag which pinned on the left breast. Later in the year when it got cold, even in San Antonio, we drew blue woolen shirts and blue overcoats with brass buttons, all quite good looking.

We "flying cadets" were a bastard rank, relatively new, neither officers nor enlisted men. We did not rate a salute but we did seem to have the respect of all the enlisted men, probably because we were all or almost all college graduates. A few of us, very few, had entered from the ranks, which was an opportunity open to enlisted men after one or two enlistments if they passed the physical exams and a rather stiff set of written tests comparable, I suppose, to college entrance exams. Our low shoes were an officer privilege instead of the high brown boots worn by all enlisted men.

A word about GI clothing. GI stands for government issue, all of the highest possible quality. Everything was bought on huge contracts to carefully drawn specifications and inspected by tough inspectors who rejected so much that it filled the nation-wide Army and Navy Stores. For example, the blue wool shirts we drew later were soft, warm and very comfortable. They never shrank although washed weekly, and they were Army surplus from the First World War. They were khaki in 1918, in storage for 15 years or so, now dyed blue as cadet uniforms. I kept mine, wearing them into the 1960s for hunting and skiing—my son has one of mine, nearly 60 years old, still warm and soft and unshrunk. Our shoes, also soft and pliant, didn't need breaking in. Later, before we began our flight training, we would be issued overalls, leather helmets and goggles, our prescribed flight uniform.

Here we were to live very comfortably, for it was all new and much better than we would find at Kelly Field later, where old World War I barracks would house us. All were double rooms with bath, iron bedsteads with mattresses and sheets, and two chests of drawers under mirrors. A regulation footlocker at the foot of each "bunk" (never a "bed") would hold our civilian clothes and a couple of Army blankets. One family picture on the chest of drawers was permitted but no other decorative object of any sort. Our clothes were folded and lined up in the drawers according to regulation—socks, rolled up with the ends tucked in, exactly so and precisely lined up, handkerchiefs folded and piled with the same corners all pointing in the same direction—so every cadet's drawer would be exactly the same as everyone else's, with not so much as a millimeter difference in the position of anything.

My roommate was a nice young chap. He had been selling neckties in Saks Fifth Avenue when his dream came true and he got an appointment to flying school. One night, much later, I heard him sobbing and gently called over to him, "What's the matter, old man?" "I washed out today". I was to learn that at the end of A Stage, our first four months, about one third of us no longer would have roommates.

"Wash out" means to be honorably discharged and provided with transportation home. In my time, I believe, it was at the sole discretion of the instructor. There was no appeal although sometimes he might ask another instructor to check his student, or even the stage commander. The reason for washing out was simply that, in the opinion of the instructor, the student would never be a good flyer.

At mess that first night, we began to experience traditional West Point hazing. An upper classman headed each table. We sat with our hands on our laps when not eating, looking straight ahead. No one could speak unless spoken to by the head of the table. If so addressed, he would put down his knife and fork in their prescribed positions on his plate, place his hands on his lap and reply, looking straight ahead. The cardinal sin was leaning on the table. Your hand must never loiter on the table. For any infraction you were told to sit on "infinity" for a while. This meant pushing your chair out of the way behind you and resuming a sitting position but eating without a chair. The toughest legs gave out very quickly and, after several collapses, you might be allowed to replace your chair under you. We, of course, took turns waiting on tables and at KP (kitchen police).

We started ground school right away. Basic Aerodynamics, Engines, Meteorology, etc. Eighteen courses in all, including War Planning and Trap Shooting.

One of the military's methods of teaching some subjects at that time was to drill the basic knowledge into the cadet's head no matter how dumb he might be. There was nothing competitive about it—at this stage. Everyone had to pass everything. Flying doesn't tolerate mistakes or ignorance. Accordingly, after lectures, study of textbooks, oral exams and class discussions, we would be given the final examination questions and the answers. The questions were many, involving everything you were supposed to have learned in the course. In taking final exams there was no question of honor system or anything like that. You could take the answer sheet into the exam and copy, if you wished, the correct answers onto the exam sheet. And the system worked! Incredibly. I have never forgotten any detail I learned in those courses and I am quite sure I could take any of those exams today, without the answers, and score nearly 100%, 40 years later. Actually, copying out the answer to a question, if it is a cleverly drawn question, is one of the most effective ways of learning.

We also had training in engine maintenance, chiefly trouble shooting. The purpose of this training was to enable the pilot to report a malfunction of his engine accurately and intelligently so the ground mechanics could repair it quickly. We flew solo in single engine planes, and we always wore a parachute. We had no radio in those days, so any malfunction faced the pilot with the immediate choice of bailing out, trying to get back into the field, or landing in the wide open spaces which are most of Texas around San Antonio. We would learn that bailing out was a court martial offense, the burden entirely on the pilot to prove it was necessary.

Of course, if anyone bailed out, the Army lost a plane and the pilot would join the famous Caterpillar Club, as he might have wanted to, thereafter wearing a little gold caterpillar lapel pin in civilian clothes. Originally parachutes were pure silk and the Irving Company who made the 'chutes started the club and gave the pins, but only for a jump to save your life. We were also taught in ground school how to pack a 'chute, but the ones we wore were always packed by the experts.

Finally, in the third week we were ordered to report to the flight line, where, dressed in coveralls, helmets and goggles, we were assigned to our instructors. Five students to each instructor. No one ever again will inspire the terror that the flight instructor did. Of course they knew this and made the most of it. They never smiled or made a personal remark of any kind; they never criticized or praised. They were picked because they were very, very tough. If you performed badly in some maneuver, the instructor would just take the controls and do it properly. But he was so good that his performance would almost seem impossible; without being told, you would realize how poor you were, and would try harder.

We were introduced to the planes we were to fly, Primary Trainers, PT-3s. These were biplanes, two-seaters, the instructor in the back, radial engines, rather primitive without cowling of any sort, fixed landing gear without brakes, and, for instruments, only an airspeed indicator, tachometer, oil pressure and oil temperature gauges. Nothing else. Dual controls, as with trainers generally, with a "joy stick" in each open cockpit. The only windscreen was a small curved piece of plexiglass in front of each cockpit —you could not fly without goggles.

Except for my roommate, hardly anyone spoke to me the first two months; but they were not hard to get along with, just very aloof. Finally, I got accepted and thereafter was called "Pop". Few Ivy League graduates had attended the Army Flying School. I know of only two, Felix DuPont and Garland Lasater from Princeton. My two best friends came to be Mitch Mitchell, who had a degree in Animal Husbandry from Texas A. and M.; and Don Ogden, a star quarterback from L.S.U. They ended up as pilots for American Airlines, Ogden later their chief pilot, I believe.

Our daily schedule was: fly half the morning and attend ground school the other half, drill on Monday and Friday afternoons, mass calisthenics and organized athletics on Tuesday and Thursday afternoons, and Wednesday and Saturday afternoons and all Sunday off. We got up at 5:00 A.M. and lights were out at 9:15 P.M.

At first we flew each morning from 30 minutes to one hour a day, later one to two hours a day. Military flying is very different from commercial or airline flying because there are no automatic pilots, and one is constantly practicing maneuvers which subject you to two or more Gs all the time. I must explain: a "g" is a unit of force equal to that exerted by gravity and is used to indicate the force which is exerted by acceleration. If you stand still on a scales and weigh 150 lbs., that is the force that gravity exerts on you, i.e., 1G makes you weigh 150 lbs. If you are on an elevator dropping freely, the scales will read nothing and the negative acceleration of dropping, –1G, will cancel the force of gravity on you. If the elevator shoots up very fast you will feel yourself pushed down hard and the scales may read as much as 300 lbs. Then you are subjected to a force of 2G. At forces (accelerations) much above 2G the blood is drawn out of your head and you "black out". To prevent this, astronauts were laced into "G suits".

One hour of acrobatics and most of us were half airsick, groggy, quite unable to stand at attention for example, and ready to lie down for the next hour. Even hardened instructors, after a long period with a poor student doing acrobatics would, once in a while after landing, climb out of the cockpit and throw up.

We soloed after three to six hours, and by the end of the first four weeks we had about fifteen hours of instruction, mostly learning to take off and land and properly to follow the traffic pattern. I suppose my previous flying experience was helpful, but not very. When returning to the line we had to park the old PT-3s in a row right next to one another, perfectly aligned on the ramp, each the same distance apart. All this had to be done with no brakes and on a grass field. The airport surface was all grass, the only paving the parking strips in front of the hangars. One had no help at all from the ground.

The next month we concentrated on figure eights and Chandelles. These maneuvers, not new to me, were all exercises in coordination, the prelude to acrobatics. They dated from the First World War, when perfect coordination was absolutely necessary to get through any acrobatic maneuver with the underpowered Camels, Spads, Nieuports, etc., and when acrobatics were essential to survival. A Chandelle is a steep climbing turn from which you come out flying in the opposite direction and having gained the maximum amount of altitude. Today a jet fighter can fly straight up, but back then it took great skill to gain 400 ft. in a Chandelle. The slightest bit too steep or too sharp a turn and you would stall out—obviously an easy prey for a pursuing enemy.

At this point we flew entirely by the seat of our pants, without the aid of instruments. Later we would have turn and bank indicators, a gyroscope operated needle to show rate of turn, and a curved glass tube containing a steel ball (like a ship's inclinometer). As long as the ball stayed in the center you were perfectly coordinated; if not, it rolled to one side or the other and you had to correct the controls to get it back in the center. The turn and bank made it much easier to learn, but we learned first the hard way, by sensations.

By then, quite a lot of us were not showing up each week, and the absences were quickly noticed—they had washed out. By the end of A Stage I was the only one left of the five who started with my instructor.

One never missed anything one's instructor said. He said little and anything was worth remembering. One never talked or fooled in his presence. We learned to keep alert in the relatively crowded air around the field where two classes were flying at the same time. We were told that there was only one fatal disease—a stiff neck, and that there was only one kind of accident from which no one walked away—a midair collision. Woe to any student so concentrating on his approach and landing that he came near another plane. It might well be his last day of flying. Your head must always be moving, your eyes looking around. Always. The instruments never got more than a passing glance.

Life in our barracks was getting a little more tolerable. We stood inspection every morning and a G.I. inspection of our rooms every

Saturday morning. An unbuttoned button on tunic or shirt was a cardinal sin, one of the worst. Standing at rigid attention outside our barracks, the inspecting officer (upper classman) would tug at a button and say, "Button it up, Mister". The only correct thing to do was to say, "Yes, Sir". Of course each of us had a sewing kit, bought at the P.X. and called a "housewife", to sew on buttons, stripes, etc. The inspecting officer might well pull out of his pocket a pair of small scissors and cut off a button which he could see was hanging a little bit loose, saying, "Sew it on properly, Mister". There was a story about the cadet who sewed his buttons on with wire to fool some inspector at the Point, but if it ever happened, I am sure he regretted having been so smart.

G.I. inspection Saturday morning might be by the post commandant, accompanied by our cadet officers. Wearing spotless white gloves, they would run their fingers along the top of the door, under the chest of drawers, anywhere conceivable, and even the slightest sign of dust would be a demerit. They might jar a perfectly made bunk creating a slight wrinkle and then say in a loud and offensive voice: "Don't you know how to make a bunk? Get someone to show you and do it right next time". "Yes, Sir, no excuse, Sir". Drawer contents would be inspected and almost always faulted—a pair of socks not rolled correctly or an eighth of an inch out of their correct place.

Our pay was $75.00 a month, net $68.75, from which we had to pay laundry (cheap), get our trousers pressed (40¢) at least twice a week, a haircut every Thursday (it would be too long for the Saturday inspection if cut on Wednesday or before) and supplies such as shoe polish and Cokes at the P.X.

About a month after our arrival we no longer had to run and could walk. Also we were at last allowed to leave the field for the first time. One Saturday, when we had our first leave, we all headed for San Antonio where, as we knew, Texas was dry and there were only bootleggers who sold two kinds of pure white hooch—either regular grade at 40¢ a quart, or fighting grade at $1.00 a quart. Some of the enterprising men in our group had learned in advance how to get around in San Antonio and soon found their way to the Elks Club, which let us in, and which had an enormous bar where we drank mostly beer. Behind the bar, the wall was covered with a huge board where all the horse races in the country were displayed and on which winners were posted. A racing form for all the races was available. We spent many Saturdays there, betting two dollars and it was fun. Not caring much about gambling or horses, I found the conversation and beer the most fun.

Acrobatics required extremely good coordination in these underpowered, clumsy trainers. Acrobatics consisted of Vertical Reversements (or *Renversements*, from the French), in which you would pull up almost vertically and then kick rudder to fall off headed in the opposite direction; Immelmans (named after a World War I German ace), in which you pulled up in a loop, but, instead of going all the way around, did a half roll at the top of the loop when you were upside down, thus coming out headed in the opposite direction but having gained altitude; loops, easy to do but not easy to do coming out at the same altitude as you began the loop; half rolls, snap rolls, barrel rolls and slow rolls. Years later, when I was flying for Pan American, I remember watching a ferry pilot taking off at Georgetown, British Guiana in a P-47, bound for Africa. He rolled slowly, round and round on his climb out until out of sight over the Amazon jungle. How I would have loved to do that and how easy it looked and was, even though these were still propeller planes.

We also worked out on spins and recoveries therefrom, stalls and inverted flight. We talked of inverted loops and spins but didn't do any. Actually, I got myself into an inverted spin one day flying between towering cumulous clouds where the canyons between clouds were exciting, beautiful, and an ever changing scene. Every now and then, as I entered a narrow chasm between rapidly growing clouds the chasm would close up and I would be flying blind but only for an instant before coming out on the other side into clear air and blue sky. We knew nothing of instrument flying at this point. But once I did not come out on the other side and continued to fly blind while I slowly lost control. Soon I was hanging by my safety belt and going round and round as judged by the feeling in the pit of my stomach. Soon I came out into the clear air but the earth was above me instead of below where it belonged and much too close above! Neither rudder nor ailerons seemed to work but at least I had enough sense to pull back on the stick, shortly regaining control around all three axes, and then could pull out of a near vertical dive and resume my normal flight altitude—but just in time. Normal altitude for acrobatics was about 5,000 or 6,000 feet. I had begun this one at about 1,500 feet. It was perhaps the most sickening sensation I was ever to feel in a plane.

To digress from flying, in addition to Randolph, Brooks and Kelly Fields, there was also Fort Sam Houston at San Antonio, a cavalry post at which the C.O. was Colonel Gordon Johnston who was married to my Baltimore cousin Julia Johnson. Colonel Johnston played polo, and captained the team. He had recently been military attaché to our embassy at Mexico City. Cousin Julia loved music and poetry, and she had a radio good enough to get "the orchestra" on Sunday afternoons. I do not remember what orchestra but on Sunday afternoons the living room was filled with folding chairs and anyone could come and listen to the classical programs. Anyone who chose could come without invitation and it was always packed, with many standing. From enlisted men to generals, they all came early. One must not be late; smoking and talking were not permitted; coughing was never heard. When the program was over, all filed out silently. The love and appreciation of good music among all those diverse, hard-boiled men was somehow very moving.

Colonel Johnston talked of Mexico, which he loved, and its then president whom he taught to play polo. Mexicans love horses and lived on them, except for the peons who only rated burros. The president, every night after dinner, when the last ceremonies of the day were over, would retreat to his private quarters with his tutor who was teaching him to read and write. Colonel Johnston was killed playing polo while I was at Randolph. He was an exceptionally fine officer and a gentleman—one of the best in the Army. Greatly missed.

We cadets would get a week's leave at Christmas and the colonel offered me letters to embassy people and friends if we went to Mexico. So I talked Cadet Radcliffe C. Clausen, the only one of my friends who owned a car, a Ford roadster with a rumble seat, into a fast trip to Mexico. Needing two more to share expenses, we got Van Gorder and Edgar Hale, fellow cadets.

On December 23rd we set off, crossed the border at Laredo and arrived for our first night at Monterrey. I talked enough Spanish for directions and that was about all. The road was not too bad at the border but deteriorated fast as it went south into Mexico. The second day took us through Ciudad Victoria, a totally enchanting old Spanish town, not changed in any way since it was founded in 1750. It is full of old churches. By night we made Tamazunchale and stayed at the Hotel Cabrera. It was little more than a village. We were now down to sea level, in a tropical climate, at the foot of the Sierra Madre up which we would climb to get to Mexico City. Below Victoria the road was unpaved. We carried cans of gasoline in the car. There were several rivers en route but no bridges. The little ones had fording places, the larger ones had one-car ferries, small barges attached at each end to an overhead cable which stretched across the river. By tightening up one rope, from what was to be the bow to the overhead cable, and loosening up the other at the stern, the barge would be swung at an angle to the cable and the river current would push it across the river. To return, the barge was canted the opposite way, and back it went. An old man operated it—there was no power, of course.

The road deteriorated to merely a single dirt lane, but we never passed more than a man on a burro. On our third day, the road climbed steeply from Tamazunchale through a pass at 10,000 ft. and down to Jacala on the other side onto a plateau at 7,800 ft. ringed by mountains, in the center of which was México, DF (Distrito Federal, used to distinguish the capital city from the country).

The road over the pass was lined with sentry boxes, each about a half mile apart, so located that each could keep in view the one next to it. They were empty. They had been manned recently by soldiers because the mountains were inhabited by *ladrones*, highway robbers, making the road quite unsafe. The president thought it not to the credit of Mexico to have one of its main roads unsafe to travel so he sent the Army into the mountains to catch enough *ladrones* for his purpose and they were hanged on poles along the side of the road, every few hundred yards, and left there. Although there were plenty more *ladrones*, no one saw them anymore, and the sentry boxes fell into disuse.

Halfway from Jacala to Mexico City we stopped for lunch at Ixmiquilpan, a sleepy Mexican town—pure Mexican or maybe mostly Aztec. Then on to the Regis Hotel in Mexico City.

From our room we looked out on, about 100 miles away, the twin extinct volcanos, snow capped, of Iztaccihuatl and Popocaté-petl, 17,887 ft. and 16,883 ft. We went sightseeing every spare moment. We ate at Sanborn's, the only restaurant where you got the best Mexican food and didn't get sick afterward. We left my letters at the U.S. Embassy and drove to the floating gardens of Xochimilco, the remnant, I guess, of the swamp which the plateau once was and which the Spaniards drained to build Mexico City on the remains of Tenochtitlán, the former Aztec capital (built in 1325 and destroyed by Cortez in 1521). We went to the Castillo de Chapultepec where Maximilian lived, the Cathedral on the Socolo (central square), and the Teatro Nacional, both very impressive, and to the *gallos* (cock-fights).

We were asked to a cocktail party by Mr. Stanley Hawks who was, as I remember, the Charge d'Affairs. He had a large and lovely house in the residential part of the city and the top brass were all there. The city was very nervous at the time. Revolutions were a part of daily life and dangerous. An official's house next door had two machine guns mounted and manned on the lawn. High walls surrounded every large place. We were somewhat awed.

We loved the Mexicans and I still do. Since none of us came from the American southwest we did not consider them "greasers" and while they may have only considered us as "gringos", we found them the politest people in the world, kind, thoughtful and always cheerful, with only a slight propensity to kill everyone in sight when full of tequila.

On our last day we went through Cuernavaca to Tasco, where we saw the picturesque Cathedral and the local American art colony headed by Bill Spratling who had a tin shop, selling lovely tin candlesticks, trays and all kinds of artistic objects made from old oil cans. A performing bear was dancing in front of the shop in the street.

The next day, the 29th of December, we took off for home. The next night was spent at Monterrey, and we were back on schedule at Randolph on New Year's Eve.

"B" STAGE

By March 12, 1934 I had survived A Stage or primary training and would now progress to basic training for formation flying, cross-country flying and instrument flying.

We had graduated to upper-classmen and we would drill and discipline the next new class. We were now to fly from a row of hangars on the opposite of the field. The planes were similar to but larger than the primary trainers. They were old Observation types, designated Basic Trainers, BT-1s and BT-2s, open cockpit, two-seaters, biplanes with fixed gear, a compass and wheel brakes. They were restricted in flight against the more violent acrobatics which would impose loads exceeding the strength of the wings.

We also had new instructors. I got 2nd Lt. Reginald C. Heber. His name happened to be the same as that of a famous English clergyman, Bishop of Calcutta in 1823, best known for his hymns, among which are "Holy, Holy, Holy" and "From Greenland's Icy Mountains". I did not ask him if he was a descendant. In fact I did not ask him anything. He did not act like the descendant of a bishop anyway. He was very straight, with red hair and always smiling; he had the reputation of never having passed *any* student and had washed out all four of his last group. I was now the only one assigned to him.

His first question to me was: "Do you happen to know anyone in the War Department in Washington?" Good God! I thought fast. Any drag with the higher ups meant almost automatic wash-

out. The Training Center was proud of its graduates. They were
to be the best in the world. No influence, even from generals on
the chief's staff was tolerated. The instructor's word was law in all
cases. And now, some well meaning fool in my family might have
made inquiries in Washington, I assumed, about my progress. Perhaps it was Captain Crawford C. Madeira of the First City Troop,[2]
of which I was a member. Looking him straight in the eye, but
trembling, I said, "No, Sir, I don't, but my family might know
some of the brass". No comment.

To digress a moment, for it concerned us, airmail services were
started in 1918 by the Post Office. The Army carried the first airmail on a test route between New York, Philadelphia and Washington, in May 1918. In August the Post Office took over the flying. Hoover's Postmaster General was Walter Folger Brown. He
was probably the father of our air transport system, but he was
unlucky. He asked for a new law and got the McNary-Watres Act
passed in 1930 making him virtually czar of air transport.

Air services at this time were mostly run by impecunious and
irresponsible dare-devils operating World War I surplus aircraft.
They only carried mail and there were many forced landings and
casualties. There was no market for new planes. Brown favored
the bigger private and wealthier operators, granting extensions of
their routes, mergers, and profitable mail pay, without necessarily
competitive bidding. He wanted the contractors to make enough
money to expand to passenger flying with new equipment and to
build the world's best airline system. The little boys yelled. They
desperately needed subsidy to survive. With Roosevelt's election
in 1932, the Democrats went after the Republicans and tried to
blow up the granting of the airmail contracts by Brown into another Teapot Dome scandal. In the closing days of the Hoover administration the Senate created the Black Committee to investigate
airmail and ocean mail contracts. Fulton Lewis, a Hearst reporter,
intimated all sorts of crooked deals by Brown but even Hearst did
not back him up.

As a result of the Black Committee report, reluctantly approved
by the new Postmaster General Jim Farley who had no idea what

it was all about except that it seemed to be good political dirt on the Republicans, President Roosevelt signed an order just as I was transferring to B Stage, annulling all domestic mail contracts as of February 19th. Two hours before signing the cancellation order, the President called in General Foulois, a veteran pilot and chief of staff of the Air Corps. The general, badly needing appropriations, said he would be glad to take over the airmail, as they had flown it before in 1918. (But in the past they had flown only one short route and only in daylight.)

Will Rogers wrote, "You are going to lose some fine boys in these Army flyers who are marvelously trained in their line but not in night cross-country flying with rain and snow". In the first week, five pilots died and six more were critically injured. Eight planes were washed out. By early in March, the public was appalled at the fearful rate of crashes. The military pilots were woefully unprepared for the task. FDR ordered immediate curtailment of the service. Farley restricted the service to daylight only. The crashes continued. On March 10th, FDR ordered the abandonment of all airmail service, and announced it would be returned to private operators. (In April Postmaster General Farley invited new bids for airmail contracts. On May 8th the first airmail was carried under the new contracts.)

Down at Randolph Field we were very directly concerned with the airmail fiasco, as our instructors vanished, many never to return. Lieutenant Heber, however, remained at Randolph but he now had a large number of students to instruct, handling them as severely as before, including myself. I suspect that the Army no longer wanted to graduate as few pilots as possible, but as many as possible for replacements. We were given a quick introduction to cross-country flying and avigation (as aerial navigation was then called), and an equally swift introduction to formation flying and instrument flying.

There were few instruments of any kind in airplanes before about 1914. Pilots said they flew by the seat of their pants, but in reality always and only by outside visual reference to some fixed object. If they boasted of flying blind through the clouds, it was only because the airplane was dynamically stable and would fly straight and level by itself, and it always turned out that in these boasted flights the pilot had just taken his hands off the controls and let the plane fly itself.

Experienced pilots did not take to flying by instruments. In fact they opposed it bitterly. Basil Rowe, one of the most experienced in the world, writing in 1956 about himself in 1928, says: "I found it hard to rely wholly upon flight instruments after so many years of feeling my way around the sky like a prowling cat, my ears tuned to the note of the wind through the flying wires, my fingers testing the feel of the controls. It was the elimination of exposed flying wires and their indication of speed that finally forced me to turn to the instruments inside the cockpit".[3]

Our instruction in blind flying began with lectures on spacial orientation—how we normally balanced ourselves—the stimuli to our senses of sight, touch, hearing and deep muscle sensations (kinaesthetic or propioceptive), and, most essentially those of the ear's semi-circular canals. The point of all this was to make us realize that our senses could lead us falsely, and that paying exclusive attention to them, as we had done all our lives where they served us well even in total darkness, might kill us in an airplane. We had to learn to depend on the instruments.

It is strange that today there is no such problem teaching students to use flight instruments as there was then. Some private pilots at that time obtained and installed gyro turn-and-bank indicators, and returned them to the factory insisting they did not work correctly. But they did. The Sperry turn and bank was developed in 1918 and was the primary instrument for blind flying, but tests conducted on transport pilots, military pilots, mail pilots and others from 1919 to 1932 found that less than 3% of the pilots tested could keep control of the airplane for more than 20 minutes under the hood. Obviously, it was not enough just to install instruments in the cockpit, and still not enough to teach pilots how to use them. Old-timers *would*, come Hell or high water, fly by the seat of their pants, and kill themselves.

Major Ocker and Lt. Crane were the fathers of blind flying and they developed the theories for successful blind flight. Jimmy Doo-little, not yet a general, but perhaps the Army's best acrobatic pilot then, did much to demonstrate and also to develop flying by instruments. Later the artificial horizon made it much easier.

Lindbergh, who was a fantastically good instrument pilot, taught himself on his bad weather mail flights. Pan American Airways was the first airline to pioneer instrument flying, but only in the Western Division where the route from Brownsville, Texas to Mexico City probably required more blind flying than any in the U.S.A. The division began instrument training for all pilots when it was formed in 1929. For many years the Brownsville Pan Am pilots were probably the best instrument pilots in the world. Their tough Yugoslav chief pilot, George Kraigher, saw to that. But it was otherwise in Miami in the Eastern Division as we shall see.

On A Stage we used to lie awake at night on our bunks and listen to the hum of motors from the other side of the field and dream of being up there. Reality was even better than expectation. One was alone in the dark with only the stars overhead, brilliant in the Texas night sky, and every now and then one little light below in the black pit of West Texas to connect one with one's fellow man below.

As soon as we could land and take off without trouble at night we began formation flights. Night formation was easy as you had the leader's wing-tip lights for orientation.

Then our first solo night cross-countries came along and we learned the meaning of "disorientation". In total blackness we be-gan to lose track of which way was up and which was down. We had to disregard our senses as we were being taught, but what would we use for a reference to keep straight and level? On a clear night one star would do, but what if it was overcast? How easy it was later with artificial horizons which continually showed the at-titude of the plane on the instrument panel. Our BTs had no blind flying instruments.

It is difficult to believe today, how hard it then was to find your destination on cross-country flights, even in daylight. It was easier at night because the Army fields to which we would fly would all be marked with rotating green beacons. But at this time, airways were only beginning to be built. There were few paved runways even on Army fields. Huge signs were appearing on the roofs of big barns showing the name of the town, or, with a big arrow, the direction to a major city or to the airport. A road map was often easier to follow than an aeronautical chart. Many a pilot landed in a field next to the airport never having identified the airport. The usual indication of an airport was a striped windsock on a pole somewhere at an edge of the field, because it was essential to know the wind direction for landing. The slow speed of our aircraft complicated everything, from dead reckoning where the drift could be very large and a head wind could reduce the ground speed to near zero, to cross-wind landings which were very difficult. Also we flew low and the horizon is only 30 miles away at 500 feet and 42 at 1,000 feet. We learned to dead reckon by observation of the ground. We noted the direction of blowing smoke from every chimney, the speed and direction of cloud shadows across the ground below.

After my first solo cross-country from Randolph to some point maybe 80 miles west of field, I reported to Lieutenant Heber. Instead of the expected question of what the destination looked like, to see if I had really been there, he asked me, "What was your oil pressure over New Braunfels?" That Texas town was near Randolph, and was known as a town where every inhabitant was a millionaire as oil had been discovered in the center of town. We were supposed to monitor our engine instruments, the oil pressure and oil temperature, continuously, so as to anticipate any engine trouble. Neither Heber nor I could possibly know what it was. With a smile I replied, "About 60 pounds, Sir". No further questions. Of course I had no idea what it was but remembered that the green area on the instrument face was between 55 and 70 pounds and that, as the engine got hotter, the oil got thinner and the pressure went down. So I picked a figure near the lower limit. On a cold morning, after starting up, the pressure would be above 70 and we did not take off until the engine had warmed up enough to bring the oil pressure down to 70 pounds. Passing over New

Braunfels would have been very soon after takeoff and the engine not yet fully warmed up, but the oil should have been nearer 55 than 70.

Traffic Control, such as it was at that time, consisted only of a man in the operations office who would flash a green light at you if O.K. to land, and a red light to warn you off to go around again. Approaches were always by the rectangle, down wind where you got the green or red light, base leg and final approach.

Our longest cross-country was to El Paso, at the extreme west end of Texas, through the somewhat dreaded Eagle Pass. Today probably few pilots know of Eagle Pass. Most are high above it. But flying at low altitude to keep out of the clouds, as we were, the west wind met us, roaring through the pass at 60 mph and more, with extreme turbulence, often raising a dust storm with zero visibility up to several thousand feet.

It was not very rough the day I flew through, but once on the ground at Ft. Bliss, El Paso, a dust storm blew up reducing visibility to a few feet. Pilots were naturally scared of Eagle Pass. Flying at 80 mph into a 60 mph gusty wind, with no instruments and perhaps no visibility, was no fun. But such experiences, once successfully completed, built self-confidence and eliminated fear, the most dangerous thing of all in a student pilot (or in an experienced one for that matter).

We all knew that fear must be conquered and that it arose from the unknown, so that successful experience and understanding would eliminate it. But the coward would duck frightening situations and never conquer fear. This fact was to trouble me much later in Pan Am when I had to check out new pilots. How to find out what they were afraid of, if anything. Thunderstorms? Ice? Then I had to make sure that they had experienced it, so as to know it and not be afraid.

The weather in Texas, and elsewhere later on, was to be a matter of great importance. In ground school we were introduced to synoptic weather forecasting, fronts, etc. We were taught what air currents might be found in clouds and what to avoid, but, at this point, we did not venture inside any large clouds. We knew just enough to be scared of them. We heard stories of Texas "northers", which were tongues of polar air that occasionally swept down from the north across Texas, dropping the temperature as much as 80 degrees in less than an hour and sometimes freezing an entire herd of cattle to death. And we experienced Texas hail, big like everything in this state, said to be the size of grapefruit at times. The biggest hailstorm I saw covered the whole of Randolph about an inch deep like snow, although the hailstones were only about the size of marbles. But an entire squadron of Army planes had been wiped out once by hail, nearby, while sitting out a passing storm on the ground. In just a few minutes all the planes were reduced to piles of unrebuildable wreckage. Incidentally the most violent thunderstorms I have ever seen with continuous lightning, violent turbulence and short duration were in Texas, in the Gulf of Mexico near the Panama Canal, in the Gulf of Guinea off West Africa, and, of all places, on Long Island Sound.

We now began formation flying. Loosely at first, then tight formation with wing tips just a few feet apart. A "flight" was three planes in a V, and such groups were the basic elements of all formations no matter how large. We might fly on cross-country in loose formation of four or five planes, but always with one flight leader out in front. The leader, at first an instructor, would signal all maneuvers or turns, with his head.

Formation flying, to be good, required the most intense concentration on the leader. In the beginning we would take off singly, the leader flying a wide turn over a rendezvous point, while each wingman, after takeoff, climbed up in a spiral inside the leader until he could catch up and get in position. Speed was maintained by the throttle and you had to ride it continuously to maintain position. The throttle, stick and rudder pedal movements had to be perfectly coordinated. The amount of concentration to be good or even safe was incredible. If anything went wrong one dropped out of the formation, *then* looked around. A goof would kill all three of you. Eyes were *never* removed from the leader's helmet ahead of you. By the time you were good, if the leader thought of a joke, both wingmen smiled, or so we said. Later with the dearth of instructors, we would do formation takeoffs and landings, and try forbidden formation acrobatics. Lots of fun, but about all that the planes would do were formation loops, and not very well.

On check flights the instructor would unexpectedly "chop the throttle", i.e., pull back the throttle effectively cutting off the engine, and placidly wait to see what the student did. The execution of a simulated "dead stick" (forced) landing was most important to your grade. There were usually clear, open fields below but they might be plowed. With the wind at 90° to the furroughs, the first decision to be made was whether to land into the wind or cross-wind down the furroughs. The instructor might let you land or apply power just before and tell you to climb out. We were drilled and drilled always to have a place in sight into which we could make a safe emergency landing.

With these early, underpowered and slow planes, we had very little range of speed. In a turn of three planes in formation, the outside plane would have to go faster, speed up to keep place, and the plane on the inside would have to slow down. But he couldn't. The outside one just couldn't keep up and the inside one might stall. So the wingmen would cross over, the outside one always crossing over on top of the leader, and the inside one dropping down a little and going under the leader, so they would exchange places, the right wingman becoming the left and vice versa. Today this is no longer necessary as there is a wide range of speed between stall and top speeds.

Turns were a nicely coordinated maneuver; but only a year later, after we had graduated and been assigned to tactical air squadrons at various fields, my best friend, Bob Streater, flying pursuit at Selfridge Field, was in a formation of P-26As when he was killed in a collision. In a left turn his right wing man came across him too close. Dropping down into position to the left of Streater, he was horrified to see Streater's head roll across the left wing and drop over the aileron. But this was in the future. So far no one had been killed or even hurt at Randolph.

We used to talk and dream of flying formation acrobatics with wings tied together. But this was before the day of the Blue Angels and other acrobatic teams of the Army and Navy—and with each new and more powerful fighter, acrobatics became easier and in time, only formation acrobatics required perfect precision and co-ordination.

One of my classmates was an unusual man, Frank Tinker, an Annapolis graduate. One Saturday inspection, the commandant, alerted by the smell, forced Tinker to disclose a fox which he had acquired. Astounded by the idea of a human capturing a wild fox with his bare hands, the C.O. did not even give him a demerit but did make him dispose of the animal. It was very wild. No one but Tinker could touch it. He had seen it running along a raised stretch of Louisiana road, water and swamp on each side, and had chased it in his car until, exhausted, the fox stopped and turned to fight. Tinker got out and picked it up—somewhat of an understatement judging by the rather severe lacerations on his hands and arms. After getting his Air Corps wings, Tinker eventually joined the Lincoln Brigade in Spain.[4] Seven victories later, he returned to the United States to write a book about it called *Some Still Live* (1938).

Life on the ground was getting better now. Inspections were less severe and it became easier to avoid trouble. Saturdays we could leave the post returning before lights Sunday night. Streater, Matthews and I had an apartment in San Antonio. Ed Matthews had been a baker's assistant in a Philadelphia bakery and could bake anything. We feasted on cakes, a pleasant change from the tacos, enchiladas, frijoles and tortillas, which were the routine fare of San Antonio eateries.

Discipline was strict. Any day we could see two lone figures far off at the edge of the field, one working and the other following slowly behind carrying a rifle. We understood that the prisoner was the only flying cadet ever to be caught stealing. He stole $6.00 from another cadet and received six years at hard labor.

Once, in our class, a cadet reported the loss and presumed theft of his watch. (He may have lost it in San Antonio.) The commandant had us all lined up in tight formation at strict attention and then addressed us with a quiet speech which not even the toughest

Mafia chief could have equalled for intimidation. He would find out who had stolen it. He never did, but then no one believed it had been stolen.

We were paid monthly in cash, $75.00 a month. But one fine day the assembly for payroll was late. The commandant, 1st Lieutenant Bevans, a West Pointer and a very fine young man whom we all liked, had a staff sergeant at Headquarters. As always in the Army, the sergeant ran the field. He ran everything. From him you could get a pass, special orders, leave, transportation, etc. He wrote the orders and the commandant signed them. The commandant trusted him absolutely. He was Jewish and one of the very few Jews found in the Air Corps. He was very, very efficient. We all swore by him. The cash for the payroll was kept in a safe at Headquarters, as required by regulations. Again, by regulation, only commissioned officers were permitted to know the combination. But this sergeant had gotten the combination from the commandant and this fine day he went over the hill with the payroll, not to be found again as far as I know. But the Army never abandons the search for a deserter even long after he must be presumed dead. The commandant was court-martialled, and dishonorably discharged for permitting an enlisted man to have access to money for which he, the commandant, was responsible, in violation of regulations. Tragic. His career was ended, and he was a fine man.

For advanced training at Kelly we had to choose a branch of the Service. I chose Bombardment only because I thought that twin-engine experience would help me get a job in an airline where nearly all planes were now twin-engine. The other branches were Pursuit (now called Combat or Fighter), Attack and Observation.

Streater and I bought a car for $100.00. A 1926 Pierce Arrow roadster. It antedated the modern fuel pump and had a vacuum tank to suck the gas from the tank to the carburetor. The vacuum leaked. We tried every conceivable kind of sealant but nothing worked for long. More hours were spent in repair than in driving. But we got places. It went two to three miles per gallon, but gas was 6¢ at the PX.

Last thing at Randolph, I looked up Lieutenant Heber to say

"goodbye, Sir". Incredibly he had graduated me. He asked me what I was going to do on my week off. "Sir, I expect to motor over to Lake Charles with Streater". A look of stunned astonishment came over his usually blank face and then he began to laugh, the first time anyone had seen him laugh, at least in public. "Brock, I have never been able to tell when you were kidding me and when not". I saluted and, without waiting for its return, about-faced and left as quickly as I could with dignity. Of course, the verb "motor" slipped out unintentionally. He may have heard it before, but to him it would have seemed appropriate only as applied to a Newport dowager setting out in her chauffeur-driven Rolls Royce.

KELLY FIELD

Kelly was still just exactly the same as when it was built as the Army's first flying school in World War I. The C.O. now was Colonel Clagett, a formidable and indeed terrifying old soldier who flew his pursuit plane with three pairs of goggles over his helmet, all with corrective lenses. One enabled him to see his instrument panel and read the instruments, one to read his map and one to look around with when landing. He had a drill master's voice, the loudest I have ever heard, and he could audibly address an enlisted man across the field, perhaps a half mile away, with engines running nearby, and the man would spring to attention.

Kelly was famous and its graduates had a standing in the flying world that no other pilots had. Lindbergh graduated from Kelly. So had Captain Bill Winston, one of the earliest Pan Am pilots, who used to call himself the pilot who taught Lindbergh's instructor how to fly, and other "greats" like Billy Mitchell and Jimmy Doolittle who were, like Lindbergh, to make history.

The barracks, our living quarters, were low ceilinged, wood shacks, built for World War I. We slept in rows of canvas cots with our belongings in a foot-locker at the end of each cot. It was now mid-summer, July, 1934. Southern Texas summer is over 100° in the shade, that is, inside our barracks, and it did not cool off in the slightest at night. One slept only fitfully and from total exhaustion. Rules were lax. The PX stayed open all night. A few of us would often get up in the middle of the night, and, retreating to the PX, drink Cokes, five to ten cold bottles to keep cool while swapping stories and casually chatting in the oven-like air. Sometimes we flew in our underclothes.

In a new ground school we learned to disassemble, clean and re-assemble the Browning .30 caliber machine gun. We also were introduced to the new .50 caliber machine gun, an awesome increase in fire power. We learned about the synchronizer, invented by the Dutchman Tony Fokker which made firing a gun through the propeller possible in World War I. Pursuit aircraft were all single seaters, and the machine gun sat on top of the fuselage directly in front of the pilot's cockpit, so he could reach up and clear it if it jammed.

It was fed with cartridges by a belt coming up from below. We learned about the trajectories of falling bombs, and about bomb sights and the importance of bomb racks and release mechanisms. Bombs, once loaded on the plane and in flight, *must* be dropped. It was unsafe to land with one still on board. A bomb was safe until it had dropped, when a little propeller on the nose of the bomb would spin around and fall off, arming the fuse. But a bomb might not drop completely clear and hang onto the rack, and the little prop would still spin off. A landing would then destroy the plane and crew, but one was not supposed to bail out and leave the plane unless over a wide desert. So the bomb racks *had* to work and work right, *always*.

Actually, we fired no live ammunition at Kelly. Gunnery was to follow later on active duty. We studied more meteorology, aerodynamics, engines, propellers and aircraft construction, etc. We soon were aware that no routine maintenance or inspections were given our aircraft at Kelly. A failure of an engine, or even a wing, would be a good thing, real experience, and, of course, we always wore parachutes.

Our mess was something! Just about the best food in the world. A super-chef as mess sergeant and all the money in the world. Eggs to order for breakfast. Muffins as you wanted. Oysters, steaks, even lobsters (in Texas!), as you wished. Just ask the sergeant. Commissioned officers, even the C.O., had to be invited. It was just for cadets.

Federal Law or Service Regulations prohibited the Army or Navy from selling their services or being paid for anything they did for the public. But Hollywood liked to film flying and, of course it was the best kind of publicity to help get bigger appropriations from Congress. The fleet could always be filmed in documentaries for very dramatic footage but, when in 1926 Hollywood produced *Wings*, it used the Air Corps Training School. The whole of Kelly Field had participated with all the students flying in great formations. In gratitude, Hollywood endowed the cadet mess—hence our superb food.

Hell's Angels had also been filmed at Kelly. Now a movie to be called *West Point of the Air* was to be filmed and we spent a lot of time drilling and formation flying for Hollywood. The place was alive with cameramen and directors. Wallace Beery and Robert Montgomery were supposed to appear.

We started at Kelly with transition training in the three other branches I had not elected, Observation, Attack and Pursuit. I had chosen, with Pan Am in mind, Bombardment but first I had to be checked out in O-19s and O-25s, A-3s and P-12Bs. The latter, pursuit planes, had camera guns installed in place of the Browning machine guns and from the filmstrips successful hits on the enemy or misses could be judged for marks. One of the observation planes I flew was powered with a Liberty engine.

The P-6D was the last great, open cockpit, single seater, fixed-gear pursuit plane or fighter. It was a dream to fly. Powered with a liquid cooled Curtiss D-12 engine which ran "like a sewing machine", it would go 250 mph straight down—terminal velocity. Full throttle or no throttle made no difference in a dive because of the drag of all the wires, struts and fixed landing gear. We've gone a long way since then in speed.

Finally I was settled in Bombardment flying B-6s. What horrors! Keystone Bombers built in Bristol, Pa.; two-seaters with a side-by-side open cockpit; slow and clumsy but twin-engined and I wanted the multi-engine experience. We used to say the B-6s took off, flew and landed all at the same speed—and it was not far from the truth. There was an open bomb bay in the belly and a rear gunner cockpit (not used in school). The two engines posed no problems at all, even in formation flying. After mastering landings and takeoffs, our flying was mostly formation flying, day and night. We also flew a lot of cross-countries to San Marcos, Corpus Christi, Gonzales, Austin, San Angelo, Abilene, Houston, El Paso, Ft. Worth, Ft. Sill, Midland and Carlsbad—some of the fields were good, some pretty rough.

Accidents began to happen, mostly in the pursuit section. We seldom if ever saw them but the word got around fast. Except for cross-countries, we flew only in the morning so an empty chair at the noon mess, indicating a missing cadet, was a bad sign. He was usually dead. It seemed to happen only on Wednesdays, and almost every Wednesday. We began to dread going to noon mess on that day and, although everyone tried not to, one couldn't help looking around for the empty chair.

One Wednesday, at least, that empty chair was reoccupied. A cadet had bailed out, losing the plane and, landing safely, had folded up his 'chute (treasuring the rip cord as a souvenir) and gotten a ride back to the field. He was promptly tried and had to prove his jump was necessary to save his life, and so escape dismissal. He persuaded the board officially but not all of us believed him. It must be remembered that a parachute jump in those days was something of a stunt. Few pilots had ever made a jump. Having done so and survived gave enormous cachet. A dare-devil pilot would make a jump, for which he could not get permission from the Air Corps, just for the prestige and to boast about it. I asked for permission once and was immediately turned down.

Finally came graduation, October 3, 1934. We were rated pilots, but we would not be commissioned 2nd Lieutenant (as always with classes before) until we completed one year of active duty at a Tactical Air Corps Base. Forty-two of the original 75 lieutenants from West Point graduated and 30 of the 75 civilian cadets (including the few Annapolis men). The Navy men were all taken back into the Navy, I believe, but three of us who continued in the Air Corps would be dead within a year. Before obtaining our appointment to the Air Corps Training Center at Randolph Field we had had to enlist for three years, but we expected to be commissioned, if all went well, after the first year which would increase our pay from the cadet's $75 a month to about $200 a month.

We were now assigned to a base of the branch we had selected, still as cadets, and I was ordered to report to March Field, California, a bomber base. I immediately requested reassignment to be near my mother in Philadelphia; the request was granted; and my orders were changed to Langley Field, Newport News, Virginia.

LANGLEY FIELD

I had recently bought a new car, a Nash coupe, turning in the nine year old Pierce Arrow, and I drove non-stop from San Antonio to Philadelphia to my mother's. I had about two weeks leave and then reported to the 20th Bombardment Squadron, 2nd Bombardment Group, U.S. Army Air Corps. The Air Corps was being changed to an Air Force, still part of the Army Department but somewhat more independent, as are the Marines in the Navy. At Langley we were to be the GHQ (General Headquarters) of the Army Air Force under General Frank M. Andrews.

Langley Field also had based on it, the 19th Lighter-Than-Air Squadron with a hangar, mast, and one TC-4 semi-rigid balloon called *Tessie*. A semi-rigid balloon has only one structural member, a metal keel along the base, from which hang the control gondola and the engine-propeller pod. Inside, the helium filled bags are attached to the keel, and the whole above the keel is covered with a loose bag of balloon cloth. Back of the propeller there is a scoop into which the propeller slip-stream blows the air to inflate the outer covering and gives the balloon its shape.

A crew of four would go off on cruises for as long as 48 hours, living nose to nose and hardly able to move in their gondola. On their return the crew would appear in our mess and sit each in opposite corners of the hall as far as possible from their former mates. But on one cruise, a very bored and tired crew let the engine idle while in the air and *Tessie* slowly collapsed inside out. It settled gently to the ground and no one was hurt as they scrambled out from under the acre of cloth which covered them. The captain was most embarrassed and court-martialled.

Langley was also the home of the NACA—National Advisory Committee for Aeronautics—an independent establishment of the government, created in 1915 to further the science of Aeronautics with representatives from the Army, Navy, Weather Bureau, Bureau of Standards and some distinguished civilians. It had come to be greatly respected by Congress and the White House and, by 1934, it was a technical research organization second to none. Here was the first full scale wind tunnel. Brilliant aerodynamicists like Theodore von Karmán, the Hungarian called the father of Aerodynamics, were pouring in, some to escape the growing fascist menace in Europe, some to partake in the great discoveries that were being made. Who supported them no one knew. But they were taken in and fed at our officers' mess, these extraordinary Einsteins, speaking a dozen different languages. They sat and chatted in mathematics language, a lingua franca for them as Latin was for Copernicus, Kepler and Galileo. We were never able to talk to any of them but they gave the USA such unrivalled supremacy in airplanes that the airlines of the world after World War II were flown almost exclusively by American planes.[5]

As flying cadets, neither officers nor enlisted men, we were something new at Langley. We simply went to the officers' mess and ate, posing a small problem as the officers contributed a small portion of their pay to the mess each month. We did not pay it and no one had the heart to dock our meager pay.

On arrival we went directly to the supply sergeant, always the toughest of the non-coms, and demanded officers' flying clothes, even taking some brand new experimental winter flying suits of wool-lined reindeer skin. They were very light, very warm, very soft and very expensive. We drew them all. None were left, not even a set for the general. Cockpits were still open to the air and winter was coming. It was now November.

We were a little cocky. We thought we now could fly and knew we had more instrument time than any of our superiors. Perhaps so, but in retrospect how much we still had to learn—and keep learning for the rest of our lives. We respected and could spot instantly the West Pointer, but we had a little less respect for the many officers who had risen from the ranks. We felt superior to them although we were not yet commissioned and they knew it but recognized their comparative lack of education. (We were, however, well disciplined and scrupulously correct in all matters of military etiquette.)

At Langley there were three squadrons, the 20th, 49th and 96th comprising the 2nd Bombardment Group. There were 10 or 11 bombers to a squadron and perhaps 15 to 20 officers normally. The C.O. (Commanding Officer) of my 20th Squadron was Captain Cronau, and Lieutenant Glantzberg, a genial redhead, was operations officer. Our bombers were the same old B-6s we had at Kelly Field or the somewhat newer model B-6As and B-6Bs, little improved.

Except for dropping some 100 pound bombs in circles on the nearby bombing range and shooting from a flexible mount in the rear cockpit at a towed sleeve for a target, we mostly practiced formation flying, day and night, locally and cross-country.

The bombers were much too clumsy to cross over in turns as we did in formation back on B Stage, and the wingmen just tried to stay in place. The leader thus had to fly slowly or the outside wingman could never keep up in a turn, but this caused the inside man to have to slow down to a near or actual stall.

This was very hairy for the inside man which I always seemed to be, especially at night. Also we usually flew quite low, under 1,000 feet and the inside man, down in the turn as the other two were up above him, worried he might brush the ground in a steep bank. It was a nightmare flying at stall speed in a steep bank close to the ground in the dark.

The end of 1934 was almost the bottom of the depression and we did not fly much at first as Congress only allocated enough fuel to the Air Corps for the armchair brass to get their three hours a month for flight pay and for us a minimum of flight training.

To round out our training as military pilots, even though we specialized as bombers, we were assigned to practice ground strafing with a few pursuit planes maintained on the field for this purpose. Strafing meant coming down in a very steep dive at full speed and sweeping low over a ground target so as to rake the area with machine gun fire before pulling up steeply. I remember only one day of this practice which ended very badly. In diving and firing on the range set aside for gunnery and bombing, a cadet named George Breck, flying a P-6D, was late in pulling up and thus mushed right into the ground with the plane in a level attitude. I landed alongside on the range and rushed over but some enlisted men had gotten there first and were standing around silently. Breck was sitting in the cockpit, eyes open, still alive. His legs had been driven up through his flying suit so the bones projected past his head. His head was driven down between his shoulder blades which were well above his ears. As I got there I heard him say, "God, I hurt", and he died.

Next morning the Newport News daily paper carried a little box saying a Cadet Brock was killed in an accident at Langley. I immediately called my mother in Philadelphia and had a nice early morning chat with her. Perhaps she wondered why I called so early in the day. Fortunately the Philadelphia papers had not picked it up.

We got to love the Virginia tidewater country. While we never got across the bay to Norfolk, we had come to know the peninsula between the James River and Chesapeake Bay, Newport News and Hampton. Almost every Sunday evening I would get a few friends and we'd go to the little church in Hampton where the Hampton Institute choir sang. We sat in the balcony reserved for whites, and the black congregation below sang with not a voice that wasn't true and beautiful. The music had to be heard to be believed. Hymns and spirituals, perfectly natural, marvellous voices—unbelievable singing straight from the heart. There was no artifice and no applause. It was pure emotion and incredibly moving.

Through February and March we flew mostly cross-country to practice navigation, sometimes in formation, sometimes night solo or in formation. To each bomber in the squadron was attached a maintenance crew with a maintenance chief, always a non-com. On these cross-countries, the crewchief always rode in the cockpit in the second seat. At all stops and overnights the crewchief looked after the plane, fuelling, servicing, inspecting and making any repairs. We always went to Army bases where there were servicing facilities. At this time there were about 25 Army fields including a few National Guard fields and about 10 Navy fields where we could get service, east of the Mississippi. There were many in the southwest where the old cavalry and artillery schools were, such as Ft. Sill, Oklahoma and Ft. Clark, Texas. We flew many trips to Bolling Field in Washington, next door to the Navy field at Anacostia.

Bolling was a treacherous little field with only one approach to a too short runway through a small gap in low surrounding hills where the wind was very gusty. An approach in rough air at stall speed and crosswind was a very hairy business and inevitably there were many crack-ups going into Bolling. We also flew to Mitchel Field in Long Island and to Hartford (Brainard Field) to call on Pratt and Whitney, now making most of the engines for the Army. Once I was entertained at dinner by Jack Horner, the vice-president, a very attractive man, and I was flattered enormously. Perhaps he thought I might be a general someday although only a flying cadet then, and it was good public relations.

My first cross-country to Mitchel Field was an event for reasons that could only be understood at that time. We flew a direct line— no nonsense about airways. Airways were used by us only for radio range practice. The straight line took us over lower New York harbor from Sandy Hook to Coney Island. Good God! Twenty-five miles over water. We *never* flew without an emergency landing place in sight in case of any engine trouble, avoiding built-up areas, schools and playgrounds. Perhaps for the first time I would be without any place to land without drowning. From the midpoint or near it, a B-6A without power would drop like a rock and nearly as steeply with only one engine.

As we neared Sandy Hook the tension mounted. I was frankly scared. The crew chief helped the situation by remarking that not long before a bomber from Langley had had an engine failure over lower New York bay and had gone down in the water, sinking immediately, with both lives lost. It was with a sigh of relief that I put down at Mitchel Field.

On March 29th I got approval for a "personal cross-country", that is a flight to a destination of my choice but listed as training. So I took off for Georgetown, S.C. where my mother was staying with my Aunt Hope and Colonel Robert Montgomery at their Mansfield Plantation. It was a showplace, rebuilt as in slave days, the maids all in colorful gingham dresses and turbans. The slave quarters were all done over and modernized, plumbing, etc. and inhabited by the families who worked the plantation, and the fields were planted with the old crops of tobacco, cotton, indigo and whatever else they grew in former times.

Cousin Bob had taken to autogiros and had a Pitcairn and a private pilot, Guy Miller, who also ran a fixed base operation for light planes and autogiros at Wings Field, Radnor, Pa. My B-6A bomber created quite a sensation as I set it down at the local airport, better suited to autogiros than bombers. I gave Guy a ride and then had to leave the B-6A at the Charleston Navy Base where Guy came to pick me up in the autogiro and take me back to Mansfield. Two days later I got my bomber from the Navy base, stopped off once more at the plantation to say goodby and returned to Langley.

In May I had a cross-country to Miami, Key West and back through Jacksonville. I remember on return to Langley from Ft. Bragg, as I headed north along the coast, an ominous front was moving in from the west. It was a typical line squall, very low base, very black, alive with lightning and traditionally accompanied by brief and violent winds and even tornados. It was terrifying. Soon it was apparent to the crew chief and me that we would not get to Langley and that it would get there first. If we went out to sea to avoid it we would never get back. As the storm got very near and we were over the beach, I swung around and landed across the wide beach into the wind just as the storm hit. We sat huddled in the open cockpit in the rain and hail with the engines running. Soon it was all over and we saw a Coast Guard crew coming down the beach in a little beach buggy. We thanked them and asked where we were. "Kitty Hawk", they said, which we well knew to be the place where Orville Wright made the first powered flight! Now there is a memorial tower there, but then there was nothing. I took off crosswind in a light breeze along the beach parallel to the sea and so home to Langley.

One time Lt. Beirne Lay, a schoolmate at St. Paul's, whose father had taught mathematics to me and to my father thirty years before that, was flying formation in a B-6A near Langley when the aileron controls failed. He bailed out after the two men with him, landed in the river and nearly drowned. On the way down, he was astonished to see the lumbering bomber coming down in a glide straight for Langley Field, where it would have made a good landing all by itself, except for a wing hitting a building on the field where his commanding officer (Capt. Cronau) was sitting at his desk watching the approach. No one was killed; no one hurt except Beirne.

On June 3rd we all moved to Mitchel Field on Long Island for about a month, where we took up most of the West Point class of 1936 for rides. Then we concentrated on daily instrument flight instruction and practice flights under the hood using the Mitchel radio range. We flew BT-2As and BT-2Bs and an occasional PT-3A equipped with hood and flight instruments. The intensive instrument flight training was the result of the air mail tragedies. Mitchel had several Link Trainers, among the first. A Link Trainer was a small simulated airplane cockpit containing the normal instruments and controls and equipped with a radio which gave you through earphones the sounds of a simulated radio range. It was just like flying except that the trainer was fixed to the floor in a classroom. By the sounds in your earphones you could steer to a leg while climbing to the prescribed altitude at the prescribed airspeed with all the instruments responding correctly to the movement of the controls, then make a procedure turn and fly the leg over simulated outer and inner marker sounds to the airport. It was very realistic and one pilot was reported to have gotten lost and so scared under the hood that he tore the top hatch off the trainer and jumped out.

In July I put in again for a "personal cross-country" to go see my sister in Lake Forest. It was the time of the Chicago World's Fair and I thought I might see that too. There was no airport near Lake Forest that I could find on any map or chart. My sister, Mrs. R. Stockton Rush, however, assured me that there was an excellent private field at Lake Forest called Sky Harbor. It was a long way from Langley. I asked: "Any lights?" Answer: "Don't know." "Well, if not, please get some friends with cars and turn on all the headlights into the wind for me to land by".

So, with my crew chief I took off on September 20 going by Bolling, Pittsburgh, Cleveland where it got dark, to Selfridge Field in Michigan and on to Sky Harbor, arriving about 10 o'clock at night. After some flying around where we thought Lake Forest might be we chanced to spot some automobile headlights in a field. I landed and, as the large old bomber careened across the field, a huge obstruction went by the wing. When the crew chief and I collected ourselves, we saw that the obstruction was an unlighted, fairly large, two-story house in the middle of the field. My sister and some friends came up and it developed that the airport had closed down and been abandoned some years before, a night club had been built on it, and that had been closed and abandoned too. Going back to the Rushs' for a late dinner, we left off the crew chief at the first bar, agreeing to meet him the day after tomorrow at the "field". I think he never left the bar until he showed up again at Sky Harbor on schedule.

On the 21st I saw the Chicago World's Fair and the next day I took off again for the return trip to Langley. On arrival after dark it was very cold. I could not get my hands off the control wheel. They were clamped on and nearly frozen. The crew chief had seen that before and was able to pry them off and get me down to the ground.

As a final comment on life at Langley Field I should say that every Thursday night was poker night at the Officers' Club, and many young officers gambled heavily, sometimes losing all their pay. Army regulations, or perhaps Army custom, required that any officer unable to pay his debts at the end of the month, even if his creditors forgave him, would be cashiered. One young West Pointer, facing such a fate, shot himself while I was there. I never gambled at poker and have never understood why poker seems to be so much more addictive than craps, roulette or even bridge.

On October 12 I flew an O-25C to Philadelphia for the wedding of my cousin Isabel Henry and Johnny Ames, and flew back the next day. It was about my last flight for now my second year was up. I was then commissioned 2nd Lieutenant Army Air Corp Reserve (rated Airplane Pilot) and I had one more year of active duty ahead of me. But I had had enough. I resigned and got out.

CHAPTER II

———————————⟨⟩———————————

Pan American Airways, Eastern Division, Miami, Florida and Port of Spain, Trinidad

JANUARY 1936 – APRIL 1937

MIAMI

I HAD obtained an introduction to Juan Trippe through friends, but I never got to see him. On my return from Langley in October 1935, I got an appointment with the chief engineer, Mr. Priester, in November. He was not hopeful but in the interview I learned that, in addition to a commercial pilot's license and 600 hours of flight time which I had, I would need an Aircraft and Engine Mechanic's License issued by the Civil Aeronautics Administration and a 2nd Class Radiotelegraph Operator's License issued by the FCC. It was understood that if hired, I would be an apprentice pilot until I had my licenses and four months of additional training.

To occupy my time while waiting I attended classes at the Philadelphia School of Wireless Telegraphy. I had been president of the Radio Club at St. Paul's School where we had had an amateur radio station. Now the real test in obtaining the commercial license was to attain a reception speed of Morse code, five letter groups, at 20 words a minute. Most of my time was spent in code practice and getting familiar with all kinds of shipboard radio equipment. I got my 2nd Class Commercial Radio Telegraph and Telephone License without difficulty.

To keep my hand in at flying I drove out to see Guy Miller at Wings Field about renting a light plane. Time passed and as my prospects at Pan Am still looked dim, I agreed to buy a Waco from a Mr. Moore and made a down payment, intending to start an instrument flying school on my own at Wings. Providentially, before I got started, Pan Am sent word for me to report to Miami on January 1, 1936. Mr. J. Turner Moore kindly accepted his plane back and returned my deposit.

New Year's Eve, I checked in at the Columbus Hotel in Miami and, in the course of the day, acquired two roommates, Ben Harrell, a friend who had been at Langley Field with me and Andy Anderson, also an ex-Army flying cadet. Harrell was a thick-set, placid soul, never in a hurry or disturbed by anything. One would not have thought of him as an athlete. I didn't think of him as such until I played tennis with him one day, losing every game. Then I found out. He had been state champion in his home state. Anderson was tall, thin and quite humorous, providing the laughs in our group.

Back at Langley when I had discussed the future with other cadets, I had found almost no one who wanted to fly for Pan American. They wanted none of this stuff about flying over the ocean and maybe having to live outside the U.S.A. Harrell and Anderson were exceptions who felt the romance of foreign fields and of overwater flying. I loved the sea and was going to see lots of it. We got an apartment in Coral Gables, one bedroom, living room and bath for $395 for one year.

At this time, 1936, Pan Am operated three divisions: the Eastern based at Miami; the Western based at Brownsville, Texas; and the brand new Pacific being put together in San Francisco using as its base an old yacht basin rented from the Navy at Alameda, California.

The Eastern Division flew only over water with seaplanes and amphibians from Miami to various points in the Caribbean, Bahamas and South America. The Western flew only landplanes to Mexico and down through Central America, stopping at each capital en route to Panama. The Pacific was getting three M-130, very long range, Martin flying boats to open a route to Manila, Hong

Kong and Macao, but regular service across the Pacific had not yet started. There was no night flying in the Eastern or Western divisions.

The Western Division pilots, all landplane pilots, were mostly ex-Army pilots. In the Eastern Division, equipped only with sea-planes and amphibians, the pilots were almost all ex-Navy, al-though a few like Bob Fatt, the chief pilot, were ex-Army because the Company had begun flying with a Fokker tri-motor landplane from Key West to Havana. The "old-timers" seemed very old to us. Some were drawing 20 year retirement pay from the Navy, but they could not have been any older than in their 40s. Two, Johnny Rogerson and George Rumill, had started flying with the Royal Flying Corps (British RFC) in World War I as seaplane pilots. The Pan Am seaplane pilots were unquestionably the most experienced in existence.

Captain Fatt was chief pilot because he was No. 1 in seniority, although Captain Basil Rowe contested it. Rowe had the most flying time of anyone in the world according to Ripley's "Believe It Or Not". On returning from Havana one day, Fatt missed Flor-ida and, thinking himself east, kept correcting his course to the west. In fact he was going farther and farther into the Gulf of Mexico. When about out of gas he landed alongside a freighter and all the passengers but one were saved.

Fatt could be intimidating. Whenever he answered the phone, without waiting to hear the identity or business of the caller, per-haps because it would usually be a pilot asking for a change in schedule, he would shout into the phone (and he had a very power-ful voice) "This is Fatt, F-A-T-T". The effect was usually to make the caller drop the phone and Fatt would hang up.

Pan Am's history has yet to be written. It begins when, in 1923, Juan Terry Trippe, with friends, formed Colonial Airlines to op-erate between New York and Boston. There was no regular air-mail then. Under the Kelly Act, Colonial got the first airmail con-tract for this route in 1925 and it became Colonial Air Transport. It must be remembered that there were very few passengers willing to fly, and little or no revenues of any kind from air services in the early 1920s, nor were planes built to carry passengers. A mail contract was the only hope of survival. There was nothing in the way of payload except mail. Trippe realized this and concentrated his time in Washington at the Post Office getting mail contracts with what influence he could muster, good financial backing and much persuasive charm.

About the same time, 1926, Basil Rowe was setting up an airline called The West Indian Aerial Express and operating between Puerto Rico, Santo Domingo, Haiti, Cuba and the Virgin Islands. He too hoped to get a mail contract, but Trippe got there first with a foreign airmail contract from Key West to Havana and, as a result, Trippe took over The West Indian Aerial Express and Basil Rowe. Actually, Pan Am was not yet ready to operate when the mail contract required it to start because, although the one tri-motor Fokker was ready, the airport at Key West was not; and Cy Caldwell was hired with his float plane to take the first flight, which was on October 19th, 1927.

Next Trippe made a joint agreement with Mr. J. P. Grace, head of W. R. Grace and Co. which controlled almost everything along the west coast of South America, forming a new airline called Pan-agra, owned 50/50 with an equal number of directors, but the president always to be appointed by Grace. There would be no competition on each other's coasts and Grace would never fly north of Panama.

About the same time, Ralph A. O'Neill, an American ace of World War I, started an airline from New York to Rio de Janeiro and Buenos Aires, called NYRBA, with fourteen Consolidated Commodore flying boats. With their equipment they confidently expected to get the mail contract when it came up for bid, but once again Trippe got the contract and, in August 1930, took over NYRBA and with it the Commodores and some very special pilots whom I came to know quite well: Humphrey Toomey, Robin McGlohn and John Shannon.

Rowe was not bitter over losing his airline as he preferred flying to running an airline from an office, and he stayed on with Pan Am until retirement, a famous and greatly respected pilot who had started as a barnstormer. O'Neill was very bitter and had nothing further to do with airlines. Toomey and McGlohn were the pioneer flyers of the east coast of South America, which was a formidable and hazardous route. In time Toomey became a vice-president of Pan Am, retired and was murdered in his apartment in Rio. Shannon went to Panagra as operations manager, later as traffic manager, and came to Pan Am after many years, eventually to retire as senior vice-president, operations.

Trippe had his sights on Mexico too. The original airline there, called Compania Mexicana de Aviacion, had been organized by George Rihl and others in 1924. Trippe bought Aerovias Centrales which ran from Mexico City to Los Angeles up the west coast of Mexico. In 1929 Trippe bought control of Compania Mexicana (CMA), obtained an airmail contract and organized the Western Division in Brownsville, Texas. Airmail from the U.S.A. to Mexico was started in March 1929.

The Western Division began with a Fairchild 71 and three Ford tri-motors. The latter were placed in Cristobal and flew to Panama City, David, San José, Managua, Tegucigalpa, San Salvador and Guatemala. Some Douglas DC-2s, added in 1934, flew from Brownsville down to Mexico City and on to Panama via the same stops.

George Kraigher, a dashing Yugoslav pilot from World War I, joined Pan Am and became chief pilot at Brownsville.[1] The Western Division routes were probably the most difficult and dangerous ones being flown at that time. There were almost no enroute facilities. Communications between plane and ground were by CW radiotelegraphy so, in addition to the co-pilot and the steward, a radio operator was carried. The only radio navigation aids were radio loops[2] on the ground from which true bearings were taken and sent to the plane. Of course, what the pilot wanted and needed were magnetic bearings which were what he flew by. The pilot had to convert, in his head, each bearing from true to magnetic, even while flying manually on instruments in a thunderstorm, but true bearings were what he got on orders from New York.

Flying in Central America was mostly climbing up or letting down through clouds among mountain peaks of which neither the exact elevation nor location were known, through violent thunderstorms which could not be seen in advance and could not be avoided anyway, and into and out of grass fields neither level nor smooth and between 800 and 1,000 meters long. One of the shortest fields, at San Salvador, had a sheer drop of 800 feet into a lake at one end, the normal upwind end. Kraigher created what I believe to have been the best trained and disciplined group of pilots ever seen, and the only accident was one in which one of the group, Archy Paschall, hit a mountain going into Guatemala. He, the co-pilot and the radio operator were killed, but the steward survived unhurt. There were no passengers.

By the time I started with the Company, Trippe had already acquired an interest in CNAC (China National Airways Corp.) flying routes in China; had set up PAA–Alaska which took over two existing lines there; and had set up or then controlled, in addition to CMA and Aerovias, CUBANA in Cuba, Panair do Brasil, Compania Argentina and SCADTA in Colombia. Avensa in Venezuela was also set up or acquired about then.

My orders for January and February were to report to Maintenance at Dinner Key, a small promontory on Biscayne Bay just south of Miami, where Pan Am had a couple of hangars. It also had a terminal building containing a globe which was said to be the largest in the world and the necessary ramps to beach and launch the seaplanes and to load the passengers and cargo. We worked on the planes in the hangars and also warmed up the planes each morning for the day's flights. We would start all the engines and run them about ten minutes until all temperatures and pressures were normal and then check the ignitions.

The planes were all Sikorsky models except for the Commodores acquired from NYRBA. There were the huge S-40s, 4-engine, high-wing monoplanes with outboard pontoons that also carried fuel; S-38s, small twin-engine amphibians; S-41s, slightly larger editions of the S-38s and very hard to land; and the latest S-42s, 4-engine, long-range models.

The maintenance superintendent in the hangar was an old Marine sergeant who acted like his prototype in the movies. He was brutal, competent, and a good instructor. The first day we had to buy tools. Sears Roebuck tools were not allowed. The only acceptable manufacturer sent a panel truck over weekly from which we bought approved tools on credit to be deducted from our pay of $150.00 a month. We would have to buy uniforms later when we began to fly. Working on the planes when not standing on the deck (i.e., hangar floor), was done from metal work stands or raised platforms with smooth double handrails going up each side of the steps on which to slide down fast in case of a hangar fire. The work platform had a shelf around it on which toolboxes were placed. The superintendent did not walk around close to a work stand. It was too easy for a toolbox to fall off on his head. He knew better.

We learned how to weld plain steel, chrome-moly steel, aluminum alloy tubing and aluminum sheet. The latter was very hard to weld when thin. We learned carpentry too, such as how to repair a wooden box spar or wing rib. We learned about glues and gluing. We learned sewing and doping, because many of our rudders and stabilizers and some of the main wings were still fabric covered. Fabric coverings were sewn by women in a section of the hangar shops. The cloth, called Flightex, was made from grade A, long staple, Sea Island cotton. It was stretched tight and made stiff and not porous to air by the application of a nitrate "dope". We learned tempering and case hardening of steel. We also worked in the instrument shop and learned how to calibrate the engine and flight instruments.

Finally we were in shape to take the CAA tests for an A and E (Aircraft and Engine Mechanic's) license, including trade tests in welding, repairing wing spars and the general expert workmanship required for work on an airplane and airplane engine. I passed and still have my license. I have known some airline mechanics to take the tests for many years and never pass them. They would remain in the paint shop or the wheel shop where a license was not required.

In March I went to Maintenance at the 36th St. Miami Airport where Pan Am had a shop for major overhaul of engines and planes. Engine overhaul takes more than an aircraft mechanic—it takes a machinist. One engine was assigned to each mechanic, and the best mechanics each had one of us assigned to him as a helper. The engine was first disassembled down to the last nut and bolt. Each part was washed and cleaned to a sparkle in special cleaning fluids. Some parts were sandblasted first. Critical parts were checked for invisible cracks by magnetism and iron filings (magneflux process) or by a dye with ultra-violet light for nonmagnetic metals (zyglo process). Then the engine was reassembled, replacing certain parts with new ones.

It took two weeks to overhaul an engine. It always took two weeks, about one week of which was taken up by the reassembly. On my last day in the overhaul shop, the regular mechanic and I were working on an engine scheduled to be completed that day. The mechanic seemed to trust me and now I was doing all the work while he sat out under a palm tree chatting with other men, drinking Cokes, and occasionally coming in to check up. He told me it was his anniversary and he would be having a big dinner at home that night. At five o'clock he came in for a last look and to put his tools away. I was very pleased with myself, with every little hex-nut beautifully safetied with new copper wire. Suddenly he seemed to go into shock. I noticed he was looking at the work bench where, unnoticed by me, lay one small gear in a corner. He grabbed a pair of diagonals and a box wrench and went to work like a whirlwind. Every one of the nine cylinders, each with about 20 studs holding it on, and each stud carefully safetied with wire, had to be removed and the entire engine had to be reassembled again. I stayed to watch and at 7:00 P.M. he was finished and left without saying good night.

I spent most of April in the Communications Department, familiarizing myself with the radio equipment on the planes. The radios had been designed by the chief communications engineer in New York, Mr. Hugo Leuteritz, and were made under his supervision. Mr. Trippe had obtained Leuteritz from General Sarnoff of RCA and he was supposed to be one of their top engineers. Trippe always obtained the outstanding experts in every field with this possible exception. The radio equipment seemed to me to be obsolete if not actually primitive.[3]

Interspersed with the mechanical training, we had a week in the downtown Traffic Office on the corner of Biscayne Boulevard to become familiar with reservations and sales procedures. We also had extensive training in seamanship with a very good ex-Navy instructor with us. We began with knots, ropes and anchors, and went on to life saving and ditching operations conducted in simulated forced landings with a seaplane out in Biscayne Bay. Finally we had written exams on the standard textbook, *Seamanship for the Merchant Marine*.

Then I was sent out on flights as radio operator and, after April 12th, I was on a daily Miami–Havana schedule, about two and a half hours each way. Along the Florida Keys, from above you could plainly see occasional giant turtles and their tracks along the beaches where they came up from the sea to lay their eggs. We would land in the inner harbor at Havana and taxi to the Pan Am Float at the Arsenal.

The station manager was Johnny Donahue. He had been Captain Ed Musick's mechanic. Captain Musick was now the chief pilot on the Pacific and, from his reputation (I had not yet met him), I believed him to be the best pilot in the world.

Musick had been a rum runner[4] as had several of the other captains, flying liquor in from the Bahamas and from the rum fleet which only had to stay three miles off shore in the early days of Prohibition. Warned in advance, Johnny Donahue would be waiting for Musick on the County Causeway at Miami. As Musick landed the flying boat and ran up on the causeway beach, a truck would materialize and, while the Coast Guard and other revenuers came tearing up in speed boats, Musick and Donahue would unload the cases into the truck. Minutes later, when the government men hit the beach, there would be no truck in sight, and a relaxed

Donahue and Musick would greet them with a present of a few bottles and a request "to lend a hand in pushing the seaplane back into the water".

In any comfortable spot in the tropics we would often find someone, frequently a gentleman, who had given up the "rat race" in the north and settled down to ease and rum. We called them TTs or Tropical Tramps. There was one such on the dock at the Arsenal in Havana, Captain Morgan. I would chat with him during my layovers there, and he got to like me. He told me he had been a Navy diver. When William Randolph Hearst publicized the sinking of the *Maine* in Havana harbor, the Navy had sent diver Morgan down to look at the wreck. He told me that all he could see was a hole. But when he came up and his diver's helmet was removed, he spoke up loud and clear and said, "Torpedoed"; and the Spanish American War was on. Another day, to show his gratitude to such an appreciative audience, he gave me a first-flight cover, an envelope from Pan American Airways in New York to Pan American Airways Inc. in Havana, Cuba, postmarked Key West, October 19th, 7:00 A.M., 1927, for the first U.S.A. foreign airmail flight.

One day on the Arsenal pier with Johnny Donahue I asked about Machado, a name still to be conjured with and maybe not even mentioned in Havana. Machado had been elected president in 1925. By 1930 he was well in control as a dictator in the best Latin American tradition. Opposed by Grau San Martín, he launched a very bloody reign of terror. Anyone opposing him was pushed down a chute into the sea from Morro Castle, where he would soon be collected by the well-fed sharks. Finally, his army revolted, and he escaped in a Cubana S-38 flown by Pan Am Captain McCullough from Campo Colombia, the military field near Havana. McCullough made it to a Bahama beach where they all spent the night, and eventually Machado went on to Miami where he lived until his death.

Captain Leo Terletzky had shown me a gold watch he had received from a Cuban official he too had flown out. I asked Dona-

hue about it. At the time Sanford Kauffman was the station manager and Donahue the station mechanic at Havana. Captain Leo
Terletzky (about whom more later) came in on the morning flight
in an S-40. Kauffman knew a revolution was brewing so he had
the captain and the crew stay on board at the mooring and warned
them to take off as quickly as possible if they saw a red flag waved
from the dock. When it was near departure time, and the passengers were being loaded from the launch, San Kauffman went out
with them to check the tickets. One passenger did not have a ticket.
San explained he could not go without one. "Oh yes I can", said
the passenger drawing a revolver. San got back into the launch. As
he and Donahue neared the dock shouts and shots were heard approaching the Arsenal. San rushed up to the second floor of the
office building and waved his red flag furiously out the window.
Down below, Johnny was still in the launch and the rebels ordered
him to go to the Clipper. "I just couldn't seem to get the engine
started", he told me. "I had removed the rotor from the distributor
and thrown it overboard".

Meanwhile the angry crowd had found San upstairs and were
deciding to hang him. Only the fortunate intercession of a brave
Cuban friend dissuaded them. Out at the mooring the co-pilot and
the flight mechanic were frenziedly trying to start the engines.
They had to be started by inertia starters which were cranked up
by hand. They got two engines started on the same side but, as fate
would have it, the other two wouldn't start. They had cast off but
the S-40 could not be steered in a straight line with only two engines on the same side. It went around in circles and each circle
brought it past the dock and under fire. Finally all four engines
were started and they got off safely. One bullet passed within six
inches of the captain's head, but no one on board was hurt. The
armed passenger, a fleeing official, was Herrera, the secretary of
the interior and chief of the secret police. It was he who gave
Captain Terletzky the gold watch.

Red flags were not unusual equipment at Pan Am stations. In El
Salvador in the Western Division there was a revolution every few

months. The Pan Am airport manager at San Salvador flew a red flag whenever a revolution was in progress and the Pan Am flight would pass up the stop.

Still flying as a radio operator, on April 21st I went to San Juan, Puerto Rico with an overnight stop at Port-au-Prince, Haiti; and two days in San Juan. We got an allowance of $4.00 for every overnight from Miami and paid our own expenses. Pan Am always reserved rooms for the crew at the best local hotel. At San Juan it was the Condado, quite beautiful, with waves crashing against the seawall at the edge of the outdoor dining terrace and dance floor. In Puerto Rico, the schools were bilingual but, even in the hotels, the Puerto Ricans would not speak English, only Spanish; and they hated North Americans.

There was a casino at the Condado as in almost every Caribbean and all South American hotels. Roulette was the usual, sometimes the only, game, and the chips were cheap. The tables were crowded all night and we learned to sleep to Latin music throbbing below our open windows. We came to love it. While the crew each paid only $2.50 or $3.00 a night for room and meals, the tourist rate began at $10.00 a night without meals.

At long last came my orders assigning me to flight duty beginning May 15, 1936. Until the start of the Apprentice Pilot program, there were only captains (that is first pilots) in the crew and the right hand seat was filled, not by a co-pilot, but by a "combination man", who was a licensed mechanic, a licensed radio operator and also held a pilot's license of some sort. These combination men had no real expectation of ever checking out as Pan Am captains. Only one had done so, Al Dreyer.

On the small twin-engine planes such as the S-38s, S-41s and the Commodores, the crew was two in the cockpit. There were no cabin attendants and there was not even a toilet in the small Sikorskys. The four-engine S-40 had a radio operator stationed in the cockpit, and the S-42 had both a radio operator and a flight mechanic in the cockpit. These larger planes which had toilets also carried cabin attendants who were all men and spoke fluent Spanish. A senior cabin attendant was called a purser.

At this time operations were always in daylight with no night flying in either division. Radio communications between plane and ground were only by Morse code, and hourly position reports were sent to the nearest of the net of Pan Am ground stations to be relayed back to Miami. Pan Am had its own meteorologists and weather station network as well as a communications system, at a time when the government was building airways in the U.S.A. for the domestic airlines. Pan Am, operating in foreign countries, had to build all its facilities at its own expense. The foreign countries provided nothing and demanded much paper work. Some stops required as many as 36 copies of the passenger and cargo manifests, for which we sometimes carried a mimeograph on board.

The apprentice pilot rank was conceived to make the small-plane flights totally self-sufficient. We carried a full toolbox, charts, radio message pads, operating manual, aircraft and engine manual, as well as a flashlight and pistol. The latter was required initially by a Post Office regulation, soon cancelled, because the pistol almost always was stolen down the line.

When the captain approached a mooring, we climbed down under the cockpit dash and into the bow, where we opened the hatch and stood by to pick up the buoy which we'd better not miss. There are no brakes on a seaplane and no water rudder; maneuvering was done by idling the outboard engines, momentarily cutting one or the other off with the magneto switch, called "blipping" it. A seaplane under way on the surface, approaching a buoy and barely moving, is very much wind-rode as well as tide-rode. There would be no going around again, nor time to anchor, especially in a narrow river where landings were usually made. Missing the buoy could mean grounding on shore.

The weakest link in the training of apprentice pilots was as radio operators. It is impossible to make a good, fast operator of just anyone. Hence the old joke "that you don't have to be crazy to be a radio operator but it helps". Strict orders from Mr. Leuteritz in New York, the chief communications engineer, forbade meddling in any way with the radio equipment and the operators were required to use the standard telegraph key and to write all messages in pencil.

At first I only operated the radio on the big S-40s. Being somewhat better at code than most apprentice pilots, I carried a typewriter on board to type incoming messages, and I brought my own "bug" key for transmitting. (A bug is a high speed key used by professionals.) I became well-known among the professional ground station operators who were patient and long-suffering, as they got messages to and from the apprentice pilots, many of whom had quite unreadable "fists". In spite of being in direct disobedience of regulations by using a typewriter and a bug, I got away with it because of support from the division communications department and because I was a pilot.

Just before I became a co-pilot officially, I went out on a familiarization trip to Mérida, Yucatán in an S-38. The S-38 was the most famous of the Sikorsky amphibians. The wheels were pumped up and down by a hydraulic hand pump in the cockpit, which was separated from the passenger cabin by a bulkhead with openings through which one could climb into the cabin. There were eight passenger seats, a mail compartment, no toilet and no washing facility. Box lunches and coffee were served by the co-pilot who climbed into the cabin from the cockpit.

The route took us to Havana and then to San Julián in the middle of western Cuba where the field was a grass strip, unfenced and occupied by cows which had to be driven off by the owner when he saw the plane coming. The refuelling there was done from a couple of 55-gallon drums with a pump worked by the co-pilot. Then we went on to Cozumel, a Mexican island just off the western end of Yucatán, and we terminated at Mérida, flying over the Maya ruins at Chichén-Itzá where archaeologists were then working.[5]

In a letter home I wrote: "They grow a kind of grass in Yucatán called hennikin or sisal from which rope is made, almost as good as Manila hemp. During World War I, when there was a shortage of hemp, the demand for this sisal made millionaires of the ranchers in Mérida. There was no railroad nor road to Mexico City, but there was a steamship line to New Orleans, which enabled the ranchers to spend their money in the U.S.A. and abroad. We saw their palaces along the Avenida Montejo in Mérida, some costing

Author in cockpit of P-12 at Kelly Field

Randolph Field, San Antonio, Texas

B Stage Hangar Line, Inspection, Randolph Field

Keystone B-6 bomber

Formation flying at Randolph

Formation flying for the movies

Loading practice bombs on a B-6 at Langley Field

Fokker F-7

Consolidated Commodore

Sikorsky S-38

Sikorsky S-40

Sikorsky S-42

Sikorsky S-43

Pan Am seaplane base at Dinner Key, Miami, Florida

Hangar at Dinner Key

S-43 at Trinidad

Frederick Street, Port of Spain, Trinidad

Caripito, Venezuela

Guanta, Venezuela

Cumarebo, Venezuela

Maracaibo, Venezuela

SCADTA hangar at
Barranquilla, Colombia

France Field, Canal Zone

Commodore at Key West

Medellín, Colombia

Fairchild 91
used between
Belém and Manaos

Pan Am base, Alameda

Goyette with sextant

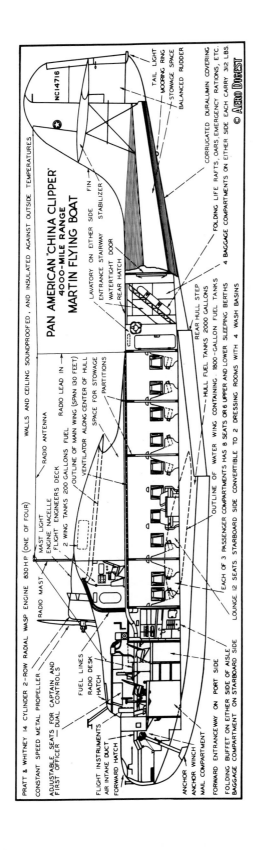

PRATT & WHITNEY 14 CYLINDER 2-ROW RADIAL WASP ENGINE 830 H.P. (ONE OF FOUR)

CONSTANT SPEED METAL PROPELLER

WALLS AND CEILING SOUNDPROOFED, AND INSULATED AGAINST OUTSIDE TEMPERATURES

ADJUSTABLE SEATS FOR CAPTAIN AND
FIRST OFFICER — DUAL CONTROLS

RADIO MAST

RADIO ANTENNA

RADIO LEAD IN

MAST LIGHT
ENGINE NACELLE
FLIGHT ENGINEERS DECK
2 WING TANKS 200 GALLONS FUEL

OUTLINE OF MAIN WING (SPAN 130 FEET)

VENTILATOR ALONG CENTER OF HULL

SPACE FOR STOWAGE
PARTITIONS

FUEL LINES

RADIO DESK

HATCH

FLIGHT INSTRUMENTS
AIR INTAKE DUCT
FORWARD HATCH

ANCHOR
ANCHOR WINCH
MAIL COMPARTMENT

FORWARD ENTRANCEWAY ON PORT SIDE

FOLDING BUFFET ON EITHER SIDE OF AISLE
BAGGAGE COMPARTMENT ON STARBOARD SIDE

OUTLINE OF WATER WING CONTAINING. 1800-GALLON FUEL TANKS

HULL FUEL TANKS 2000 GALLONS

REAR HULL STEP

EACH OF 3 PASSENGER COMPARTMENTS HAS 8 SEATS OR 6 UPPER AND LOWER SLEEPING BERTHS

LOUNGE 12 SEATS. STARBOARD SIDE CONVERTIBLE TO 2 DRESSING ROOMS WITH 4 WASH BASINS

PAN AMERICAN "CHINA CLIPPER"
4000-MILE RANGE
MARTIN FLYING BOAT

LAVATORY ON EITHER SIDE FIN
ENTRANCE STAIRWAY STABILIZER
WATERTIGHT DOOR
REAR HATCH

CORRUGATED DURALUMIN COVERING

FOLDING LIFE RAFTS, OARS, EMERGENCY RATIONS, ETC.

4 BAGGAGE COMPARTMENTS ON EITHER SIDE EACH CARRY 312 LBS.

TAIL LIGHT
MOORING RING
STOWAGE SPACE
BALANCED RUDDER

NC14716

© AERO DIGEST

Vic Wright at navigation station

Bob Fordyce in cockpit

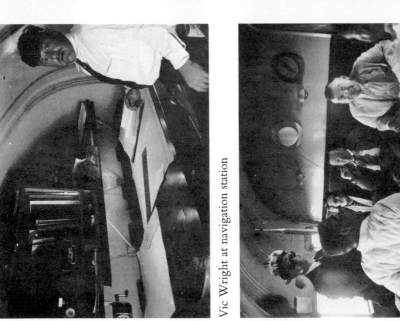

Purser with passengers in main lounge

Howard Cone at flight engineer's station

a million or more dollars each, with beautiful tiles, tapestries and paintings, and their owners spoke English, French and Italian as well as Spanish".

After an overnight at a good hotel in Mérida where the menu featured quail and little else, even for breakfast, we flew to Belize, the capital of British Honduras, a small jungle town on the Gulf Coast. Guatemala, an independent Central American republic, claimed its boundaries included British Honduras and printed a map on all its postage stamps which included British Honduras, but the British did not recognize the claim.

I had one other familiarization flight as a radio operator, which was across the middle of the Caribbean to Barranquilla, Colombia. We flew a Commodore to Havana, then to Cienfuegos on the south shore of Cuba, and then across to Kingston, Jamaica where we stayed overnight at the Myrtle Bank Hotel. We always took off at sunrise so as to be sure of landing before sunset. It was against regulations to land after sunset and, when it was close, violent altercations would arise between the station manager and the captain as to whether the sun had or had not set before he landed. Any infraction was reported to Mr. Priester in New York.

Our longest overwater hop from Kingston to Barranquilla required dead reckoning with great precision. The northeast trades blow hard across the Caribbean so that, by flying low at perhaps 500 feet or less, and with skill in estimating the wind direction and velocity from the whitecaps, we could usually hit Barranquilla on the nose. We carried little reserve fuel and there was no alternate, and we had to get in before sunset.

Barranquilla is at the mouth of the Río Magdalena, a huge river which comes down from Bogotá far up in the Cordilleras. Bogotá is at 8,660 feet—a peak nearby rises to 17,717 feet—the rivers on the east side of the mountains run down to the Amazon. There were neither house numbers nor street names in Bogotá. But the intersections were always named plazas, and mail was addressed to the family near such and such a plaza. Barranquilla is the Colombian port on the Caribbean and SCADTA, a German airline, was based there, manned entirely by Germans. Trippe had acquired control of SCADTA in 1931 but we did not know this at the time. It flew corrugated metal, single-engine Junkers on floats around some of the roughest terrain in the world. With the coming of the war, the Germans were considered a threat to the Panama Canal and SCADTA was closed down and disbanded. Incidentally, alone among foreign airlines in South America, it had a concession which allowed it to issue its own airmail stamps.

Large, wood-burning, paddle-wheel steamers travelled the Magdalena like Mark Twain's Mississippi, and great rafts of logs and islands of driftwood floating down made aircraft landings fairly hazardous. We stayed at a good hotel, and the next day flew the Commodore to Cristobal, Canal Zone and returned to Barranquilla. At Cristobal, a Western Division base, I met my first Brownsville associates, Captains Ham Smith and George Doole who were operating a shuttle across the Canal which they called the Critty-Pitty-Critty run for Cristobal, Panama City, Cristobal, with a tri-motor Ford which was even then becoming a museum piece.

Each end of the Canal has twin cities, one in the Canal Zone under U.S. jurisdiction, and the other across the street in the Republic of Panama. On the Caribbean which is the west end, believe it or not, because of the S shape of the Isthmus, and is on the same meridian of longitude as Miami, the cities are Cristobal (U.S.) and Colón, and, on the other end, they are Balboa (U.S.) and Panama City. The shops and shopkeepers in Panama were almost all East Indians, with a few Chinese. Before the Canal, a railroad was built across the Isthmus (1848–1855) with imported Chinese coolie labor, and one Chinese is said to have died for each tie in the railroad. The almost daily afternoon thunderstorms in Panama must be seen to be believed—it rains so hard that visibility is literally zero. The maximum wind and average wind in the Canal Zone are said to be three miles an hour.

My very first flight with Pan Am had been as a passenger to Havana when on vacation from Yale with my friend Ernest Brooks in 1929. It was on a tri-motor Fokker with Captain Bob Fatt. I remember being enchanted with Havana. We stayed at the country club, promenaded on the Malecón at twilight, smoked Coronas, danced on marble floors out of doors to a rhumba with girls we met at the club, and lost our hearts to the Latin American tropics. But the city had its sad side. Hordes of beggars, mostly urchins, tugged at your clothes everywhere you went. Havana then had more and more persistent beggars than any city in the world.

On May 22, 1936 I was returning to Havana again, this time as co-pilot on a huge S-40 with Captain Leo Terletzky. Terletzky was a Russian of medium height, slender, always immaculately turned out, with a somewhat olive complexion and a small, neat moustache. He always wore a supercilious half-smile which suggested a Russian aristocratic background. We left at ten in the morning and would return from Havana at 3:00 P.M. The captain landed in Havana harbor and we taxied up to the float. At three in the afternoon we cast off to return.

I had already learned that the discipline exacted by the Pan Am captains was about what it was in the British Navy under Nelson. They did not speak to co-pilots and treated them with practiced contempt, especially Terletzky. On the return flight from Havana when we went into a large cloud on instruments, Terletzky completely lost control of the aircraft and, to make it worse, was obviously scared. I remained indecisive. Terletzky had not spoken to me all day, not even to reply to my "Good morning, Captain". If I took over the controls I might expect to be shot. Some moments later we came out of the cloud headed in the opposite direction. Terletzky recovered and we proceeded safely to Miami. The passengers out of Havana were much too full of Bacardi to notice anything.

After arrival and checking in, I was trudging up the hill from Dinner Key to Mr. Critchley's office (he was the operations manager) to resign, when I met a very good looking, cheerful young man coming down the hill. He did a double take when he saw my expression, stopped and said: "I'm Tex Walker. What's the matter?" I knew of him, another and very popular apprentice pilot senior to me. I said: "I'm on my way to the operations manager's office to hand in my resignation. I'm quitting". "Ah", said Tex,

"First flight with Terletzky. Don't", he went on, "We've all been through it. You'll survive". (As will be seen later, neither Terletzky nor Tex did survive.) So I changed my mind and stayed.

Back in New York my top boss was the chief engineer, André Priester, another extraordinary man. Trippe had obtained him indirectly from Dr. Albert Plesman, the head of the Dutch KLM Airline, the most respected airline in the world at that time. Priester, a Dutchman, spoke English with a thick, not easily understood accent. He was a complete dictator in flight and ground operations, ruling pilots, mechanics and station managers with an iron hand. He was said to keep a picture of every pilot in his office to refer to if his name ever came up. No pilot could be hired or fired without his approval. It was Priester who goaded the principal airplane manufacturers to produce the planes Trippe needed to cross the Atlantic and Pacific Oceans.

Every Christmas each pilot received a Christmas card from Mr. Priester. Rather obscurely on the card could be found two little numbers, perhaps .87 in the upper right hand corner and .55 in the upper left. For the many pilots with some aeronautical training, the meanings were obvious. The upper right referred to propeller efficiency and the upper left to specific fuel consumption, efficiencies not yet obtainable. Just as the Wright brothers had known that successful heavier-than-air flight would depend on a lighter engine and a more efficient propeller than any then in existence, so Priester would predict the specific fuel consumption (pounds per brake horsepower per hour) and the propeller efficiency which the manufacturers would have to achieve to make Trippe's dream of a world-wide airline possible. I suppose he hoped the little figures would encourage designers who saw them.

Priester was a dedicated American, fanatically so, and like so many others among our most valued citizens who were born abroad and never lost their foreign accents, he was sensitive to insult as they all were. They were never permitted to criticize anything American without promptly being told, "If you don't like it here, why don't you go back where you came from?" This common, hard hat, middle class comment was like a red flag to a bull.

Priester felt deeply that the foreign born were discriminated against and that there wasn't going to be any such discrimination in his department.

Terletzky once told me that he was afraid of flying but the only thing he feared more was telling Seppy, his wife, who had been dean of women at Sarah Lawrence College. He had escaped from Russia by joining the Americans under General Graves, then commanding the American forces in Siberia. They withdrew via China from where Terletzky got to the U.S. through American connections. He worked as a mechanic for General Motors and, in time, presumably having had some flying instruction in Russia, he ran an airport at Armonk, New York, taking people up for rides. Mr. Priester hired him as one of the first pilots.

During the first four and one-half months of training on the ground, never touching the controls of a plane, I pined to fly something. So did some of the others. There was a local Army Air Corps Reserve field called Chapman Field near Miami. I persuaded Andy Anderson, another ex-Army apprentice pilot, to have his Army records, along with mine, transferred to Chapman Field where the only plane they had was an old PT-3A. Anderson and I sort of took it over from the commanding officer who had used it for his private airplane and made it ours. Then I bombarded the chief of the Air Corps in Washington with demands for the latest pursuit plane to be based at Chapman to maintain the proficiency of the numerous Air Reserve pilots in Pan Am. I received courteous replies, but we got no new plane.

Throughout June, July, August and September I flew with Captains Titus, Rowe, Ekstrom, Adams, Cluthe, Person, Swinson, Pat Nolan, Craine, McGlohn, Culbertson, Clark, Keeler, Lorber, Nixon, Dewey, Doxey, Snow and Harold Gray. Many of these were shortly to go to the Pacific where I would see them again. I also made two more trips with Terletzky and grew to like him. He was a gentleman and it was hard not to be fascinated both by him and his background, although he would talk little about it. Terletzky, who was now an American citizen, was similar to other less fortunate escapees from the Russian Revolution whom I was to meet later in China. You could find out nothing about their past. They never talked of it, even among themselves, as far as I know. Devoted to their motherland—their entire world collapsed around them—they had abolished the past, cut it off completely and totally from their minds.

I went to Key West and back, our shortest run; to Nassau where I felt I might some day retire; to San Juan via Antilla on the north coast of Cuba, Port-au-Prince, and San Pedro de Macorís in Santo Domingo; to Barranquilla and Cristóbal; and to Belize in British Honduras.

We stopped on demand at Cat Cay, the next cay south of Bimini on the way to Nassau. It was a famous club for game fishermen who fished the Gulf Stream for sail fish, blue marlins and even giant sharks. It was then famous as Ernest Hemingway's residence. Once we took his son over and Ernest Hemingway came out to the Commodore in an outboard, as we had no dock, and just hove to in the brilliant blue and green water. Hemingway never even slowed down as he came alongside, but fortunately hit a pontoon which survived and stove in the outboard which sank. We hauled Hemingway and a friend aboard and then beached the Commodore to unload.

A trip with Harold Gray was always an event. He had one of the finest engineering minds I was ever to know. Gray plied you with mathematical puzzles and engineering problems that kept you very much on your toes mentally. Working with Admiral Rickover on a nuclear submarine many years later was said to be a similar experience.[6]

In the cockpit, above the loud drone of the engines, Gray would put simple mathematical problems to his co-pilot simply to try and teach him to think like an engineer, if he wasn't one. A very simple example is this one: If you are driving along a highway averaging 60 miles an hour, and you come to a 2-mile hill, one mile up and one mile down on the other side, and you are slowed down to 30 mph on the climb, how fast must you drive down the other side to regain your average of 60 mph? The engineering mind would answer immediately that it was impossible, but the non-engineering mind would argue about 90 or even 120 mph. Gray would say nothing, leaving it always up to the co-pilot to figure it out for himself.

A more appropriate problem might be: Suppose you are flying a shuttle between LaGuardia (N.Y.) and Logan (Boston). Does it make any difference to the round-trip time and the fuel required if you have a 30 mph wind directly on your tail one way, and directly on your nose on the return? The non-engineer would say: "Certainly not. The wind would cancel out". The engineer would just laugh, knowing that it always took longer on a round trip with any wind from any direction than with no wind at all.

We rarely had any trouble with a passenger although I was always a little alarmed when a Federal marshal would remove the handcuffs of a boarding passenger at Cristobal in the Canal Zone, and turn him over to me, the co-pilot, to be delivered to another marshal in Miami. There was no Federal prison in the Canal Zone, so felons were sent back, via Pan Am, of course, to prison in the States. The only remembered case of a drunken and really troublesome passenger occurred with Captain Gray in a Commodore. Gray got out of the cockpit, went aft and slugged the culprit, knocking him out and also, unfortunately, nearly knocking him through the side of the plane which required extensive repair before its next trip.

Captain Slim Ekstrom was a Swede, tall with striking blond hair. I remember once in Havana a Swedish cruise boat was entering as we were taxiing out for takeoff. The cockpit hatch in the S-40 was overhead. So he opened it and, standing up like a Viking, discoursed in Swedish with the steamer captain who came out on the bridge while every living soul on board crowded the rail to watch us. There was a little drama on every flight. Slim stuttered badly, very badly. There was a story that one day, about to land in a restricted area, he called to the co-pilot for flaps, as usual. His order went like this, "Put down putputputputput Oh, Hell", and he landed without flaps.

In addition to all the training, mostly mechanical, in Pan Am's shops, we also had to take an extensive series of courses set up by the International Correspondence Schools for Pan Am, 33 in all. We were indeed busy the first year and even more so thereafter when we got to the Pacific. Our chief engineer, Mr. Priester, was determined to see that Pan Am pilots were the most knowledgeable anywhere.

I had been told by Mr. Critchley that I would soon be transferred to either Trinidad or San Francisco. There was no pilots' union then, no bidding on assignments and no choices for apprentice pilots who were always on probation. One went where one was told. On October 7, 1936 I was transferred to Trinidad to go down on the first S-43 being sent there. With the transfer my pay would be raised to $175.00 a month, and I would also get a $25.00 a month foreign station allowance, one-third of the allowance to be paid in local currency. After arrival I would get $5.00 a day for the maximum of seven days to find a place to live. I would replace apprentice pilot Lloyd Osborne who had been there about six months, leaving George Davis, Bob Gibson and me.

The Sikorsky twin-engine S-43 amphibians just being delivered to Miami to replace the old S-38s and S-41s, were much more complex and so we had to spend a lot of time training on the new equipment. The S-43 had a complex hydraulic system to operate the landing gear and flaps, electric trim tabs for ailerons and rudder, and an adjustable stabilizer. Newest of all, it had the first controllable pitch propellers.

Of course the captains were checked out on flying the planes, but it was doubtful if most of them knew exactly how the new gadgets worked. Certainly the station mechanics down the line knew nothing about the S-43s. For the first time the co-pilots would be vital to the operation, trouble shooting and maintenance of the new planes.

I flew to Port of Spain, Trinidad with Captain Craig on a ferry flight of the first S-43. We left Miami October 17, spent the night in San Juan and arrived the next day.

PORT OF SPAIN

Trinidad was a British possession with the majority of the population East Indians, many Negroes and a few Chinese. The Pan Am seaplane base was at Cocorite, a coastal suburb just north of the city. Four crews were based there and we had three S-38s and an S-41 in addition to the first S-43. By January, 1937 we had five S-43s.

There were no apartments in Port of Spain, so I moved into the same boarding house at 5 St. Clair Street with another co-pilot, George Davis. The landlady was Sheila Nothnagel, a plain, middle-aged and kindly widow who gave us tea mornings and afternoons, making five meals a day. An egg for breakfast was sixpence extra. The main meat at dinner was offal. I was afraid to ask what it was for quite a few weeks, but finally found out it was the insides of a cow, sheep or goat—just the entrails. As a change we often had turtle.

The house had no windows or screens, just jalousies. It was very hot, and we slept under nets. The local black servants were scared of hot water because they thought it would give them a cold or pneumonia. Only the tea water was ever boiled. I do not even remember having hot water to shave with. Cooking was always done in a pot on a tripod out of doors over a small wood fire. The other boarders included a British Public Health doctor who constantly complained about the Rockefeller Institute doctors who were making much of South America healthier and more habitable. He thought it should be healthier but only for the British— the more natives who died the better. There were also two boys who boarded at the house while going to the university in town. Sometimes we played cricket with them.

I wrote home, "The country looks quite lovely until you get to know it. There are mountains and all over grow orchids, bougain-villea, flame trees, giant poinsettias, jasmine, palms and great mahogany trees. But beneath are so many venomous bugs, snakes, vampire bats and mosquitoes, etc., that you don't dare to step back off the roads into the country, and it's folly to sleep, even on hot nights, without a net over the bed". One of our pilots had become paralyzed not long before in Trinidad. He was said to have paralytic rabies, carried by vampire bats who would come in at night and suck your blood. Also, when we took the trolley car downtown, the rear seats were reserved for the lepers; and it made us nervous until we got used to it.

I once had William Beebe, the naturalist and herpetologist, as a passenger on a flight from the U.S.A.; he was coming to Trinidad to catch a bushmaster. He told me it was the only snake known which would chase a man, following him in the bush by the side of the road until it was ready to strike. On such authority one was reluctant to explore the back country. When Captain Ford was out one day, Davis and I did talk Mrs. Ford, a very pretty blonde, into taking a walk with us to the top of the mountain range on the north along a jungle trail. There were no roads. We saw no snakes but did see two large furry rodents, a manicou and an agouti, harmless local animals.[7] Hot and tired when we returned to the Ford's house, we prepared for a swim off their dock. Betty casually mentioned she had caught a seven foot barracuda off the dock the day before. We did not swim.

Port of Spain had an English country club with tennis courts and a golf course. One played golf with three caddies each, very small boys—one to run ahead and shoo away the goats and live stock which kept the grass short, one to find your ball and one to carry your clubs. Similarly at tennis which we played often, we always had ball boys. It was very hot and there was rarely even the feeblest breeze. Even though we were all very fit, I doubt if we would have played tennis if we had had to pick up the balls.

The Pan Am route was across the top of South America to the Canal Zone and back, three times a week at first. We stopped at Caripito, Guanta, La Guaira, Cumarebo and Maracaibo in Venezuela, and at Barranquilla in Colombia where we spent the night. Next day we went to Cristóbal, past Cartagena where I landed once. I longed to see it because it was the departure point for the Spanish galleons going home, laden with Atahualpa's gold.

Most of the Venezuelan stops were at oil camps and the fields we

landed on were rough. We landed on the water only at Port of
Spain, Guanta, and on Lake Maracaibo where we landed in a forest
of oil derricks which were drilling or pumping day and night in
the shallow lake. It was then considered, I think, the biggest oil
field in the world.

In Venezuela most of the talk was about oil. La Guaira was the
port for Caracas, the capital, to which a road ran from sea level
almost straight up to 3,000 feet. At that time it was one of the most
dramatic mountain roads in the world, paved, with hairpin turns
and two-way, but guarded by no fence, with an almost vertical
drop on one side. At Barranquilla the talk would run to the Bar-
quisimeto pipeline in Venezuela, an engineering miracle whereby
oil from the fields was pumped up a pipeline over the mountains
and down to the sea. This was the engineering forerunner of the
Trans Arabian pipeline and the new one in Alaska.

Pan Am was the only transportation along the north coast. Local
people waited months for our air freight delivery of a stove or re-
frigerator. When they boarded us to travel, they moved with all
their household pots and pans, chickens, children and relatives.
Sometimes it was only a small S-38, but we packed them in and
we, the co-pilots, fed them their box lunches and coffee. They
were indescribably dirty and, lacking any toilet on board, they just
used their seats. They stuffed the seat pillow between the legs of
their children as sort of an over-stuffed diaper. Thank God natives
cleaned the planes for us.

One day, to sightsee, we diverted a little south of our course
along the coast and went by the top of Santa Marta coming into
Barranquilla. It was 18,947 feet (according to the map) and we had
no oxygen. The top few thousand feet were snow covered, and as
we flew close alongside it was a beautiful and exciting sight. I remember it took the S-43 a long time to get up there. The captain
and I kept a close watch on the passengers who luckily were still
alive and well when we landed in Barranquilla.

Other than the few natives, most of our passengers were oil field
workers who were always extra large and extremely strong. Furthermore, when on their way home to the States or on leave, they

would get very drunk. As passengers they made me and others rather nervous, but we never had any trouble. They were meek, cooperative, obedient and always smiling.

In January a new extension was tacked onto our route so that, from Panama, we flew back and down to Turbo on the coast where Colombia meets Panama and then flew straight up to Medellín at 5,000 feet. It was maximum rate of climb all the way and a mountain close by rose to 13,396 feet. Medellín sits behind the Cordillera Central in the interior of Colombia. It was old Spain, ancient and beautiful, unchanged in several hundred years; and there were thousands of orchids everywhere. These trips were fun, but if one engine ever failed, we had nowhere to go but down and probably nowhere to land. We could never have gotten back to the sea.

At Port of Spain our days off were spent at the nose hangar working on the planes. The only local mechanics were East Indians. The chief was a very cheery young man named Toolsie and, since none of them had licenses and the CAA required a licensed mechanic to certify all major repair work and major services, on our days at work we would have to inspect, sign for and be responsible for all the maintenance.

President Roosevelt stopped at Port of Spain on his way south to the Buenos Aires Conference on the cruiser *Indianapolis* but he did not come ashore. However, on his way back he did. It was on a day off for me and I was down at the waterfront to see the show. The cruiser anchored close in, in sight of the crowd, with Roosevelt standing at the rail. He came ashore in a launch and got into an open car for the parade. It was incredibly done. At no time during his movements from the deck into the launch, or from the launch into the car, could anyone see that he was crippled. No one would have ever known that he had braces and couldn't walk. When he moved, a group of Secret Service men, Navy officers and others would surround him and he would become invisible for a few seconds.

The day of his visit was hot and sweltering. The Trinidad guard of honor was mounted on beautifully polished horses, every bit of brass and leather gleaming. The mounted black men had plumed helmets, and not one of them, nor one of the horses, ever moved. Not a flick of a tail, all were as motionless as statues. It was most impressive. I pushed through the densely packed crowd, the biggest Port of Spain had ever seen, and suddenly noticed some other men were pushing through the crowd, slightly ahead of the car carrying the waving Roosevelt. They were unusually big men. Suddenly a black man in the crowd near me reached into his hip pocket for a handkerchief to mop his dripping brow. One of the big men just ahead of me glided over as the arm reached for the pocket, moving as fast as if there hadn't been a crowd, and took the arm. The black man, also large and powerful looking, turned around surprised. One look and he just relaxed, for he saw someone who could break his arm or his neck without trying, and he knew it. In the 1932 election campaign at a political rally in Bay Front Park in Miami, an assassin had fired at Roosevelt and missed, but hit and killed Mayor Cermak of Chicago who was next to him. There wasn't going to be any repeat in Port of Spain.

I had visitors occasionally. My mother and my Aunt Julia Henry stopped by on a cruise, and I was very glad to see them as by now I was appreciating home more every day. I had written my mother my impressions of South America and she had sent me everything she could find on it. I particularly enjoyed Prescott's *Conquest of Mexico* and *Conquest of Peru*, *The Pageant of Cuba* by Hudson Strode, *South America* by James Bryce and *Sunlight in New Granada* by McFee.

My last trip was to Pará (Belém); it marked the end of my Trinidad tour of duty. The captain was A. G. Person, and we stopped at the three Guianas, Georgetown in British, Paramaribo in Dutch (Surinam), and Cayenne in French Guiana with Devil's Island just off shore. Next to Ile du Diable, were three little islands called Père Ile, Mère Ile, and Enfant Perdu. The three Guiana capitals were incredibly dirty and hot; we landed in rivers and refuelled from gas drums on Pan Am barges. Still, the Guianas had a certain mystique about them because of Devil's Island and the stories of diamonds and emeralds dredged from the rivers by the bucketful.[8]

The route into Pará, on the south side of the Amazon estuary, crossed Marajó Island, which lies in the 200 mile wide mouth of the river. The Amazon is 4,000 miles long and the drop is only 100 feet from Manaos to the mouth. There is little current but the huge volume of water coming down from the Cordilleras, only a hundred miles from the Pacific, makes the ocean drinkable for over 100 miles out to sea, as the earlier explorers discovered.

Pan Am was then operating a service up the Amazon with Fairchild, single-engine amphibians flown by a singularly colorful group of captains, chief of whom was Steve Bancroft. The flight followed the river from Pará to Manaos, the old rubber port 800 miles up from the sea. Manaos had been built by millionaires who made their money by having a monopoly on the world's rubber when automobiles were becoming plentiful. It boasted a famous opera house built of Italian marble where European companies performed. But one day the rubber seed was taken to Indonesia where it flourished, and the bubble burst. The Ford Company tried to cultivate rubber along the Amazon and a town called Fordlandia grew up, but the project failed.

Captain Bancroft, now a legend in this part of Brazil, was a Pensacola trained pilot, totally fearless and very tough. Annoyed for some reason by Customs at Miami, he packed in his bag a cardboard box stuffed with tarantulas, rather venomous and particularly terrifying looking spiders. "What's in the box?", said the inspector. "None of your Goddamn business", said Bancroft. Inspectors were not used to being talked to that way, but Bancroft didn't look like the kind who could be arrested easily, so the box was opened and a dozen or so of these huge, hairy spiders crawled out and onto the floor of the Customs area. In no time the place was evacuated. Customs officials, passengers, porters and guards all vanished. Customs never opened Bancroft's bags again.

One day, taxiing upstream on the Amazon to a barge to take on more gas, he saw a very large anaconda swimming. Cutting off the engine, taking off his coat and shoes and leaving the plane and passengers to the co-pilot, he dove out and took off after the snake. No piranhas (a very vicious fish found in the Amazon) would bother Bancroft. Catching up with the anaconda, he seized it by the neck and attempted to pull it to the dock. The snake was help- less, needing a tree to wrap its tail around and it headed for the bank. But Bancroft was more powerful and made it to the barge with his anaconda which he later took to Miami to live with him. The Miami police forcibly removed it one day with a hand picked squad of officers, and rumor says that it took more of them to handle Bancroft than the anaconda.

Pará was not a nice place to live. No breeze ever blew, and an occasional thunderstorm would only make it hotter. A sweet smell of rubber pervaded the waterfront from the piles of bales. We would sit at little tables on the street in front of the hotel, under the towering mango trees which lined the main street, carefully keeping at the outer edge because a mango would fall occasionally and would crack your skull if it hit you. We drank only beer which was served in pitchers or newly corked bottles from the brewery nearby. Water, bottled or otherwise, we never touched. Meals in the dining room were always accompanied by music. A piano and two violins played, except at breakfast; and the dining room didn't open until the music started.

The captains never drank on duty, and I never saw one of them the slightest bit inebriated in flight. Only a very few drank heavily, whiskey or rum, after arrival, going to their rooms and not ap- pearing again until the next morning at breakfast, when they showed up fresh and bright. One could hardly blame those who did, considering the violent tropical storms from which they never turned back, considering that dead reckoning was their only means of navigation and that an engine failure over many parts of their routes might mean death for everyone. There was no air-sea rescue service then in existence, nor any other rescue services like the U.S. Coast Guard in South America. We, the co-pilots, had com- plete confidence in them and we didn't worry much; but they must have. They had wives and children; we didn't, and it made a difference.

Only once, in Port-au-Prince, did I have to wake up the captain in the morning, get him shaved and dressed and down to the plane and into his seat with the help of the station manager. Once there he went sound asleep again. After the passengers had boarded, I got the engines started—always hoping he would wake up—and I made the takeoff. I shook him most of the way to San Pedro de Macorís and he woke up for the landing which I wasn't too sure about if I had to do it myself. I do not remember any trip ever not going through on schedule, and I doubt if any other airline in the world could have said that then.

Every six months we had booster inoculations for typhoid, paratyphoid, tetanus; and later on for typhus, cholera and plague. In addition, we would go to the U.S. Public Health station every two years to have yellow fever shots. We survived dysentery because, I suppose, we followed the rules which were strictly drilled into us: no uncooked vegetables, no raw fruit except what we peeled ourselves, no water and no ice. I would rather not remember some of the hotels at small towns along the way. The bathrooms would be no more than a piece of cement floor with a drain in the center which served as a toilet. A small spigot overhead might or might not dribble cold water for a shower. Used toilet paper was always put in a box in the corner and was valued for fertilizer. I was not to fly this coast again until 1940 and there had been many improvements by then.

The company doctor in Miami, Dr. McDonald, must have been very good. Except for the one case of paralytic rabies in Trinidad, no one was ever sick. Once quite a few pilots did get an ear fungus which was painful and very hard to treat and cure. It was thought to come from the swimming pool at the Condado in Puerto Rico and all pools were proscribed for a time. A few years later, Douglas Moody, then an apprentice pilot and working on the beaching crew at Dinner Key, had his hand hit by a still rotating propeller. It was badly mangled. Dr. McDonald had him rushed to the hospital while he sought a competent surgeon. He needed the best and happened to know of three long-retired and living in Miami. One was too full of martinis and didn't dare to operate. The second could not be retrieved from a golf course. The third was gotten in from a golf game and operated on Doug. It was an extraordinary job, several jobs, and what at first looked like a certain amputation finally looked normal again with no movement impaired.

Pan Am, with its company doctors as with everything else, took exceptionally good care of its employees. Such care was unique for persons sent to the remote parts of the world where we worked. When I first left Philadelphia to take the job with Pan Am I asked my family physician, Dr. McCloskey, to get me the name of a reputable doctor in Miami. After several days of investigation, he told me if I got sick in Florida to get out of the state as fast as possible. But Pan Am had the exception.

Our jobs as pilots involved special problems. There were, of course, sailing charts, hydrographic charts and the coast charts issued by the U.S. Coast and Geodetic Survey. These ocean charts were of little use due to the lack of details of the shores of the adjacent land. We were reduced to maps issued by the National Geographic Society and school-book atlases. Mostly, we drew in prominent features of terrain as well as courses and distances on any maps we could obtain. My mother used to send me ones she got at a map store in Philadelphia. The USC&G chart which I used on this first Pará trip was only a strip cut from the full chart. I noticed on it a landmark which said, "Big Tree", on the dotted shore shown between the Orinoco and Marajó Island. Obviously there were no trees along this coast, only mangrove swamps and no identifiable shoreline for hundreds of miles. When I got to Miami, I looked for and found a copy of the entire chart (we always cut them into strips as they were easier to handle in the cockpit) and promptly sought the lower, left hand, bottom corner where the legend was, and under it, in fine print, the source was given as "From Surveys by Magellan".[9]

Back in Miami I got orders transferring me to Alameda, California, which meant the Pacific Division. My overdue vacation was cancelled, and I was to report to Captain Wallace D. Culbertson, as first officer, to go in a Commodore needed on the west coast for instrument flight training and navigation practice. A quite new world would be opening up to me, and it was exciting. But how on earth would we get there in a Commodore flying boat?

On April 13th I left Miami with Captain Culbertson, a flight engineer, and a radio operator. The captain decided to cross the continent at the Isthmus of Tehuantepec, the narrowest part of Mexico, only about 135 miles wide, where the continental divide is not very high. A valley cuts across the Isthmus and it is known for violent wind storms called Tehuantepeckers.

Our first night was spent at Carmen, Mexico, just below Campeche on the Yucatán coast. It provided a nice sheltered lake and had Compania Mexicana personnel to look after the plane. At this time Mexicana operated from Mérida, where we stopped, to Campeche, Vera Cruz and up to Mexico City. From there Aerovias Centrales, also owned by Pan Am, operated up the west coast of Mexico to Los Angeles, providing a through flight from coast to coast for Pan Am, albeit a rather roundabout one.

Going via Tehuantepec was about 2,000 miles shorter than going via the Panama Canal Zone, and was about 1,600 miles shorter than crossing Nicaragua, which has a big lake in the middle that would have shortened the overland distance to only about 65 miles.

Our second day, crossing the Isthmus of Tehuantepec uneventfully, we turned north and came to Acapulco for our second overnight. It was as beautiful then as now but not yet discovered by the Hollywood crowd. We stayed in the only hotel, a first class one, just above the cliff from which boys made spectacular dives into the ocean far below to retrieve peso coins we would throw down for them.

Our third night was spent at Mazatlán, a sport fisherman's resort, where the talk was all of giant fish, especially the manta rays which grow to several tons there and which, rumor had it, could leap right out of the water, land on a small boat and crush it and its occupants. I was never quite sure if they were pulling my leg with that one or not.

The next day we planned to make San Diego, but Captain Culbertson, like myself, saw no reason not to enjoy our cruise; so instead of going north outside Baja California to stay over water all the time, we flew up the Gulf of California for lunch at Guaymas.

From Guaymas we crossed Baja California and turned up the

Pacific Coast to San Diego. Baja was a miserable desert then with no roads, towns, hotels nor any conceivable reason for there ever being any. We arrived and spent the night uneventfully at San Diego.

Early the following morning, April 17, 1937, we left and proceeded north along the coast. Once beyond Catalina and Santa Barbara it was hazy, and kept getting hazier. Long Pacific rollers crashed against the rockbound shore from which the coastal range of mountains rose up steeply. It should be remembered that we were in deep trouble if either engine began to miss. We could not fly on one engine.

Soon we were in fog, thick fog. Flying in an ocean fog was something new to me although we were used to early morning fog, sometimes only a few feet thick over the water in Biscayne Bay. Captain Culbertson was down on the water, flying at 20 feet or less above the "deck". I was assigned to keep careful track of the navigation. We could no longer see the shore. There were no radio aids—our radio had nothing to communicate with. We could see nothing outside the cockpit except the water straight down, and only then if we stayed very close. Captain Culbertson showed no sign of being bothered in any way; but I did, hoping there were no boats along this coast and remembering that Sir Francis Drake sailed right by the Golden Gate and never saw San Francisco Bay.

After about four hours in the fog it began to lighten and we could see, right on our E.T.A. (estimated time of arrival), the Praesideo and the towering Golden Gate Bridge under which we flew, happily indeed!

Captain Culbertson, always known as Cubby, was a delightful person to be with and one of the best pilots. He was an old-timer, an ex-Marine officer and very much of a sailor. The hotels where we always stayed had swimming pools, and we lived by the pools when on shore. At the pool Cubby would be a surprise, much respected by the junior pilots who were all very good athletes, for he could dive better than anyone and seemed like Olympic material, which perhaps he had been.

CHAPTER III

------------------------------‹›------------------------------

Pan American Airways, Pacific Division, Alameda, California

APRIL 1937 – FEBRUARY 1939

THE Ocean! A magic word, as it was to Magellan so it was to me. From now on the sun would set every night in the ocean. At least this ocean's reputation was one of peace and quiet, a reputation not entirely deserved as I was to find out.

Now it was back to school again to master new subjects and for very advanced work in old ones. It would be ten days before I got in an airplane, and studies would go through the next year. My salary was still $225.00 per month but I would get a raise to $275.00 the next January 1st. It would go to $300.00 if I qualified in Ocean Meteorology, Celestial Navigation, Engineering and Communications. Once again we would have another set of International Correspondence School courses to take at our expense, one-half refunded by the Company upon completion. Meanwhile I would be in classes every day from morning to night.

Our base in Alameda, across the bay from San Francisco, was an old yacht club basin on the east side of the bay just below Oakland. The basin was inside a breakwater with only a narrow entrance from the bay, a precarious taxiway for the new flying boats, in any wind.

Within three months I qualified in Cruise Control,[1] developed by John Leslie, an engineer back in Mr. Priester's office in New York and then division manager of the Pacific. Some seven or eight years later when the Air Force B-29s were making raids on

Tokyo from Tinian and Saipan, the military pilots had all been sent to Pan Am's Navigation School in Miami, as had the navigators on General Doolittle's Tokyo raid.

I qualified once again in Communications and Radio Direction Finding.[2] Proficiency in these subjects might now be a matter of life and death. In these first months I also qualified in Meteorology, much the hardest subject. In addition to the I.C.S. written courses we had regular classes at the base. We started with Humphrey's *Physics of the Air* and went through Jerome Namias, then the foremost authority. We learned all about lapse rates, adiabatic and otherwise. We drew weather maps. We made upper air soundings with balloons and theodolites. We learned thoroughly all that was known about the weather at that time, especially frontal activity, cumulonimbus structures and forces, hurricanes and typhoons.

Pan Am had excellent weather service and perhaps top meteorologists—Allan Clark in the Atlantic, W. H. Clover in San Francisco and others now forgotten but still highly regarded by us.

Pan Am made its own weather observations across the Pacific from the island stations and later across the Atlantic from the flying boats in flight.

The first day we started on navigation. The instructor and chief navigator was Judd Ingram, an experienced navigator from the merchant marine. He was a tough taskmaster. He would say, "Navigation is easy. It is learning never to make a mistake that is hard". We started with Bowditch's *American Practical Navigator*, still the bible of navigators nearly 200 years after publication in 1799. We got to know this book forward and backward. We learned the adjustment and use of a sextant and of our bubble octants and all the methods of determining latitude and longitude at sea. Finally we came to the Sumner line of position and how to obtain fixes from the intersection of two or more of such lines. I was soon to have my first flight in one of the giant Martin M-130 flying boats.

Just after my arrival on April 26th, I was scheduled out, as one of several observers, on a local test flight with Chief Pilot Edwin Musick. The usual crew on a local flight would be the captain, first officer (pilot), flight engineer and radio operator—the basic crew of four. But there would be many others, maybe five or six, going along for familiarization, as there was a lot to become familiar with.

To a man we in Pan Am considered Captain Musick the greatest pilot alive. He was slender, of medium height, clean shaven with the telltale shadow of a dark beard. His cap was always squarely centered on his head. He spoke little but when he did, everything was punctuated with profanity. He was utterly cool under any circumstances, quiet and low key. Boarding the plane his eyes would miss nothing. He would settle comfortably in the left cockpit seat, adjust his seat belt and straighten the perfect crease in his trousers. Then he would lightly touch the setting on every instrument and check every control for ease of movement and position. Finally after a meticulous and unhurried inspection of absolutely everything, he would say quietly, "Start number one". The flight engineer would reply, "OK on number one, captain" and press the starter button.

The M-130 was built and designed by Glen L. Martin in Baltimore. Only three were ever built, all for Pan Am. At its center point the high wing was attached to the fuselage by a cabane strut which enclosed the flight engineer's station. On each side two big struts came down from the wing to stub wings, called seawings or sponsons which were also gas tanks. The sponsons rode on the water and gave lateral stability. The plane's fuel was carried in four wing tanks, from each of which it ran into an engine, and in the two seawings, from which it could be transferred to any of the wing tanks. The flight engineer in the cabane had, in addition to the usual engine monitoring instruments, an elaborate fuel transfer system of valves and pumps to get the fuel from the seawing tanks up into the wing tanks.

In addition, the Pratt and Whitney Twin Wasp engines were especially equipped for Pan Am with propeller brakes. If an engine failed in flight and continued to windmill, it would produce so much drag that the range to dry tanks would be greatly shortened. In plain English, if an engine quit near the middle of any of the legs across the Pacific, the plane might not get back or ahead to its destination. So we had brakes, just like automobile wheel brakes, a drum and a brake band around the output shaft of the engine behind the propeller. The brake was pumped up by the flight engineer hydraulically, and tests showed that this had to be done with great care at the lowest possible air speed or the entire assembly would melt and fall off into space. With the brakes, at least we had a chance of making it; without them we had little chance. Only a few years later propeller hubs were designed to permit full feathering of the blades so they would stop rotating by themselves in the position of minimum drag.

On May 10th I again went out with Captain Musick, on a courtesy flight from Alameda to Avalon and back. Glen Martin, the designer of the boats, was on board and there was a reception at which he made a speech at Avalon, the town on Santa Catalina Island, about thirty miles offshore from Los Angeles, one of the Santa Barbara Islands. It was a beautiful place, with cliffs rising from the sea and a small harbor full of yachts, into which we taxied after landing in the lee of the island. As the junior officer, I stayed on board as a guard and didn't hear the speeches.

The Pacific Division had been operating since 1935 when the first survey flights were made in a Sikorsky S-42B which had been modified with cabin tanks for additional range. The first M-130 arrived the same year and the inaugural flight across the Pacific to Manila was made by Captain Musick, leaving on November 22, 1935. The three M-130s were named the China, Hawaiian and Philippine Clippers respectively, although the press usually referred to any of the three as the "China Clipper".

The once-a-week schedule left every Wednesday at 3 P.M. from Alameda, arriving at Pearl Harbor, Honolulu, early the next morning. Passenger service had begun in October 1936. The crew and passengers spent the day and night there, leaving next morning for Midway Island. Except for the overnight flight to Honolulu, each island leg of the route was flown in daylight with an overnight at the Pan Am hotel on each island. The next island after Midway was Wake, then Guam and the end of the route was the U.S. Navy

Base in Manila. There the crew would spend two days before heading back home.

Before each departure from Alameda the crew and plane always made a predeparture flight the day before, of not less than three hours, and everything on board, particularly instrumentation, was checked by the flight engineer and an inspector. The compasses were swung also. On the test flight, the airspeed indicators were checked against a specially calibrated "bomb" (a streamlined box containing a special test airspeed indicator) suspended far below the plane in air not disturbed by the aircraft's wake. Because gasoline quantity could not be measured with anything like sufficient accuracy by existing types of tank gauges, the tanks were filled from accurately metered fuel pumps. The fuel consumption in flight was measured by fuel-flow meters which were accurate. In addition, all cockpit instruments were calibrated regularly in the instrument shop. The compasses were not compensated by little magnets, but a Napier diagram or table of compass errors would be drawn up for each compass. There were two cockpit compasses and a special one at the navigator's table. The CAA required two compasses. Pan Am required three. (It is said that the Chinese junk captains always carried three compasses asking, "Which of two would you use if they pointed in different directions?") The crew would get to know each other and look each other over on the predeparture flight.

After I had been in the division a month, I felt at home. We were a small and dedicated group. Everyone was at the base every day and the senior co-pilots (I remember Bill Masland and Howard Cone especially) helped a great deal in teaching navigation. Many stories passed around. Fred Noonan, a tall, dark Irishman, had been the first and chief navigator for the division—Musick relied heavily on him—was famous, but Fred Noonan had one problem: drink. Musick had him followed and watched the day before departure, but once the shadow failed and well on the way to Honolulu, Noonan was found asleep and unwakeable. Fortunately, one of the pilot crew was Harry Canaday, an Annapolis grad who turned out to be as good a navigator as Noonan; and Musick's problem was solved. Noonan left soon after and was employed by Amelia Earhart.

"As a boy Fred had attended public schools in Chicago", I am quoting from *The Search for Amelia Earhart* by Fred Goerner, "then a private military academy and the London National College, but at fifteen, his restlessness drove him to the sea. In 1910 he served aboard the *Compton*, largest square-rigged ship under the Union Jack. On one voyage from the Pacific Northwest to Ireland, the vessel was weatherbound for 152 days. During World War I, Fred became an officer aboard a munitions carrier between New York and London, and then joined the Royal Navy, surviving three torpedo sinkings. On one trip from London to Montreal, he helped rescue five French soldiers adrift on an ice floe. On another, he was credited with saving the crew of a foundering Portuguese fishing schooner. In twenty-two years at sea, he made the trip around Cape Horn seven times, thrice in a windjammer".

The navigating techniques we used had been set up by Noonan after consultation with Harold Gatty who with Wiley Post had circumnavigated the globe in a single-engine Lockheed in 1931. Gatty was considered the foremost authority on air navigation and was a consultant to Pan Am. He was an Australian born in Tasmania. Gatty wrote what is by far the most extraordinary book on survival at sea, *The Raft Book*. It should be the bible of anyone going to sea in a small boat and should be in every life raft on a seagoing boat. It describes how to survive and get ashore again, how to steer by the stars, what information you can get from birds and even insects found at sea, how to find your position—that is your latitude—with no instruments, and your longitude if you have a watch set on Greenwich time.

After many test or training flights, I was at last scheduled for my first crossing, leaving Alameda on May 20th for Honolulu. The captain would be Terletzky, but Musick would be along to check him out.

Terletzky had preceded me to the Pacific, as a senior captain, of course, but he had not yet made his first trip in command. Musick was said to have serious misgivings about his competence and to have tried to ground him. But Priester, back in New York, still had absolute authority over all flight operations and took the position, we may assume, that even Musick had the prejudice against foreigners that Priester thought all Americans had. Priester ordered a thorough flight check for Terletzky, which he passed with good marks. Of course Musick knew there was no way on a local check flight to check on the qualities of courage, emotional and mental stability or any of the traits of character which were considered so crucially important in the Army or Navy flying schools.

At 3 P.M. we cast off from the dock in the Alameda yacht basin, Terletzky at the controls, Musick in the right seat as check pilot. A small crowd had gathered to see us off, mostly the wives of crew members but also a few sightseers. The crew were all too busy to notice the crowd, checking and rechecking and again rechecking everything on board—we did not yet have the lengthy question and response checklists which came later. But, being only a supernumerary and somewhat in the way, I was able to notice the crowd. There was no cheering or even waving, mostly women pulling out handkerchiefs to dab their eyes. It was to be that way every Wednesday afternoon.

We left on Wednesday because the Matson Line's *Lurline* and *Matsonia* left every Monday from Honolulu and San Francisco respectively, alternating weekly, and they would both be about in the middle of the route when we passed them Wednesday night. This whole passage took them five days and four nights; it took us about 18 hours. At least there would always be these two ships along our route on this leg. East of Honolulu we very seldom ever saw a ship or got a position from one, although the U.S. *Meigs* ran a regular schedule between Honolulu and Guam.

Besides Musick and Terletzky, the crew consisted of four copilots, one navigator, one pilot being checked out in navigation, one flight engineer and one radio operator. Then there were two cabin attendants, both male. That made a total of 12 or so. The two extra co-pilots, the third and fourth officers, were qualified as both radio operators and flight engineers. They stood relief watches for the regulars.

The main cabin was divided into compartments which made up into lower and upper berths on each side, and there was a lounge amidship for meals and drinks, with tables and chairs which seated fourteen, leaving room to walk around. The furniture was secured to the deck; it had been specially made for Pan Am by Gump's in San Francisco. It was bamboo and rattan and weighed almost nothing.

Forward of the main cabin was the galley and forward of that, the navigation compartment with the navigator's table, chronometer, compass and chart rack on the starboard side with two single seats facing each other on the port side. The off duty crew would usually occupy these seats. The navigator was very seldom off his feet although eventually we got stools for the chart tables. We stood watches, four hours on and two off. There was no pressurization yet in any aircraft. Fortunately one became so exhausted, partly from nervous strain, that one could always sleep; but the navigator never did. It was seldom necessary to call the next watch —they would appear on time looking not much the worse for wear.

Landfall would be Diamond Head shortly after dawn and we would turn up the coast past Waikiki, into Pearl Harbor and dock at a float at the Pan Am terminal across from Ford Island. There would be a crowd of Hawaiians with leis to greet everyone. A crew car would take us to the Moanna Hotel where two cottages were rented for the crew. Washed and cooled off, we would be in bed asleep by ten or eleven in the morning.

After a few hours rest, we would get up and go down to Waikiki to swim and chat with the beach boys. The most famous surfer was Duke Kahanamoku, then sheriff of Honolulu.[3] Other famous ones, like Colgate and Panama, would gather around, for we were more or less celebrities, and take any of us out, for free, through the surf on their 16-foot, hollow surfboards, and back in behind them, on the steepest part of the waves just beyond the curl. Late in the afternoon, we would go in town to the Alexander Young Hotel where the best Hawaiian music was played and Hawaiians danced. It was seldom necessary to pay anything, and the manager would always come up to us, recognizing the crews who, even in civies, were easily distinguished from tourists, and say, "Just forget the check".

Often, if we slept late in the afternoon, we would awaken to the sound of guitars and find a Hawaiian band serenading us out on the grass in front of our windows. Harry Owens played at the Royal Hawaiian, next door to the Moanna. Although an American, he was the composer of almost all the Hawaiian hits then current, like "Sweet Leilani". Only a few old war chants were original Hawaiian music. The wahines appeared to us the most beautiful girls in the world, especially the Bray sisters, promoted by Mother Bray as the most beautiful in the Pacific.

One day when we had a layoff for a week in Hawaii, we were having a beer in a local restaurant when Duke Kahanamoku and several of his brothers passed by our table. I asked him to sit down and have a beer with us. With a soft and dignified smile, he stopped and said, "We never drink". The "we" encompassing, it seemed, his whole island race. But he stopped, introduced his brothers and chatted pleasantly with us. Having met the Duke, one never forgot him—his incredible build, his height and look of royalty.

Friday morning at daybreak we left for Midway. On Wednesday, the flight from Alameda to Honolulu had been 2,080 nautical miles, nothing but dead reckoning and celestial navigation all the way—but at least we had had the *Matsonia* and *Lurline* on our route and we had talked to them and gotten their positions (by CW, of course) en route. The flight to Midway would be only 1,126 nautical miles and easy because we passed Kauai, Nihoa and French Frigate Shoal, good checkpoints, and also various reefs and tiny atolls stretching along the course to Midway.

The highest point at Midway was 34 feet above sea level. High clouds do not form over atolls to mark them from far off as with volcanic islands. A sailor could pass by within 10 miles (according to S. E. Morison) and never see one. The first thing one saw from the air was a lighter patch of sea, becoming light green when the lagoon, ringed by sand, could finally be seen. The atoll was entirely made by coral and would be more or less in a ring around a shallow lagoon with coral heads in it. The sand beach surrounding the lagoon was made from coral ground up by the surf and was pure white. In the bright sunlight it was blinding and dark glasses were a must. Amazingly enough, as the sand contained no silica, a usual constituent of sand which retains heat, the beach was always cool to the feet. No sneakers were required, even on the hottest day.

The water was cool and incredibly clear; it looked drinkable; it was brilliant green, shading to very dark blue as the red was absorbed from the sunlight more and more with the depth. The colors were even more brilliant than in the Bahamas.

The station manager greeted us at the dock. We had swimming trunks and he lent us face masks from Japan where they were used by pearl divers. Snorkels had not yet been invented. We were warned to stay away from morays, and to watch out not to step on any giant clam. The huge tridacna clam will close quickly on anything that touches it, imprisoning a careless foot so only amputation can get the unfortunate one ashore again. The clam is too big to pull ashore or pry open.

There was a cable station at Midway with three lonely souls who manned it, getting mail and provisions only twice a year. Now they would feel nearer their homes with two seaplanes a week, one from each direction.

Midway was the home of the Gooney birds (Laysan Albatross), large albatrosses that nested only at Midway and left for the Arctic when their young were raised. The island was covered with them, but they had become accustomed to the arrivals and departures and posed no problem by getting in the way of landings and takeoffs. We came to know the Bosun birds and Man-o-War birds (Frigate birds) which fascinate all deep-sea sailors on the Pacific. We never saw a Man-o-War on the ground or the water. They appeared to live in the air. They would feed by diving viciously on any other bird that was carrying a fish, force it to drop the fish and then would catch it in midair and swallow it.

The next day, after a good dinner at the Pan Am hotel, a night's rest and breakfast, we were off early for Wake, only 1,034 nautical miles, our shortest leg. Now we navigated in earnest. There was nothing within a thousand miles of Wake and not enough fuel to get back to Midway once we passed the point-of-no-return which Navy carrier pilots call the "Splash Point".[4] During the middle of the day sun-sights gave us good checks on our latitude, but what could we use for a distance check? How far had we gone? It was clear at a comfortable 8,000 feet and we got a good observation of Venus behind the sun in the east. An observation of one heavenly body works out to a line of position on the chart upon which you are located somewhere. A second sight on another body gives another line, but the lines must cross at a good angle to give a reliable fix. It is necessary to get two bodies, one ahead or behind and one abeam, to get a good fix. A third body to give you a three-line fix is desirable, but what three bodies could you see in daylight? We had the sun, sometimes the moon and occasionally Venus, and nothing else.

But we could get Venus—for a while. Our Bausch and Lomb (specially made for Pan Am) bubble octants gave us an inverted field. We complained about the difficulty in identifying the stars; so one day we got nice, new, improved octants with right-side-up fields, and we never saw Venus again in daylight. A simple lens inverts the field. To reinvert it requires a prism and the extra glass of the prism absorbs enough light so that one can no longer see Venus in daylight. We learned our first lesson in writing new specifications for an improvement: First be sure you know what you've got and won't lose it!

On this leg the navigator took frequent drift sights, opening a little trapdoor and throwing out a glass flask filled with aluminum powder which, when it hit the water below, made a large splotch. Sighting this splotch with a pelorus mounted by the hatch enabled one to measure the drift.[5] If the plane was drifting sideways above the surface due to a crosswind, the drift bomb mark would not stay directly behind the plane but angle off slightly to one side. That angle would be the drift angle. Taking drift sights on two different headings gave two drift angles from which wind and ground speed could be calculated.

Of course it was not all that easy because the plane was not a stable platform and it would roll and yaw, continuously introducing large errors into the drift readings which had to be averaged to get a useable figure. The M-130 was anything but stable. Musick used to say it was the only plane he ever flew that was very stiff and unstable around all axes. The Sperry autopilot was almost useless as it normally hunted so badly in yaw that it would make the passengers in the tail seats sick, and it also produced a dutch roll making it very difficult to get a good octant reading. During the taking of sights, the plane was always flown manually. If we had serious doubts about our position, we would get a sun line when the sun was low in the sky in the late afternoon, as when nearing Wake, and then advance the line to have it run through Wake on the chart. Then we would make a definite turn to the north or south and dead reckon up to the line, so as to be reasonably sure we were north or south of Wake. Then we would turn to fly down the line till we made landfall. It was somewhat nerve wracking. Radio bearings would have made it all so easy—had good ones always been obtainable. Often they were not.

The British called this method "Aim-Off". Chichester used it in his crossing of the Tasman Sea to find Norfolk and Lord Howe Islands. He used a sextant, flying at 100 to 150 feet, having found it impossible to use a bubble octant in his little light plane. He used precomputed sun altitudes to give him L.O.P.s (lines of position) running through his targets.

When nearing your destination, it was very easy to think you saw the atoll and very hard to stick to the course posted by the navigator on a little clip on the dash. Under no circumstances could you change course to take a look at a light green spot or a cloud shadow just to see if it wasn't the island. It would throw off the navigation. Positive identification was essential. We never changed course until we were absolutely certain.

Wake was inhabited by birds called Flightless Rails, and also by rats and sand crabs. They lived off each other. All rails and the rats vanished, presumably eaten by the Japs who occupied it during the war. There are none today. The water was crystal clear, the colors even more beautiful than at Midway. Here we found glass balls used as floats by Asiatic fishing fleets. Their nets had been broken or otherwise damaged and the floats drifted loose for years. Sometimes there was water in the glass and we speculated as to how it got there. No one knew. It seemed a little too much just for condensation. I once picked up a rarity, one marked with a hammer and sickle.

The station manager at Wake was Bill Mullahey, an ex-lifeguard at Jones Beach (L.I., N.Y.) and at Los Angeles beaches. He loved underwater swimming and was fearless. He carried a razor sharp knife at all times and had no fear of sharks, although he admitted he never antagonized anything bigger than he was, and he was pretty big. He would take the crews out to the outer reef where they could stand and look over the edge into nearly 5,000 feet of water.

A moray bit him on the ankle once, before he carried a knife, and he couldn't get it off; so he swam ashore and dragged the moray to the dispensary where the doctor cut it off and treated him. We never feared a shark with him around. He seemed more at home in the water than the shark. He had built himself a heavy, rubber-band, underwater spear gun which we all copied when we got home, and he fished for the beautiful angel fish and parrot fish. Mullahey was greatly admired by the crews. He was sort of an American Duke Kahanamoku.

Once later on, at Wake with Bob Fordyce, another junior pilot and close friend, when we had been walking around the islands which enclosed the lagoon and had to swim about two hundred yards across an inlet to get back to the hotel, I noticed a shark swimming alongside Fordyce and me. It was about five feet long. It didn't bother Fordyce at all, and he reassured me that, as Mullahey had said, it wouldn't bite us because it was smaller than we. I still wished Mullahey had been along.

On this trip with Musick and Terletzky they seldom spoke to each other and Terletzky, who must have known that his future was on the line, did a flawless job, showing no signs of strain. He appeared confident and relaxed and Musick let him make virtually every landing and takeoff which were all smoothly and perfectly executed. Nevertheless, I thought even then and I know today, as Musick must have known, that Terletzky was relaxed and proficient only because Musick was there beside him to take over if anything went wrong.

Early the next morning we left for Guam, 1,305 empty miles away, where we landed after dark—our first night landing. Guam was the southernmost island of the Marianas, a chain of islands running north and south about 140°W longitude and 20°N latitude. Just about 60 miles north of Guam (U.S. territory) was Rota (Japanese territory). There was nothing for a long way to the south, so it was a human tendency to stay north of the track, or at least to make sure you were really north of it. North of Rota you would come to Tinian and Saipan (Japanese), meaningless names to us at that time, but due to become famous as bases from which our B-29s took off for Tokyo in the war.

We might get radio bearings from the U.S. Navy Station at Apra on the island of Guam, and even from Japanese Rota, to get a nice fix on approaching, but then again we might not. Anyway, no bearing was possible until we were far beyond the point-of-no-return. As always, we were essentially dependent on celestial navigation and dead reckoning.

The navigator never rested. It took about ten minutes to take and plot a line of position, and nearly 30 minutes to get a three star fix. We could usually get these only at night between Honolulu and San Francisco. On this trip on May 24, 1937, about 20 miles out from Wake one engine got very rough and we returned to Wake, glad it happened early. As usual, the roughness was caused by bad spark plugs which would require a complete change of plugs on that engine.

Early the next morning we were off again for Guam, about a ten hour flight; so we left very early for a daylight landing. The landing area was in a smooth inner harbor with plenty of room (Apra Harbor). Guam was taken from Spain in the Spanish-American War in 1898 when an American gunboat arrived in the harbor and fired a shot across the town. It was answered by a boat coming alongside carrying an invitation to dinner from the Spanish Governor and a profuse apology for not answering the salute because he had no powder on the island.

Guam has a peak 1,344 feet and making landfall was not as difficult and uncertain as with the last two islands.

The local natives, Chamorros, were very cheerful and friendly and supplied the Company with servants for the hotels on Midway and Wake. They were replaced whenever they got lonely and we would take back a new contingent on our return flight. We (the crew and the two paying passengers) overnighted in comparative luxury at the Pan Am hotel in Agana.

Next day we departed at dawn for the long leg, 1,384 miles to Manila via the Strait of San Bernardino. We always stayed over water so we went through the strait and up the coast to the U.S. Naval base at Cavite where we had a hangar, shops and an office.

Captain Musick, who made the inaugural flight arriving at Manila on November 29, 1935, a year and a half before this, was still famous; and a crowd greeted us—everyone who could get in the Naval base. The arrival of the first Clipper had been quite an event in Manila. President Quezon had just been inaugurated and the independence of the Philippines had been declared on November 15th; so the departure of the Clipper from Alameda on November 22nd had attracted little attention in the press. But the arrival on the 29th was something else again. It is worthwhile quoting Pan Am Vice-President Harold Bixby's private memoirs, as he was there:[6]

"On the morning of the 29th of November, we kept the populace informed as to the progress of the flight from Guam by means of a large sign board over which we flew a miniature Clipper, moving it up with each position report. The committee had also arranged for, and widely advertised, the blowing of a large whistle, used as a warning for typhoons during that season, as soon as the Clipper reported the sighting of the west coast of Luzon. This would be some two hours before its arrival at Manila. Mr. Quezon had issued his first proclamation as President of the new Commonwealth, announcing a half holiday for the occasion. When the whistle blew, it seemed as though every man, woman and child in Manila, and many who had come in from provinces for the occasion, started for the Luneta. The crowd became bigger and bigger until some two hundred thousand people had congregated. The Clipper radio reports indicated that the ship was approaching. White fluffy clouds floated at six thousand feet. At Admiral's Landing we stood by with high ranking officials of the Philippine and American governments. The crowd took on a hushed expectancy. Finally overhead we could hear the motors of the Clipper but the plane was not in view. It was circling above the white clouds gradually losing altitude over Manila Bay. Presently through a hole in the clouds the clipper suddenly burst into view, its silver wings shining in the bright afternoon sun. It seemed as though the crowd—strangely silent under the spell of this historic event—all spotted the plane at the same instant. There was a mighty murmur of voices followed by a din such as I have never heard before. Every automobile horn was sounded, all the factory whistles in town cut loose, and all the boats in the harbor emptied the steam from their boilers through their whistles.

"It was a thrilling moment for all of us. Next to me a tough 'old timer', who had come to Manila in 1899 toting a gun, was so choked up with emotion that he could not speak. His eyes filled with tears.

"Musick brought his ship down in a slow graceful glide, came in low over the Luneta, levelled off and skimmed the surface of the Bay to a perfect landing. The crowd went wild with excitement. He taxied up to the buoy and the crew came ashore to be greeted by the Reception Committee. The Postmaster General was present with a cancellation chop which he promptly impressed on a letter that Captain Musick had brought from the President of the United States to the President of the Commonwealth, the first trans-Pacific airmail letter to be delivered. Captain Musick, with the head of the Post Office, left for the Palace to complete his mission and deliver the letter to President Quezon".

On this later flight we waved to the crowd at the Cavite terminal and then took a crew bus to the Manila Hotel. We had rooms in a new air-conditioned wing, and it certainly was needed. Generally, hotels, department stores and even movie houses were not yet air-conditioned.

Buying white shirts, shorts and "silk" suits in downtown Manila was pleasant, but somewhat embarrassing. Even though not in uniform, the shopkeeper would always recognize a Pan Am crew member and mark the things down, sometimes refusing to take any money at all.

We had two days off and would leave the third day on the return trip. During the layover, I went sightseeing in town and was impressed with the Cathedral, built with foundations of stone in the shape of a boat hull underground, to withstand earthquakes. It did ride out several severe quakes as well as did Frank Lloyd Wright's Imperial Hotel in Tokyo.

Back at the hotel, we played tennis and swam in the pool most of the day. We played even at noon when we had the courts to ourselves as it was very hot, and we drew comments adding Pan Am crew members to "mad dogs and Englishmen who go out in the mid-day sun". No one ever did get a sunstroke, but we all swore by Skol and coated all our exposed portions very carefully with it.

On the third day we got up at about 2 A.M. and had breakfast at the crew table in the main dining room while the late floor show was going on. We took off from Cavite well before dawn in an utterly still, hot night. The high temperature robbed the engines of power and the glassy water sucked at the hull like a leech so that the takeoff run seemed forever and went far beyond the float lights put out by the launch, which had patrolled the area to shoo off any boats. Small boats, and there were many, would not have lights so that on the run, after the last float light was passed, the pilot just prayed. Terletzky at last got us off the water, the engine cylinder-head temperatures, up against the pegs, finally started down to some reasonable figure and the navigator busied himself with a good visual fix on a point-of-departure, probably Corregidor, as we climbed slowly, at about 300 feet a minute, on a southerly course till we had enough altitude to turn into the strait and get on our course to Guam. Performance might have been a little less than the manufacturer's engineers guaranteed, but then the gross weight was probably not quite what our manifest showed. As always the flight engineer had a little extra fuel, "pocket gas", just in case. No captain would ever object. We did have a maximum gross weight for takeoff but not until years later did regulations compel temperature accountability, meaning that you had to reduce your allowable gross weight for high temperatures. When we had the whole ocean ahead of us, we just roared along at full power, hoping the cylinders wouldn't blow up, until we got off or it became apparent we were not going to. The worst condition for a boat was glassy water and no wind.

As we left the strait, the sun was about to appear, and dawn over a tropical ocean is something special. No sunrise anywhere else in the world is ever as beautiful and dramatic. On the crew deck total silence reigned. If the captain addressed anyone, he would have to poke him first to get his attention and be heard. The navigator, after getting his point-of-departure leaving the strait, would have nothing to do until the sun rose high enough to provide a good line of position for a distance and speed check. Over land the clouds dissipate at night and the sun rises in a clear sky except in storms. Not so at sea. Whereas the land cools off at night, the sea does not and the clouds remain with maybe some new ones forming before sunrise, but the air is always crystal clear, much of the pollution such as salt spray having settled. The brilliance of a tropical ocean sunrise is spellbinding and always has remained so to me. We were to see many over the Pacific but few on the Atlantic. The return trip was uneventful.

Upon my return to Alameda it was back to school, six days a week with the seventh spent at home studying. I had begun by rooming with another pilot in a small apartment at 530 Santa Clara Ave. in Alameda, but I soon ran into an ex-schoolmate, college classmate and friend, Edwin Olaf Holter, who had moved to the west coast to run the family Sage Land Improvement Company, which owned forests of redwoods in the north. He and I got together in May and took the ground floor of a house at 1800 Vallejo Street which was furnished, owned and inhabited by the landlady who lived upstairs. Toward the end of my second year, Olaf got married and I moved to 1338 Filbert St. with a local friend, non-Pan Am, Johnny Potter. We got a very small, attractively furnished house on a street which ran up Russian Hill. Potter was very good looking and a more than expert skier and tennis player. He had grown up at Biarritz next door to the Basque Davis Cup champion, Jean Borotra, and had played with him almost daily as an exercise boy. As a skier he had acted in the first ski movie, an international hit called "The Chase".

I had occasional instrument flight practice under the hood in the Commodore which Culbertson and I had brought out from Miami, but the lack of any solo flying bothered many of us. So with Andy Anderson, again as at Miami, I got us OK'd to fly whatever equipment we could get our hands on at the Oakland Airport where there was an Army Air Corps Reserve unit. Thereafter, whenever we had some spare time between trips, we would take up the PT-3A or the BT-2B which were all they had, and explore over the Sierras. Later I would mostly go skiing between trips for we could find snow eight months of the year and I had finished ground school and had had enough flying to need a little change.

June 29th I was assigned to my second trip, with Captain Terletzky, this one to be his first solo flight. He was OK on the Tuesday pre-departure flight and the next afternoon we left, flying over both bridges, and arrived safely in Honolulu. On July 2nd we flew from Honolulu to Midway. The radio carried news of Amelia Earhart's round-the-world-flight with Fred Noonan, and she was due to arrive at Howland Island the same day from New Guinea. As soon as we got to Midway, we rushed to the radio shack to see if there was any news of Amelia and Fred. The operators had maintained a continuous watch on her frequencies and had overheard

her last message, on phone on 3105kc, to the U.S. Coast Guard
Cutter *Itasca* stationed at Howland to meet her. The Pan Am radio
operator at Midway thought she sounded hysterical and mumbled
about being low on gas. *Itasca* kept asking her to switch to 500kc
and just to hold the button or key down so they could take a
bearing on her, but she never replied. (A good bearing could have
been gotten on 500kc but not on 3105kc.) Amelia was not too familiar with the radio, and may not have known how to change
frequency. When we arrived in the shack on Midway it was long
past the limit of her endurance. *Itasca* was off to search the vast
area of the mid-Pacific, and we all knew she and Fred were down
at sea and probably would never be seen or heard from again.

As we learned later, President Roosevelt ordered the greatest sea
search ever conducted, but nothing was ever found. Much later we
learned that the White House had been concerned over the Japanese
activities in the Pacific. Amelia had been well briefed to stay away
from the Marshalls, Marianas and Carolines which the Japs held
under mandate of the Geneva Convention since the First World
War. (Historians say that the Japanese did not begin fortifying the
mandates until 1940 but, at this time, we all heard and believed
that it would be very dangerous to fly near any of those islands.)
The Navy, wholly and sadly unprepared, had only Guam, Wake and
Midway in the North Pacific and were seriously worried about war
with Japan. They had sought to have an airfield built on Howland
Island, U.S. territory, a speck in the mid-Pacific for which
Amelia was heading from Lae, New Guinea, en route to Honolulu.
Howland was under the Interior Department which declined to build
an airport for lack of money, so Roosevelt had used Amelia's need,
and went ahead and built an airport on Howland with special funds.

As we were to see the following year, the public will not tolerate
a mystery. They always sense a conspiracy. They will never believe
in a coincidence or even a predictable tragedy.

The papers made the disappearance a "mystery". Suggestions
were made that she was spying on the Japanese for the Navy. Then
stories appeared that they had been picked up by the Japanese and

imprisoned and that Noonan had been beheaded in Saipan. Mysteries sell newspapers and provide stories for writers which often turn into bestselling books. There is money in a mystery. Amelia Earhart's disappearance was written about for 29 years. Toward the end, a reporter named Fred Goerner conducted a search from 1960 through 1966, backed by CBS, "tracing" Amelia and Fred to Saipan. The Second World War was over now and the U.S. held Saipan but the Navy wouldn't let anyone explore it. Obviously to Goerner, the Navy was covering up the story of Amelia and Fred. Actually the CIA was conducting a top secret school for undercover agents and saboteurs to operate in China against our then No. 1 enemy, the Red Chinese. But Goerner was tenacious, and found "reputable" old-timers, Chamorros, on Saipan who showed him the prison cell where "the lady flier" was held and died of dysentery, and told him she had been brought in on a Japanese fishing boat with a white man who had been beheaded. Finally, the "important" Chamorros showed him the graves. He dug up the remains and, after obtaining the necessary church and other permissions, including that of Amelia's sister, the remains were shipped by Pan Am back to California to be examined by a doctor who had known and treated Amelia and Fred. After the most meticulous care, refusing to send a bill for his work to CBS who gave him some money anyway with which the doctor set up a student scholarship, the doctor's report, questioned by no one, said that the remains were those of four Chamorros dug from a common grave.

Sad at the almost certain end of a fellow pilot, and a glamorous one, we left Midway for Wake, Guam and Manila. In Manila we picked up Captain Musick and returned with him in command.

Back in San Francisco Holter and I would play tennis every day on the indoor municipal courts. One day I was summoned to dinner by Admiral Hepburn, the senior admiral on the west coast whose headquarters were on Yerba Buena Island, midpoint in the Bay Bridge then being constructed. He was unmarried and, needing a woman as hostess because his duties appeared to be mostly entertaining, he had gotten his niece, Louise, from Philadelphia, whom I happened to have known back home. Fairly soon, I, Holter and Alfred·Bell were regular attendants at the admiral's and attempted to liven up the otherwise dull dinners.

On August 4th I left on my third trip with Captain Jack Tilton, a Naval Reserve officer, a top pilot and a great gentleman. It was uneventful on the way out although my log shows a day at Wake and a day at Guam which I must assume were due to mechanical troubles. I remember few weather delays. On the return trip we took on the station manager at one of the stations who was returning to the States. As I was still 3rd or 4th officer, the captain assigned me to keep the manager company. I took a seat in the cabin beside him and listened with rapt attention to his stories of building the island base from the *North Haven*. Unable to anchor in a rough sea, they unloaded onto barges to be towed into the beach by a tug, also brought on the *North Haven*. To the horror of the crew, one barge with all the fuel drums capsized.

But they noted that the drums floated so the tug could just push them all ashore. Right in the middle of one spellbinding story, he said to me, "Excuse me please" and then, leaning on the window and looking down, he shook his fist and said loudly, "Leave me alone you bastard". Then he turned to me confidentially and said, "That son-of-a-bitch down there is shooting needles in my balls". Then he went on with the stories, interrupted occasionally by the "person" below where there was only 8,000 feet of air. Shortly I went up to the captain to ask, politely, if there was anything wrong with our passenger. "Nothing that I know of", said the captain, which was not true; but the first officer spoke up and said he heard the station manager had got into and consumed all the medicinal alcohol in the dispensary. I never saw him again after Honolulu.

My fourth trip was with Captain LaPorte, an ex-Navy CPO, later to be operations manager of the Atlantic. This time we had a six day layover at Manila. Previously we only had two days rest there, then turned around and came back on the same plane. Those two days were, presumably, built into the schedule to allow for extending the route to Hong Kong for which permission had not yet been obtained from the British. But now there would be a crew waiting in Manila to take our plane back and we would pick up the next arrival. The schedule once a week from Alameda required three planes, which were all there were.

I had with me a letter of introduction to a Mr. White and his wife who were friends of my Cousin Julia Johnston. He was an English businessman and an old Manila hand. Well-known in the Philippines, he was nicknamed "Shiny White" and owned a house on a little island in the middle of the Pasig River on the outskirts of the city. Having been asked to dinner I took a taxi to the address given me which turned out to be the end of a very lonely dirt road at the river's edge. It was pitch dark, no light anywhere, and I was scared to even get out of the taxi, thinking of the various kinds of snakes I knew about, to say nothing of scorpions. I had been stung on several occasions by a scorpion and I know of nothing more painful, but the ones I knew were only about an inch long. Now I had just seen a preserved one in a Manila museum which was a local specimen nearly eight inches long. Soon there appeared noiselessly along the river two Philippinos paddling a long, dugout canoe with a bench running down the middle covered with a narrow awning. In the dark it looked extraordinarily unseaworthy. But I got in, sat down and was paddled a little way upstream where I disembarked in total darkness and walked, or perhaps ran, through the jungle to where I saw a light. Admitted by a native butler clad only in a loincloth, I entered into one of the most fabulous houses I had ever seen. It was a large house, with no electricity and no windows—only jalousies. In the glow of many candles could be seen incredibly carved and polished furniture of native woods, and all sorts of oriental art, jade, silks and pieces of Philippine gossamer called "piña" cloth. The Whites were charming and presented me upon my arrival, without any preliminary questions, with a large, ice-cold martini. They well understood my then desperate need for just that.

A very good dinner was served at a table perhaps 12 feet long and two inches thick, with a top made of one piece of wood, polished to an incredible brilliance. I was interested in tropical woods, and Mr. White explained how large pieces could only be used locally. He told of an American who had bought and taken home to the States a table like his only to be awakened one night by an explosion like a cannon shot which turned out to be his new dining room table splitting down the middle.

Over the table where we ate, there hung a punkah, pulled slowly back and forth to create a gentle breeze by a servant clad like all the others only in a loincloth. A loincloth is a long piece of narrow white cotton. The Philippino servant, usually a Tagalog, wraps it once around his waist, knotting it in back and leaving a long, loose end which he then pulls between his legs and up in front where he tucks it into the sash. Mrs. White explained that she had never been entirely successful in stopping the boys from untucking the loose end in front and using it to hold a very hot plate or to mop up if a guest spilled something.

It was very, very hot, as tropical nights can be. Often it seems to get hotter after sunset. One only wore white in this part of the world. It took a lot of suits, several changes a day, to look neat and clean, which meant a lot of servants to look after one's clothes. Cotton got rumpled almost as soon as you put it on, but synthetic materials were just appearing. They held a crease, did not rumple easily and stayed clean. Almost all of us would get several synthetic suits. The material was very shiny and looked cheap but it was cool and would stay clean and unrumpled all day.

My interest in Philippine woods prompted Mr. White to arrange a trip to a lumber mill for me and my friends on the crew. First we were taken to a place on the river where we got into a native boat and shot rapids of swirling white water, which was exciting and fun. Then we went to a mill built in the jungle which had a huge circular saw perhaps six feet in diameter. The manager explained that most of the woods had a specific gravity of more than one, i.e., would not float, so logs had to be dragged to the mill by water buffalo. Then he explained that due to the extreme hardness of the woods, the teeth of the huge saw had to be resharpened every few days and the saw itself lasted less than a year. He dreamt of much tougher tool steels which were not yet available but which were to come in a few years.

Another day on this long layover, several of us got a car and driver and went up to Baguio, a mountain resort north of Manila, about 5,000 feet up in the mountains. The Americans had built a long road up the mountain to make the city accessible, and it became the summer capital. It was lovely and cool, about 65 degrees compared to Manila's usual 80 degrees. It was also a gold mining center and we went into a mine where the shaft ran horizontally several miles into the mountain.

Back at the Manila Hotel, one evening General MacArthur appeared at his table to watch the late floor show which was going on. Noticing us nearby, he came over to our table and asked if he might join us. Of course, we were honored. Then, after learning where we originally came from, he began to lecture us on the Pacific. He spoke with a practiced delivery in what was almost biblical English. He was enormously impressive, although he had not become as famous then as he was to be in a few years. He knew the Far East as well as any westerner in the world, and he spoke of a subject to which he was dedicated. He had served in the Philippines and Japan right after graduating from the Point in 1903. He told us he was never going home again. He had retired from the U.S. Army, having been the youngest chief of staff at 50. He was building and training the Philippine Army full speed ahead then, getting what he needed from Washington; and he was apprehensive about the Japanese. He had served in France all through the First World War so he knew Europe too, but now he told us in measured prose that the center of all future history, the center of the world, would be in the Pacific Basin and that the Atlantic Basin and the Western World countries that surrounded it were through. Nothing in Europe would be of importance again. If nothing else, he made us look west to the Orient, something few on the east coast of the United States ever did.

On one leg of the trip we had a very rough engine. The captain decided to stop it. As explained before, stopping required braking the propeller to keep it from windmilling, which would slow the plane down. Seldom, if ever before, had a prop been braked except for a few demonstrations on test flights where the procedure had not always worked very well. This time it didn't work either. Cutting off the ignition, the captain slowed down to near stall. The flight engineer, with the "Operations Manual" open in front of him, began pumping the brake. The prop slowed somewhat; but the brake mechanism, partly visible in back of the prop hub, got very hot. Pressure was released, but it got hotter; soon it was red hot, then melted and fell off. The prop continued to turn. We began losing altitude, but Captain LaPorte found he could hold altitude at 500 feet. It made us all a little nervous, but few of our half dozen passengers showed any concern. We made it to our destination safely.

On a subsequent trip on which I was not aboard Captain Mike LaPorte got into a typhoon in mid-Pacific and lost control. Losing altitude in what the crew all thought was spin, they came out in clear, smooth air at about 5,000 feet. But it was only the eye. Just as they got well trimmed in level flight, they hit the other side and violently rough air. Again the clumsy and unstable M-130 was out of control and losing altitude with LaPorte and his first officer both on the controls together. They came out and recovered at 500 feet with the whitecaps plainly visible and continued on schedule. That time the passengers did show concern.

I think, in retrospect, it would be hard to exaggerate the fatigue on these long flights.[7] Fatigue was caused by the very high level of vibration, the noise, the loss of water (sweat) on a long flight at low altitude when the cockpit temperature might be over 80° continuously, and from lack of oxygen if we flew long at any altitude. While domestic airline pilots were limited by law to eight hours a day and eighty-five hours a month, we flew up to 24 hours in a day and were limited only to 250 hours in three months. Of course, a Pacific crew was a multiple crew; everyone stood watches, four hours on and two off, but there was no way to get out of the environment. It was just as tiring off duty as on.

The navigator worked hardest because sighting any celestial body with the bubble octant involved ten readings of the altitude, each written down in degrees and minutes, noting the time you started and stopped taking the sights. Then the ten readings had to be averaged, meaning that they had to be added up and divided by ten, and this was a column of degrees, minutes and seconds, no nice decimal system here. The time for the sight would be taken as the halfway point in the time recorded which would then have to be corrected for any error in your watch vs. the plane's chronometer. *And you must never make a mistake.* Averaging the ten altitudes would have to be done several times to check the addition. When very tired, it would sometimes seem as though no matter how many times you added up the column, you could never get the same answer twice. We tried using little mechanical pocket adding machines and still couldn't always get the same answer twice.[8] One might even have to lie down for a minute and then try again. We did not carry oxygen and we had been told that 8,000 feet was the maximum for any prolonged period if normal alertness and speed of thought were to be maintained.

On one return flight, during the week off at the Moanna cottage, I toured Oahu, saw the Pali where King Kamehameha ordered his well-trained army to march off the cliff, and I called on and was entertained by Mr. Northrop Castle, a friend of my family. I also went out to Wheeler Field to see an old friend from Langley Field, Lieutenant Duke DuFrane. He told a fascinating story. Pele was the Hawaiian goddess of volcanos who lived in the crater of Kilauea. Mauna Loa had erupted violently recently. The Army Air Corps was asked to help as molten lava was pouring down toward Hilo. Lieutenant DuFrane was assigned to lead a flight of bombers to bomb a path down the mountain to deflect the stream of lava. When he got up that morning, the Hawaiian maid was in tears, although she wouldn't give the reason; so he got his own breakfast. The flight consisted of three planes, DuFrane leading. During the bombing, Pele let out a blast and all three planes collided. DuFrane parachuted and survived, but his bombardier and the pilots and bombardiers of the other two planes were killed. Through the local grapevine the maid knew of DuFrane's mission that day and believed that Pele wouldn't let them survive.

My next trip was with Captain Tilton, January 20, 1938, and it was to be my first as navigator. I was now fully qualified and checked out. It was a dark night with a high thin overcast through which I could occasionally shoot a planet such as Jupiter, which was a nice bright one. But the overcast was thickening. Halfway to Honolulu the flight engineer came down to the navigation compartment which was the forward compartment on the main deck. "Trouble," he said, "may I get in there?" So I moved out from the navigation table where all calculating and plotting was done. He began to remove the navigation table and the deck beneath it to get to the main fuel transfer pump below in the bilge. This pump pumped the gas, most of our fuel supply, from the big tanks in the sponsons up into the four small wing tanks. Each engine was totally separate from each other engine, so trouble with one could not cause trouble in another, except for the fuel transfer system. In fact the only other connection between the four was a master ignition switch in the cockpit so all four could be shut off simultaneously and instantly before a crash. But most of the fuel supply had to be pumped up from the sponsons to the individual wing tanks, and now the pump wouldn't work.

We were about seven and a half hours out from Alameda and had not yet reached our point-of-no-return. I gave the captain a new course back to Point Reyes, but I had misgivings. I had had no star fix and few drift sights on the water flares which I had dropped, for there were broken clouds below and the flares could only be seen momentarily and for a very short time until they disappeared. I expressed my misgivings to Captain Tilton who was unperturbed as we were getting some fuel from the seawings, enough to make the coast. The engines were purring nicely but, in a few hours, all four would stop. It was pitch black above and below. I moved into the co-pilot's seat with the octant and hoped for any little break in the clouds that would disclose a celestial body. There was no moon.

Suddenly the overcast thinned a little and the glimmer of one solitary star appeared. I took as many shots as I could, noted the time, and went to work on the flight deck with pencil and paper, Dreisenstock and the Nautical Almanac. The problem, of course, was star identification. The star had vanished never to be seen again that night. I could approximate the azimuth. I identified it to my satisfaction for the time being, as Dhube in the Big Dipper. But when the line of position was plotted, it was a course line that showed us to be several hundred miles south of our course. What to do? Captain Tilton continued on unperturbed. The radio operator was frantically tuning back and forth across the whole spectrum available to him, trying to get any broadcast station from Alaska to Mexico on which to take a bearing and trying to raise a boat with a CQ from whom to get a bearing and position. But the radio waves were singularly quiet, and the night only got darker. We remained in touch with Alameda on high frequency CW, but no bearings were possible.

Because San Francisco was foggy, Alameda directed us to head for Long Beach where Mr. Leslie, the division manager, had arranged with the Navy for a lane of battleship lights by which to land. We came down under the clouds to look for the coast. Suddenly we saw a light on the surface. A lighthouse? It did flash irregularly. We knew that marine lighthouse beams were directed at the horizon, so the full strength of the focused beam would be visible to a ship coming over the horizon. Airways beacons, however, were directed up three degrees above the horizontal so a plane at altitude would get the full brightness, whereas a person on the ground below the plane would barely see the beacon. Soon we saw several more flashing lights, presumably not boats. Finally we all agreed we were seeing various lighthouses on the Santa Barbara Islands off Los Angeles. By then we could see the glow of Los Angeles against the sky and shortly after we could see the coast plainly and locate ourselves accurately.

As San Pedro came into sight we could see the double line of warships, all precisely aligned and forming a lane between them wide enough to land in. Every searchlight on every ship was on, pointed down the alley at the surface, illuminating it like Broadway. Tilton landed smoothly down the brilliantly lit avenue. A Navy launch appeared to lead us to a mooring. Apparently the Clipper had attracted a little attention. Soon a large admiral's gig came alongside and on board came a procession of brass, stripes, scrambled eggs and even medals such as we had never seen before.

I tried to hide, barricading myself in a lavatory, not wishing to be identified as the navigator who had been so far off course. But as bad luck would have it, I soon heard my name called and was discovered. An Admiral William Carleton Watts heard I was on board and wanted to see me, introducing himself as Cousin Billy Watts. It was about six A.M. by then and we were unshaven and dirty. A sorry, most unnaval sight, I fear, but Captain Tilton looked as shipshape and naval as the commandant of Annapolis.

All the next day the flight engineer, with help from the Navy, worked on the fuel transfer system, but could neither find the trouble nor make it work. We could get enough fuel from the tanks to get to Alameda and we did so the next day with our loyal passengers. All that day, all night and the next morning maintenance crews worked on our ship. The transfer pump was all right. The sponsons were removed and one was found to be corked up so no fuel could get out of it. They had been inspected and painted just before our trip; and during spray painting, all disconnected and open lines were always corked up to keep out the paint. In this case a cork was painted over with aluminum paint like everything else and went unobserved when the sponsons were reinstalled.

Now, everything was OK and off we went that afternoon, three days late. Only one passenger left us; and the remaining seven were determined to start out all over again, and three new passengers were added. It was an uneventful but very long flight, 22 hours and eighteen minutes to Pearl Harbor. I was still navigator and now everything was working like a dream.

As I have mentioned before, the *Matsonia* and the *Lurline* sailed on the same day each week from Honolulu and San Francisco respectively and passed each other in mid-ocean about midnight the second day out with all lights on and passengers lining the rail in evening clothes to wave at each other as the two orchestras played Hawaiian music. The radio operator got their positions and I noted that at midnight we would be pretty close to them. I gave Captain Tilton a slightly changed course and asked him to reduce the air speed by a knot or two; and, sure enough, as midnight approached, we could see the converging lights of the two ships. Tilton dropped

China Clipper Crippled at Sea With 15 Aboard

ALAMEDA, Calif., Jan. 22 (UP).—The China Clipper which left for Honolulu with eight passengers and a crew of seven developed a failure in its fuel system 700 miles at sea and sped back to California early today. They ordered it to land at San Pedro harbor, near Los Angeles, instead of the Alameda base because the distance to San Pedro was less and there was a heavy ground fog here.

The airline was in communication with the Clipper by radio. Capt. J. H. Tilton, the Clipper's commander, reported that the fuel system had been repaired temporarily in the air. He said he expected to reach San Pedro about 4 a.m.

CHINA CLIPPER AT BASE

Craft Is Made Ready at Alameda for New Start for Honolulu

SAN FRANCISCO, Jan. 23 (AP).— The China Clipper, far behind schedule because of manoeuvring incidental to a clogged fuel line, returned to her Alameda base today from San Pedro and was made ready for a take-off for Honolulu tomorrow, three days late.

Pan American Airways announced that the plane had carried her eight passengers in the back-trailing trip to Alameda and that all would continue on their transpacific journey tomorrow.

Although the fuel trouble was remedied after the plane had landed at San Pedro yesterday, company officials said the craft would receive a rigid check-up before starting again on the 2,400-mile flight to Honolulu.

Six hundred miles out over the Pacific the big skyliner developed gasoline-line trouble late Friday night. Because she was less than half way to Honolulu at the time, Captain J. H. Tilton turned the ship back toward the California coast, landing at San Pedro.

Hawaii-Bound Air Boat Puts In at San Pedro— Was 600 Miles Out

San Pedro, Cal., Jan. 22—(AP)— The Pan-American Airways China Clipper, forced back from a flight to Honolulu by gasoline line trouble 600 miles at sea, alighted safely in the Los Angeles Harbor here at 6.35 A. M. (9.35 A. M. Philadelphia time) today.

The giant seaplane's four motors were functioning perfectly as it swung in over Long Beach, circled Reeves Field, Naval port on Terminal Island, and then settled into the water.

The craft was taxied promptly to Cabrillo Beach, where it dropped anchor with a group of Naval barges following in its wake.

Six men passengers boarded one of the Navy boats and were landed. The crew and the two women passengers did not leave the plane immediately.

The passengers said that when they were awakened about 5 o'clock this morning and were informed they were going to land at San Pedro they thought it was a joke, as they had thought they were nearing Honolulu.

They said the steward informed them the gasoline line trouble developed between an auxiliary tank and one of the motors, and although there was no emergency, the crew felt it would not have a sufficient fuel supply to make Honolulu without use of the gasoline in the spare tank.

Hawaii-Bound Airplane Gives Up Hop While 700 Miles Out

8 PASSENGERS SEE FUEL SYSTEM FAIL

Gigantic Flying Boat Lands Safely in Los Angeles

Los Angeles, Jan. 22.—(UP)— Besides Captain Tilton, the crew included A. O. Fisher, first officer; H. L. Brock, navigating officer; G. J. Wernett, engineering officer; S. F. Marrell, junior flight officer; R. G. Dickson, radio officer, and Peter Sarrels, steward.

Fuel transfer failure between San Francisco and Honolulu.

down to two or three hundred feet so that we flew low over both ships exactly as they passed each other. We could see the excitement below for a few brief seconds, and then we saw the puffs of steam meaning whistles, from the stacks of both ships.

As soon as we got to our Moanna cottage everyone slept. No surfing that day. We slept right through, lulled in our dreams by the Hawaiian band which played softly on the lawn outside our windows, serenading us at about tea-time.

The next morning we departed on schedule for Midway, now with 14 passengers. About two hours out the fuel transfer system once again would not work. Captain Tilton whipped around and shortly we were back in Pearl Harbor. This time all our passengers left us for good, or at least we refused to take them back to San Francisco with us where we would have to take the plane. On February 1st we flew the jinxed plane back to the maintenance men at Alameda once again. The flight engineer assured us we would get there; we believed him without question—and we did. Back in the hangar at Alameda we observed a new face; no one commented and we guessed he was FBI. The problem was discovered, attributed to a loose cork floating around in the fuel pipes, but there was no evidence of sabotage.

On March 19th I went out with Captain Tilton on what was to be the first flight to China. Mr. Trippe had obtained permission from Portugal to land at Macao and the British then caved in and gave us the right to land in Hong Kong. I was to be the navigator and would remain so on all the rest of my Pacific flights. We would have a seven day layover in Hong Kong, a replacement crew having been put there by an S-42 from Manila to bring back our Clipper while we would return on the next one. The Pan Am flights with the Sikorsky S-42 which had operated between Hong Kong and Manila were flown by Captains Chilie Vaughn and Pop Sellers. We would now have Chilie along as check pilot between Manila and Hong Kong. Chilie was an old China hand, having gone there as an ex-Army pilot for Pan Am in 1930. He was said to be Madame Chiang Kai-shek's personal pilot and had been flying in China for several years.

What actually happened to Chilie was this. T. V. Soong, a brother-in-law of Sun Yat Sen and also of Chiang Kai-shek, was the finance minister and he had ordered an S-38 from Sikorsky. The company had delivered it to Soong and had had it assembled in a field next to his house. But there was no one to fly it. Soong called CNAC and Chilie volunteered. One day T. V. Soong gave a ride to Chiang and Madame who were so enchanted that Soong gave them the plane. Thereafter, Chilie was on call at CNAC for the Generalissimo or his wife.

After one day's rest in Manila, we left the next day with Chilie for Hong Kong. The war between China and Japan was well under way at this time having started with the bombing of the Woosung Forts at Shanghai by the Japanese in 1932. By 1937 the Japanese controlled Manchuria and, with the start of the Second Sino-Japanese War in 1937, Bixby and the Pan Am Far East operation had moved out of Shanghai to Manila.

Chilie turned out to be all we expected. Attractive, good looking, very funny and, in addition, a very good pilot, one of the smoothest I ever knew. There was a story about him which appealed to me, and this is what he told me many years later:

"When I was at Shasi on the Yangtze enroute to Chungking, I and my co-pilot observed a coolie woman fall into the river from a float upstream from where we were. Her head kept bobbing up and down as she swept by our float. I asked the co-pilot to pull her out but he said: 'No, you get her, my watch isn't waterproof'. So I dove in and pulled her out. She appeared dead but we held her upside down until a lot of water ran out her mouth and then laid her down and administered artificial respiration by the classical method. Finally she gasped and resumed breathing. When she stood up we observed for the first time that she was pregnant, nine months or more by appearance. So I quickly got a ricksha and sent her to the hospital at the Seventh Day Adventist Mission. The Mission doctor gave her an aspirin, sent her home and sent me a bill for $4.15 Mex. I was mad at being charged by a missionary for his services, but when I told Bixby, he thought it was funny".[9]

We took off from Manila Harbor, NNW to Hong Kong across the China Sea, and it was pure dead reckoning again. It was not very far—only 638 nautical miles—to Macao where we would land first, but with each mile the visibility got worse. We knew the coast was dotted with steep little islands which rose unexpectedly from the sea and were inhabited by pirates. There were no radio bearings to speak of nor lights nor checkpoints along the way. Flying on the deck at an altitude of 200 feet or less, peering into the haze, Chilie was in a familiar environment, and we thanked God for him.

Suddenly a little peaked island showed up a few hundred yards ahead. With a steep bank we barely avoided it. Chilie then knew where he was. We passed Victoria Peak looking down on Hong Kong and turned west to Macao. But then we saw to our surprise much of the Japanese fleet off Macao including several small carriers with fighters buzzing around them, over the middle of which we would have to fly. The carrier planes were bombing Canton, unopposed and not doing much damage. Through all this activity we landed at Macao and took off again later, a little nervously, but no one worried with Chilie aboard.

Back at Kai Tak Airport, secured to our little facility, we went to the Peninsula Hotel at Kowloon. Kai Tak is in the New Territories, the area on the mainland held by the British on a 99 year lease. It is immediately across from the Island of Victoria on which is the British Crown Colony of Hong Kong. That very evening Chilie took us over to Hong Kong and then out to the Lido in Repulse Bay for a drink. It was on the far side of the island, overlooking the China Sea. The bar was crowded and, as usual, we needed no introduction to anyone. We were immediately recognized as Pan American and on the first flight from the States to China; and everyone came up to say hello. We would be in Kowloon for five or six days.

We learned what "White Russians" were. Many of these unfortunates, fugitives from the Communist Revolution which swept them out of their homes and country, were stranded on the coast of China, stateless and without passports, with nowhere else in the world to go. Speaking almost every language in the world from Mongolian to Hungarian, there were few drunks and all were well-mannered, well-educated, self-respecting and long ago drained of any and all emotions—they were fascinating people. Some had been titled, but no one knew and no one cared, least of all themselves. Their world had vanished for good; nothing comparable existed or ever would again. They knew it and just made the best of what they had. A Mr. Popoff ran the bar and wouldn't let us pay for anything. We got a free lunch from tables of smorgasbord, on the house.

The next day we all went sightseeing, and the following day Everard Bierer and I decided to go to Canton. Ev was the first officer, a Navy-trained pilot, somewhat senior to me and soon to become one of my best friends. We knew that our passports were not valid in China and that Bierer's had expired anyway, so we decided not to tell Captain Tilton. The next night, having gotten tickets somehow, Bierer and I went to the railway station and boarded a train leaving for Canton, 70 miles up the Pearl River. It was after dark. The train was totally blacked out, not even a cigarette was permitted, and it was stuffed with soldiers. We chugged through the night having second thoughts about our expedition. A conductor of sorts came through the car, took our tickets, peered long at each of our passports, holding Bierer's upsidedown, returned them to us and we chugged on. Sometime in the night we got to Canton and promptly found ourselves in a place where no one spoke a word of English. Bierer said he knew some Chinese, having learned it from the laundry man at home in Utah where he grew up. He tried it on a Chinese but the normally impassive face had a peculiar look as he walked away without replying. A second try was equally unresponsive. We never learned what he said.

Out in the street we got two rickshas and they had sense enough to take us to the Hotel Oi Kwan. It was first class but the personnel spoke no language except Cantonese. By pretending to sleep, we indicated to the clerk what we wanted and he showed us a room.

We saw no signs of the bombing but, due to the war, Canton had been invaded by several million refugees for whom there was no shelter of any kind. We arose early in the morning as I wanted to buy some jade and knew that a Chinese shopkeeper always tried to sell to his first customer because, if he goes away without buying anything, it means bad luck for the day.

The ricksha ride in the very early morning was memorable. We went down the streets along a narrow path between the bodies which covered every other inch of sidewalk and pavement. I did get some jade and we spent a second day shopping; and we got passage on a river steamer down the Pearl River back to Kowloon.

It was a slow and lovely trip down the river, passing an occasional junk or sampan and, in the distance, white puffs would appear in the air, followed later by a boom, where Japanese planes were bombing the airport and other installations around the city. Back in Kowloon we confessed to Captain Tilton who did not reprimand us. After an uneventful return trip we were back in Alameda on April 10th.

May 18th I was out again and once more with Captain Terletzky. I was beginning to like him and I think Terletzky liked me, although I did not think much of him as a pilot because of his temperament. He was a gentleman, well-educated and very good company to be with if he accepted you as he now did me, for we had flown a lot together. The crew schedule had been changed again and we just stayed overnight in Hong Kong and returned to Manila where we again had a week's layover.

One afternoon, resting in bed, I watched the clouds building up over the glassy water outside. Suddenly I saw one of the huge CBs (cumulonimbus or thunderstorm clouds) start to bulge out at the bottom. The base was not very high off the water and soon a small whirlpool developed on the surface of the bay. This whirlpool then began to show a light column going up toward the cloud and a similar column starting down from the bulge under the cloud. The columns connected and then a core began to get much darker as solid water began to be sucked up. All at once I noticed a freighter coming around a bend into the bay and heading directly for the waterspout. The captain appeared to ignore it and made no change in course. The spout moved a little and the freighter passed very close by without apparently disturbing the spout in any way. After a few minutes the spout quickly died out and the bay was flat and glassy again.

The trip back as far as Honolulu was very pleasant, and all went well. Back in California on June 8th, we still had spring snow up at Soda Springs and on Mt. Lincoln behind it. I forgot the Pacific for a while and got in some flying in the Commodore. About this time, one of my best friends from school and Yale, Dean Sage, Jr., came back from China where he had been hunting big game like the Ovis Polii (Asian mountain sheep) with Brooke Dolan. He had caught or bought a baby Giant Panda in Szechuan or Thibet and had brought it back with him. He left it with Olaf Holter, his first cousin, and me while he went back east to arrange for its reception by the New York Zoological Society. Olaf and I took care of it in the apartment, feeding it bamboo shoots easily obtainable on Grant Ave., and we both agreed that it was the stupidest animal we had ever seen. He became quite a sensation in the zoo.

My next trip would leave on July 15th with Captain Nixon, a very genial ex-Navy CPO and a man of prodigious size and strength. This trip was uneventful on the way out except for a broken oil line between Midway and Wake, which caused us to return to Midway and have a day there for repairs, giving us a day to explore and collect more glass balls. I found a large chunk weighing perhaps a pound, of a thick, yellow, waxy substance. After much discussion, most of the self-styled experts on the island assured me it was a congealed lump of oil from a steamer at sea. I threw it away. Later, telling of it in San Francisco, I was assured it was ambergris and worth many thousands of dollars.

Having gone to Macao and Hong Kong, we were back in Manila on July 24th for a week's layover there, awaiting the next flight which would arrive on the 27th en route to China and back to Manila where we would pick it up. The captain would be Terletzky, with Tex Walker as first officer and with George Davis, my ex-roommate in Trinidad, as second officer. It was said that Terletzky always requested Tex now, because anyone else tended to ask for a schedule change or might even refuse to fly with him, which was embarrassing. Tex was carefree, happy and afraid of nothing.

On the 27th, ominous rumors came to us at the hotel that the Clipper's last position report was about halfway from Guam to Luzon and that it was no longer in communication. We went out to Cavite to stand by. We had no other plane as the S-42 had been removed. By now the Clipper was well overdue. Soon the time of its maximum endurance had gone by. We knew it was down in the vast empty spaces of the Western Pacific between us and Guam where a quick check determined there were no ships except the *Meigs*. Captain Nixon took local charge of the attempt to conduct a search. The Navy at Cavite sent out what boats they could; but it would be days, going south and through the strait, before they could be in the area of the last position report. The Army Air Corps at Clark Field could not help. We were up all night at our Cavite base. Every radio receiver in Luzon was alerted to maintain watch on our frequencies so as to cover every frequency we had on board.

The next morning, on my own authority, I took a taxi to Clark Field and called on the commanding officer. Such was the name of Pan Am that I was immediately taken to him. "Sir", I said, "why can't you send a squadron of your B-16s out towards Guam. They might just find something, even an oil slick". He was a senior and a very tough, old general, or he seemed so to me. Obviously, not liking interrogation by an impertinent young man who, however, was not under Army jurisdiction, he said patiently, "I believe I told your Captain Nixon that we have a problem with very high oil consumption and the B-16s do not have the range to go anywhere near where you want". I said nothing and continued looking him straight in the eye. Obviously I didn't believe him. He was not used to this. Finally, the general sighed and said, "Son, my men have families too, wives and children. They have no navigation experience. I doubt if any one of them could find his way back".

During the week, waiting for the next Clipper, we were hounded by well-meaning people. People followed us down the streets in

Manila telling us how they had figured out that the Japanese had gotten the Clipper. Our Twin-Wasp Pratt and Whitney engines were the most powerful aviation engines then in existence. Even long, long after the war, reporters would write that copies of the Clipper engines were found in Japan.

There is no question but that Terletzky had run into a very bad storm; there were passengers aboard and no trace of the plane was ever found.

The weather was something else again. There were no weather reports from the Pacific wastes. The Pan Am island weather stations were the only weather observation points. On a recent flight between Guam and Manila we had seen a huge cloud mass to the north. To try and measure its size, I took a careful bearing as we came abeam of its eastern edge and another on its western edge. Using our track distance covered in the same time, the cloud, a typhoon we supposed, was 125 miles long. Next I measured the height. Measuring with the sextant the angle from the cloud base of the storm to the shadow on the surface beneath, and then the angle from the top of the storm to the same shadow, and knowing the height of the cloud base from the surface because we were flying at the same height, the top of the storm figured as 60,000 feet. This was something of a shock at that time when we generally believed that the top of most clouds would be less than 20,000 feet and that the biggest cumulonimbus or even a West Indian hurricane would never be over about 30,000 feet.

During our layover in Hong Kong in March, we had gone down to the waterfront to see Richard Halliburton and his large junk in which he sailed shortly thereafter for the States. He was never heard from again. The junk was a beautiful boat, maybe 50 to 60 feet long, all teak rubbed with tung oil, no bottom paint, fully equipped with the latest radio gear, and complete down to the eyes painted on the bow so it could see. Joss sticks were burning in the huge and elaborately decorated main saloon and all Chinese rituals to ensure a safe passage were rigorously complied with. We supposed they went into some weather such as we had seen and measured, which seldom appeared on any weather map.

Back in San Francisco I was asked to join a special pilots' club which had been organized by a Chinese lady, Dr. Margaret Chung, a surgeon with offices on Grant Avenue and a house on Telegraph Hill. She called the club members her "Beloved Bastards" and gave each one a jade, watch chain pendant. My number was 421. The membership was made up mostly of young naval aviators at the Naval Air Base at Oakland, but Captain Musick and a few other Pan Am pilots were members.

Dr. Chung was a reputable surgeon, and I believe that some of the members had surgery performed by her for free. It was odd enough in those days for a woman to be a surgeon, to say nothing of a Chinese woman. We were all fond of her and called her Mike.

On the last trip I had been out one month and now had a month and a half off. I was through with all school courses for a while, and instead spent most days teaching navigation to newly transferred pilots.

On October 5th I left with Captain Joe Barrows. He had transferred from the Pacific-Alaska Division which was based at Seattle. We were a little surprised at the new influx of senior captains who had never been on a flying boat and had no seaplane experience whatsoever. It was Company policy now to transfer and promote pilots in strict order of seniority, subject only to completing all the exams and checks.[10] He had vast experience in the Arctic and his record was proof of a good, resourceful pilot. Joe Barrows was a redhead, and he had been bitten with the gold mining bug that so many had or developed in the far west. He lived in a trailer, unusual in those days, and his wife, at his request, had obtained a degree in geology and was a licensed assayer. Between trips they roamed the Sierras prospecting but never finding a fortune.

Through my mother, I had been commissioned by a friend in Philadelphia, Rodolphe de Schauensee, to get him a specimen of a Wake Island Flightless Rail for the Philadelphia Academy of Natural Sciences. Rodolphe was the curator of birds. The rail in question was found only on Wake.

On an earlier trip I had asked the manager to get me one, but he had said he couldn't. The island was under the jurisdiction of the

U.S. Navy which allowed nothing to be removed. He was sure that permission to take a rail would be denied. On this trip, after dark and in total secrecy, I netted a rail with a sheet and promptly plunged it into a small jar filled with alcohol, just small enough to fit in my pocket and the right size for a bird a little bigger than a robin. There the bird went through Immigration, Customs and Public Health unobserved and arrived safely at the Academy in Philadelphia. In due course I received an engraved testimonial to my gift but it was not named after me. It is Rallus Wakoloensis.

Navigating between Midway and Honolulu, there is, on the chart at least, a line of shoals—Pearl and Hermes Reef, Lisianski, Laysan, Gardner Pinnacles, LaPerouse Pinnacle, French Frigate Shoal, Necker and Nihoa. However, we never saw any of them, except very occasionally French Frigate Shoal. We did not even have them printed on our work charts as most did not project above the surface and were practically invisible from the air. The first clearly visible landmark would be Niihau, the first of the Hawaiian chain in the northwest. Now, as we neared Niihau, not yet visible, Captain Barrows summoned me to explain the island which had suddenly appeared dead ahead. He kidded me about my navigation but I was fairly sure of our position and insisted nothing was supposed to be there. He decided to go down and look. We circled the "island" and saw no birds or vegetation as we flew around it at about 500 feet. We gave all the passengers a good look too. No one had a camera. The entire crew, pooling our little knowledge, finally decided it must be an iceberg. After all, Captain Barrows knew icebergs well. The rest of us had never seen one. We knew, however, that an island in the ocean *always* has a ring of white surf around it, no matter how calm the sea. Only a floating object could be on the open seas with no sign of any surf. There was no surf anywhere around this one. Barrows agreed it must be an iceberg, only commenting that it was a bit dirtier than usual. It was of an irregular shape between one-half and a mile long and half as wide. Of course we talked of the Trojan Horse and seriously speculated about the Japanese. Although it sounded a bit silly, Barrows radioed in and reported the sighting of an iceberg. When we resumed course, Niihau appeared exactly as forecast, to the fraction of a minute. My navigation was vindicated.

Upon arrival at Alameda there was a larger than normal group of people to meet us, many in uniforms. The senior Coast Guard official said bluntly that we were crazy. Since our message, he had been thoroughly researching the problem and there was no possible way an iceberg could have gotten to where we reported it unless it had been towed, and even then it wouldn't have lasted. Did we have a picture? No. A Coast Guard cutter was sent anyway and searched the area but found nothing. Were we nine crew and all eight passengers crazy? Perhaps a submarine volcano had pushed up through the surface and then settled back, but the experts were certain that was impossible because, among other reasons, of the short time between our sighting and the Coast Guard's inability to find it. As for a Trojan Horse, it had been just too big, much too big, to be a camouflaged boat. So the mystery remained unsolved.

One sees strange sights in the sky at night when one watches the sky all night. But who ever does except a bedouin who very likely will be inside a tent? A sailor on watch will keep his eyes ahead and on the horizon. Only an airplane pilot or two, side by side in the cockpit, and especially on the long, all-night flights across the Pacific, will do so. We did not speculate about Martians and the term UFO had not yet come into use. But we saw a lot of "things". Showers of shooting stars in August were like fireworks. Something was always moving in the sky at night.

We knew how the sky must have looked to Marco Polo and other travellers along the old silk route to China (which I flew over as a passenger in a Russian plane years later). One night, as I was sitting in the cockpit, suddenly a large ball of fire overhauled us and went past "close" by, disappearing out ahead. How big was it? How could one tell? No reference. How fast was it moving? How far away was it? Both of us in the cockpit and the radio operator behind us had observed it. We had each felt our hair standing on end or trying to. It appeared to have been travelling horizontally at the same altitude and on the same course as we were. It looked like a red ball of fire about the same diameter as a rising full moon.

I saw a school of whales moving from south to north one time which must have stretched 30 or 40 miles, somewhere west of Midway.

While I was becoming qualified and concentrating all my interest on the mid-Pacific route, much was going on which I did not even know about in preparation for a South Pacific service. At the beginning, Australia showed no interest in service from the United States but New Zealand did. Two possible routes were investigated; one through Canton Island and New Caledonia, the other through Kingman Reef and Pago Pago. The latter was selected because at least part of Samoa belonged to the U.S.A. However, no one was quite sure where Kingman Reef was. It did not appear on any ocean charts until 1925. I was told that Pan Am, on the first survey flight, found it about 100 miles from where the Hydrographic Office had located it. That was about 1,000 miles southwest of Hawaii with nothing else around, and the shortest route was via Kingman Reef. Kingman was 120 feet long and 90 feet wide and was only three feet above water at high tide. Submerged reefs, however, enclosed a lagoon with smooth water and large enough for the Clipper to land and take off on.

This is the general area in the South Pacific where the great typhoons form and sweep west to the Philippines and Asia. A weather station as well as fuel was badly needed at Kingman, to say nothing of a radio signal on which to home. Kingman was the smallest target, perhaps, ever to be sought by an air service. A ship, the *North Wind*, was chartered and it proceeded to Kingman, anchored in the lagoon, and stood ready with fuel for the survey flight. Pago Pago, on Tutuila, the largest island of American Samoa, was set up as a station.

The survey flight left on March 23, 1937 when I was in Miami, with the long-range S-42B which made the mid-Pacific surveys. The 1,100 miles to Kingman, the next 1,600 to Pago and the last 1,800 to Aukland were uneventful. Mr. P. St. John Turner, writing 35 years later in the *Pictorial History of Pan American World Airways* said, "The precision of Pan American Clipper's navigation owed itself entirely to the virtually unique Pan American long-range direction finders, which gave an almost continuous stream of bearings from Honolulu behind and from the steamer *North Wind* ahead at its Kingman Reef anchorage". Pan Am's long-range direction finders owed their fame mostly to Van Dusen's super publicity, but they may have worked well here. (Van Dusen was Pan Am's public relations man.)

Regular service was started successfully with the S-42, now the *Samoan Clipper*, on December 23, 1937. I was at home on my first vacation. Returning from vacation I tried as hard as I could to get assigned to the second schedule which was to leave on January 9, 1938. I was rejected for more senior pilots who wanted to go. I never asked for a special schedule again for no one came back.

Pago Pago was a beautiful harbor but ringed by mountains which rose sheer from the sea on the landing and takeoff sides to about 1,500 feet. On January 11th, departing Pago Pago with passengers aboard and Captain Musick in command, an oil leak developed and he turned back. Now faced with a landing in a very restricted area at full gross weight which was in excess of allowable landing weight, Captain Musick wisely decided to dump fuel to lighten the plane. We heard that the dump system of the S-42 had never been tested with flaps down. We believed at the time—and I still believe—that, as the flaps went down, the fuel being dumped was sucked up over the trailing edges of the wings and into the engine exhausts.[11] The Clipper blew up and went down like a flaming comet. Stories came back to us as stories do, mostly pure invention. One was that a shark was caught after the crash with Musick's uniform and his gold flight pin inside.

First we were enraged, the rage directed at Sikorsky for not testing the fuel dumping system in every possible configuration. But we were young and knew little; and we were not yet aware of the compromises and tradeoffs, sometimes anguished, which every great designer and aircraft manufacturer has to make. But most of all we were subdued. The death of a pilot was nothing new to us, but this was special. Gone for a long time were the usual jokes and banter among the lighthearted men of the flight crews, many of whom were very funny. But there was no humor now. Captain Musick was deeply mourned.

My next, and what was to be my last Pacific crossing was with Captain Kenneth Beer, a quiet-spoken pilot from Salt Lake City, ex-Army and a crack tennis player. We left January 13, 1939 and were back on February 9th to find headquarters buzzing with the expected delivery of the first Boeing B-314, a giant and very luxurious flying boat which would be ferried to the Atlantic. Captain Harold Gray had gone to take delivery at Seattle and ferry the new plane to Baltimore where the Atlantic Division had its base and was now flying a service to Bermuda with an S-42 known as *Betsy*. A British Imperial Airways service which used a Short-S-23 Empire flying boat, the *Cavalier*, matched us flight for flight.

On my last trip through Wake Island I had just read *Hurricane* by Nordhoff and Hall and raised the question what the station personnel would do if one was on the way. They had planned well. I found that almost everyone stationed at Wake had read *Hurricane*. James Norman Hall, a pilot from the Lafayette Escadrille and Charles Nordhoff had settled down in the South Seas, had made a fortune with *Mutiny on the Bounty*, both the novel and the film that had made Captain Bligh and Pitcairn Island world famous. They later wrote a powerful novel, *Hurricane*, the authoritative book on what happens to a small Pacific island in a hurricane. In 1940, after I had left the Pacific, one hit Wake Island. Flights were cancelled. The wind picked up. The sea rose. Much of the island became covered with water. All personnel took refuge in the power station. A huge diesel driven stationary generator provided electricity for the station and was housed in a concrete blockhouse on the highest point. The hotel went, followed by all the other buildings except the power station, which held. The water came up. The generator failed. Personnel huddled in the water with what food they had brought with them. Most were familiar with hurricanes in Miami and also knew the book with its vivid description of the sea rising from a very low barometer until it covered all the atolls in the area. Probably everyone took it for granted that they were going to drown. But the hurricane moderated, the radio was made to work again, and the word went out to those at home that all were safe and well.

As an example of our early instrument approaches, once Harry Canaday was on a night training flight with Captain Jack Tilton and was making an approach to land in San Francisco Bay off Alameda. There was a not unusual, very thin fog lying right on the water, perhaps 50 ft. thick, with a lovely clear night above. The lights of San Francisco and Oakland showed plainly. Being low on the downwind leg and just before turning on base leg, both Tilton and Canaday saw the marquee of the Alameda movie theater right below them, with the name of the feature plainly readable. A second later, Harry saw the face of his wife peering out their window, attracted by the noise, no doubt, and she saw him. The landing was otherwise uneventful and perfectly executed.

In February 1939 I learned that I was being transferred to the Atlantic and assigned to Captain Gray's crew for the ferry flight. Right away, Gray, with his usual thoroughness and attention to detail, had us working on a route manual all day and every night. Every conceivable route across the country and Central America, from San Francisco to Baltimore, was explored. The plane always had to be within landing distance of an adequate water landing area if two engines were out on the same side. Route altitudes were figured to clear the terrain with one outboard out.

Every conceivable contingency was planned for so that, no matter what happened, the correct steps to take were plainly laid out on a given page. The maps would show where to land safely on any en route water such as Lake Tahoe or the Salton Sea, as well as the landing speeds and distances for various gross weights, winds and temperatures at the altitudes of the water areas. Working for Gray was an experience one never got over. It was an incredible training in thoroughness and foresight.

We left on February 19th after four days of crew familiarization with the B-314, and spent overnights at San Diego, Galveston and

New Orleans, arriving at Baltimore on February 24, 1939. Bob Fordyce was the first officer and I was second, being junior to him. There were about ten others in the crew including flight engineers and radio operators. Bob was a close friend of mine on the Pacific and we planned to live together in Baltimore.

CHAPTER IV

―――――――――――――――― ‹›‾――――――――――――――――

Pan American Airways, Atlantic Division, Baltimore, Maryland

FEBRUARY 1939 – APRIL 1940

I ARRIVED in Baltimore February 24, 1939 with Captain Gray on a ferry flight of the first B-314 from San Francisco. "Dutch" Schildhauer was the operations manager of the Atlantic run—as he had been of the Pacific when it was being organized—and it was now operating three times a week to Bermuda with an S-42B.

Soon after arrival Bob Fordyce and I found a two-room apartment in a new development in Dundalk, a section of Baltimore. Its only recommendations were its cheapness and proximity to our base which was a rented hangar on Logan Field, the Baltimore Municipal Airport. Bob and I were unfamiliar with Baltimore, but I had some cousins, the Robert Garretts, and a great-aunt, Mrs. Robert Johnson, living there; my cousins, the Garrett boys and girls, were very kind to us and I was soon exposed to the very real charms of Baltimore and its inhabitants. One never forgets the crab meat and mint juleps. Soon I knew most of the people in the famous Green Spring Valley starting with the Jack Symingtons who were old friends of my mother and father, and the Curzon Hoffmans who were also. The Symington's son, Fife, was our Pan Am traffic and sales manager; Harry Snowdon, a huge Adonis from Yale was our station manager. Trippe's family came from Baltimore. Even the Governor of Maryland thought of Trippe as a Baltimorean who had based the Transatlantic Flying Service in Baltimore out of loyalty—which was not exactly correct.

119

Bob Fordyce and I lived in Dundalk most of 1939—until he left me to marry Dorothy McElree in West Chester, Pa. I then found a new non-Pan Am friend, Eno de Buys, a young gentleman from New Orleans, employed by a local trust company, also looking for a place to live, and we got an apartment at 4327 Marble Hall Road in the city. It was through Eno that I met the girl I was to marry, Hope Distler, as told a little further along, and it was through her and her family that I was to become familiar with the *Preakness* and the *Maryland Hunt Cup*.

Now that the B-314, the Super Clipper, had arrived, there was a big push to get it into service across the Atlantic. On March 13th we took it to Port Washington, Long Island, to show it off to the New York office and distinguished visitors. Such occasions produced a cloud of beautiful girls, mostly Powers' models for fashion magazines. Our vice-president of traffic and sales, Vic Chenea, believed in photogenic females as the best kind of publicity.

The B-314 was the largest flying boat and perhaps the largest airplane in the world at that time. The main deck consisted of compartments which made up into upper and lower berths. Forward of the passengers was a galley, then a small stairway or companionway up to the flight deck. The latter was very roomy by aircraft standards—the pilot and co-pilot seats behind the instrument panel were all the way forward, the radio operator's station was right behind the co-pilot and consisted of a table with the radios and an upholstered swivel armchair; next, behind the radio on the starboard side, was the flight engineer's station with a similar chair by a table backed by a huge instrument panel and various engine controls extending up over his head. Across the way, behind the captain and extending the length of the port side, was the navigator's table and chart cases. The entire flight deck was high enough to stand up in comfortably and had two comfortable seats at the rear for extra crew.

At that time our flying boats used a float with a runway to it from the edge of Logan Field on Baltimore Harbor. Our transatlantic passenger service was to be from New York to Europe, but there was no suitable place around Manhattan for an operating base for a giant Clipper. A float and runway from a small building on shore had been arranged at Port Washington which was to be the New York passenger terminal for several years. For every Bermuda flight we flew the empty plane from Baltimore to Port Washington where the passengers were loaded outbound, and unloaded on the return trips.

I made my initial trip to Bermuda as first officer with Captain Charles Lorber, and in Bermuda we used a facility on Darrell's Island in the Great Sound as our base. We shared it with Imperial Airways which used our terminal at Port Washington and our main base at Baltimore. In those days there were no cars on Bermuda; only horses, buggies and bicycles. Royal cedars covered the islands. All the roads were shady, and the islands were even more beautiful then than they are today. It seemed as though every available acre of land was planted with onions or lilies—export crops of which we carried as much as we could on the planes. Before Easter, every cubic inch of space not occupied by passengers would be loaded with cut lilies for the trip back to New York.

After my first trip to Bermuda the next week was spent in training and practice flights on the B-314. We had received a second one from Boeing, and Captain Gray was soon to take off on a B-314 survey flight for the coming passenger service across the Atlantic. Captain Gray, with Bill Masland as first officer, had surveyed the Atlantic routes to Horta and Lisbon the year before. Now, several flights would have to be made with the B-314 before the CAA would approve the carriage of passengers. The first would be called a survey flight and would carry only Pan Am personnel. If all went well and the ground stations appeared ready to go, the second flight would carry the first airmail and some CAA inspectors. After that several more proving flights might be made with mail and cargo until the CAA certified the service for the carriage of passengers.

On the 26th we left from Baltimore with Gray in command after a one day delay awaiting Portuguese and French permissions. Captain Mike LaPorte was an alternate captain being checked out on the route by Captain Gray. The second officer was Kalkowski; my friend Jimmy Walker was navigator and third officer and I was the fourth. Chan Wright, Ray Comish and Shelby Kritser were the flight engineers, and Bob Dutton and Addison Beideman were the flight radio officers.

Harold Gray was of medium height, lean, athletic and very blond. Normally he was smiling and very pleasant, but a steel will was discernible in his personality. He was an aggressive winner at almost anything; later when we passed our time during long delays in Bermuda waiting for the Horta swells to subside, we would play ping-pong. Although not very good at it, Gray always won. You couldn't beat him.

We went straight for Horta in the Azores, skipping Port Washington and Bermuda. Horta is a very small harbor on the Island of Fayal providing good shelter behind a seawall. Fayal is the next most westerly of the Azores. None of the islands provided any stretch of smooth water, sheltered and large enough for our seaplane operations, and we lacked the range to go to Lisbon.

We were met and guided to our mooring by the Pan Am launch. It, like the Pacific island ones, was built by Matthews and was an exceptionally seaworthy boat. In accordance with Portuguese custom, the skipper of the launch—any motor craft—could not speak to the "engineer". All orders were by bells which he rang; one for ahead, two for stop and three for reverse. These commands were executed by the engineer who was also the deckhand and who stood in the cockpit right beside the skipper.

The non-stop flight from Baltimore had taken 18 hours, and we spent two days at the comfortable hotel at Horta while Gray surveyed the facilities and discussed the very real problems of open sea operations with the local weathermen and seamen. I remember learning how to design a mooring which would have ample scope on its anchors to hold and would still stay in place, as there was barely enough room in the harbor for the Clipper to swing around in its own length. By using three anchors, equally spaced apart, the buoy would shift very little with the tide, just up and down in the same place.

Horta was enchanting. Almost all of the local islanders spoke English, having spent much of their lives at New Bedford, shipping out on whalers. When they made enough money they went back home to the Azores.

The food was good and we especially enjoyed the "melao", or Portuguese melons grown on the islands. These were shipped all over the world, picked green and each one packed in its own little basket woven around it. The melons hung in their baskets from the ceilings in local food shops throughout the Portuguese Empire. They ripened, maybe months after shipment, into the most delicious fruit, similar to but better than Persian melons.

A monk, head of the local monastery, made the most exquisitely carved sailboats out of the pith of some local fig tree. It was pure white, very soft, and very, very light. The remarkably delicate little ship models could be bought and, in exchange for a donation to the monastery, I got one which I treasured for many years. It was destroyed 35 years later in a fire. On the way back we picked up and brought home quite a large model in a glass case as a present from the monastery to President Roosevelt.

It was on this layover that Captain Gray calculated that the critical wave height for takeoff was three feet. There is a relationship between the height of waves and their length, theoretically. The relationship is affected by the depth of the water, winds and any conflicting swells. Gray prescribed that three-foot swells or greater at Horta meant "no go" at Bermuda or Lisbon when bound for Horta, and similarly for any plane at Horta. We did not worry too much about landings. When you got to Horta there was nothing to do but land, so land we did regardless of the sea. The problem was takeoff with the heavily loaded seaplane, and there was no good reason to leave Bermuda or Lisbon for Horta if you could not take off again and were going to be stuck there. In the future we would only clear for Horta with a forecast of swells less than three feet.

By way of explanation I might say that a takeoff in a heavy chop posed no problem. You just bounced off successive waves, faster and faster, until you were finally airborne. After each bounce you were going a little faster. But as the waves increased in height, they became farther apart, and, as you hit each one, the bounces got harder and harder until they were so severe that each bounce knocked off the air speed gained since the last bounce. You could never get enough speed to be airborne. That was the critical wave height and it worked out to three feet. Of course, long swells were quite different. With very long swells, which might be 20 feet or more in height, one could land crosswise parallel with the crests, or even in a trough, but it was only done in an emergency. A very thin-skinned flying boat is certainly not designed for rough water, and a more unseaworthy boat would be hard to imagine.

Leaving Horta on March 30th, we had a smooth takeoff and arrived at Lisbon in 7 hours and 48 minutes. The river Tagus (Tejo) is narrow, deep and swift where the city of Lisbon is built. Just above the city, however, it widens out into a large, smooth area where we landed. The current ran several knots and we could not taxi up to the float, so we went to a mooring and unloaded the passengers and cargo into large rowboats which took them to the float.

Our terminal building was at Cabo Ruivo. It was a small, very old stone building at the head of the gangway from the float. As the sun set and darkness fell, one weak electric light bulb provided the only light, and the four-feet thick stone walls made it easy to imagine oneself back 400 years ago. A couple of old taxis took us down dark, quiet streets, past cavernous wine cellars which smelled of the fermenting grapes, to the mid-town Avenida Palace Hotel.

We spent two days in Lisbon while Gray checked the facilities and directed the setting up of equipment and methods for handling the Clippers; and we stood by to learn what we could, or we went sightseeing.

The operations office had been looking for an alternate in case our European seacoast terminals were fogged in. One might assume that if one's departure-point weather was good enough for takeoff, one could always come back if destination weather got bad. But too often, with a deteriorating departure-point weather and good destination weather, one may have both ends close down while in flight. We had lived without weather alternates in Latin

America and on the Pacific, but now we were entering Europe with quite a different weather situation.

A large lake in France used by some of the big French flying boats had been selected as a possible alternate. It was at Biscarosse, about 35 miles southwest of Bordeaux. We had planned to fly from Lisbon to Marseilles, but the weather was very bad and so we flew out the Tagus and up the coast past Cape Finisterre, along the lovely north coast of Spain (always staying over water), past enchanting little landlocked harbors, past Biarritz where Bob Fordyce had grown up and Johnny Potter, our San Francisco friend, had played tennis with Borotra, and on to Biscarosse. The lake was an ideal operating area, large, unobstructed, free from swells and approachable from any direction.

We stayed in my first "relais" or small, French, country hotel. It was quite cold and, after a wonderful dinner, we took a walk through the town where all the local girls, under their mothers' watchful eyes, came up to practice their English and ask us to send them back some American *jazz disques*. In the hotel the beds were very thick feather ones, with china hot water bottles, coarse linen sheets and peculiar small comforters which only covered one's middle. We never saw Biscarosse again, as it was not equipped for nor ever used as an alternate.

From Biscarosse we went across France to Marseilles where we landed and moored at Marignane, the seaplane base on the Etang de Berre, about 15 miles west of Marseilles. This was to be the terminus of our mid-Atlantic route from Port Washington to Bermuda, Horta, Lisbon and Marseilles.

It had only been a three hour flight from Biscarosse to Marseilles and the base at Marignane was well set up with a station manager, mechanics, radio and weather stations. Gray gave us the rest of the day off. Jimmy Walker and I promptly found an Air France flight to Cannes and we got a ride in the cockpit with the pilot. We flew on a Dewoitine D-338 tri-motor, flown by one pilot and a mechanic. The cockpit was very wide with a co-pilot seat usually occupied by the mechanic, but now by one of us, and a jump seat which the other occupied. The mechanic crouched on the floor. The pilot non-chalantly drank champagne (we accepted all offers) and smoked, something never done in any Pan Am cockpit. When the pilot finished a cigarette, he flipped it casually over his shoulder and the mechanic would leap to get the butt and put it out. The cockpit was not clean of spilled gas, oil and fumes.

At Cannes we headed for the Negresco bar where the best looking cocottes in all France congregated to be picked up by the remarkably sinister looking Balkan millionaires who also congregated there, looking for them. Early in the evening we went back to Marseilles on a super-train which ran at 160 kilometers an hour.

That night I was assigned to stay on the plane as guard. Although it was April, it was bitterly cold and I learned how cold it can be on the water in a metal hull. The wind often blows down the valley of the Rhone at gale force. Such wind is called a "mistral". I was to start two engines if the mistral came up, to take the strain off the mooring. It didn't, but even wrapped up in blankets I couldn't sleep for the cold.

Our North Atlantic route would also go to Ireland and England, but still with flying boats, the only aircraft that could cross the Atlantic. We were denied Paris and London because there was no place to land. Pan Am had considered, I believe, Cherbourg, Le Havre and other places, but all were operationally unsuitable. Now we were to check our facilities at Southampton and Foynes.

Next day we left for Southampton, a five hour flight. Captain Gray had found our takeoff performance unsatisfactory and the takeoff pitch setting had been changed to a flatter pitch at Marseilles. There were, however, only two settings: "Takeoff" and "cruise". The takeoff setting was a flat pitch and gave a high r.p.m. and the cruise setting gave an increased pitch and a slower r.p.m.

On the takeoff from Marignane, Gray found the takeoff performance improved—we leapt into the air—but then the plane would not accelerate. At full throttle we staggered through the air at takeoff speed, and there the speed stayed. If the props had been changed to cruise pitch at stall speed, we would have gone down. So we sat and prayed. There was not enough speed to climb and we were going across the countryside at maybe 50 feet and full throttle. There was a steep escarpment straight ahead and we would hit it as we were going. Very, very gradually Gray made a turn and we climbed slowly until he could change to cruise; then we were on our way to Southampton. It had been a close call flying through a 90 degree turn at 50 feet and at stall speed. Gray was not a particularly smooth nor good pilot by Army standards, but with a mind like a computer and probably faster, there was no one we would rather have had flying us on this hazardous flight. It was an engineer's nightmare.

The area below Southampton, past Portsmouth, is called the Solent and the channel goes both ways around the Isle of Wight and out into the English Channel. Where we landed was between Southampton and Hythe across the river. The *Queen Mary* was berthed across from Hythe which was also the home of British Power Boats Ltd. We could watch their small torpedo boats on trials running at 40 to 50 knots up and down the river Test. They were the precursors of the British E boats and our PT boats.

We stayed at an old inn, the Langdown Lawn Hotel, at Hythe. Imperial Airways' main base was near there, and all the famous English transatlantic pilots came there to talk to Gray. I remember Kelly Rogers, later to be the president of Aer Lingus as Gray was to be of Pan Am, Wilcockson and Don Bennett of the *Mercury* which was a piggyback[1] plane flying mail between Ireland and Canada. Flying with a radio operator, Bennett navigated with pre-computed altitude curves and a cylindrical slide rule in his lap.

Imperial Airways had several Short Sunderland Flying Boats nearby and each had a kerosene stove on board for the watch at night. Gray very kindly allowed us to borrow a stove that night when I stood watch on board, although it was strictly against Company regulations to have a fire of any sort. It was bitterly cold.

On April 5th we left for Foynes on the river Shannon which was to be a stop on the soon-to-start North Atlantic service, but we returned due to a violent storm en route and deteriorating weather at Foynes. We spent the next five days at Hythe keeping one of the crew on watch day and night at the mooring. On April 11th we left for Foynes again. When we left the delightful little inn at Hythe, the proprietor, a very proper Englishman who had gotten used to the noisy Americans, made the mistake of pointing out that the beautiful oak on the lawn was over 600 years old. His comment only provoked ridicule from a Californian in our crew who asked, "When is it going to grow up?", and then explained that our Sequoias were well over 1000 years old. I think the innkeeper was glad to see the last of us.

Foynes on the river Shannon is about 20 miles downstream from Limerick, on the south bank. The river is very wide and Shannon Airport was yet to be built on the north bank almost opposite Foynes. Foynes was to be the first European stop for our seaplane route across the North Atlantic. The town consisted of only a few small stone houses along each side of the road to Limerick. At least half of them seemed to be pubs. Gray landed smoothly on the river and we secured to a mooring in midstream. The station manager approached in a small power boat to take us to a dock, but Gray was uncertain about the security of the mooring and sent me back in a rowboat to run a line from the bow to the shore as an extra precaution. I secured a one inch line to the bow and was taken ashore to where a huge old oak grew near the water. As I was putting a second half hitch around the tree, the door of a nearby house opened and out came the owner of the house and the tree. He was bright red in the face, proceeded most unsteadily on his feet, and carried a double-barrelled shotgun pointed right at me. I spoke quickly before he might think I was an Englishman. "Thank you, sir, very much, for allowing us to secure to this beautiful tree. We don't trust our mooring in the river and the current is strong". "Who said you could do that?" he replied rather thickly but threateningly. Not deigning to reply I quickly inquired, "Perhaps we could buy you a drink?" "Perhaps", he said; and, leaving the gun on the lawn, he staggered on farther and we helped him into the boat where the oarsman, who knew him, rowed us back and left us at the riverside rear door of the nearest pub. Mr. Fitzgerald, as he was named, happily consumed most of a bottle of John Jamieson's best, and so we made a friend to say nothing of an armed guard for the Clipper. We spent one night at Foynes, nearby at the Dunraven Arms run by a Miss O'Callahan. It was part of the Earl of Dunraven's estate, and the whole crew was invited to tea at the castle to meet the Earl and his son, Dickie Adare, who was married to a lovely American girl named Nancy Yuille.

It was bitterly cold, and while the Arms had hot water, there was no other heat except a very small grate in the living room to which, if she favored you, Miss O'Callahan would occasionally add a lump of peat. For those who are not familiar with peat fires, let me say that peat is the only known combustible which gives out almost no heat whatsoever when burning.

The next day we returned to Southampton in three hours, staying overnight there; then to Lisbon in nine hours, staying overnight again; then straight to Bermuda with a short stop at Horta for fuel; an overnight at Bermuda after 27 hours of flying; and then home to Baltimore the next day.

I carried with me on the first B-314 survey flight, two envelopes, one addressed to myself at Hythe, England and one to myself at Baltimore. At each overnight stop I took the appropriate envelope to the post office, bought and affixed a stamp and got the postmaster to cancel it, and then took it back and kept it. By International Postal Union regulations, international mail had to be sent through the post office. We were often asked to carry letters from Bermuda to the States to expedite delivery in the States, but we would firmly refuse.

For the balance of April, while preparations were going on for the second transatlantic trip, captains were being checked out on the B-314 instead of the usual S-42. During the first part of May there was intense training at Baltimore on the B-314 and Captains Sullivan, Blackmore, Ford and Winston were being checked out. They had been operating the S-42 to Bermuda since June 18, 1937.

I remember Sullivan making practice landings at Baltimore. Sully was one of the most experienced seaplane pilots. I was standing on the dock with Gray watching. There was a strong wind across the harbor. As we watched, Sully bounced on one landing. It was a high bounce. The B-314 hit a second time and bounced again, higher. Sully applied full power. In a full power stall the plane sank again and hit the water, bounced again, but by now the water had given out and the next bounce would be over land. This was the "porpoising" tendency, feared by all seaplane pilots. The plane could become completely out of control, bouncing higher and higher till it crashed, regardless of whether it was with power off or with full power on all engines. Now Sully was settling under full power into a freight yard, clearly in sight across the harbor. But this time, with just enough air speed, the keel seemed to skid along on the ground. Sully was able to drop the nose a very, very little, pick up just enough air speed to stay in the air, and then to climb out, barely missing the rolling stock in the yard.

Seaplane pilots would talk far into the night about the causes and prevention of porpoising. It appeared evident that it was a fault in the hull design, the length or height of the "step".[2] The Sikorsky had a slight hook in the aft step. The Commodore was the most stable hull on the water and therefore easy to land. The S-42 was very difficult to land safely.

I talked at length to Gray who probably had a better understanding of the forces involved than anyone. Much work was being done, he said, in the tow tank at the Stevens Institute in Hoboken, N.J., but that was the only tow tank in the world that could handle the high speeds of seaplane hulls. Whatever was being learned in the Stevens tow tank didn't filter down to us. Gray explained to us that the angle of trim upon contact with the water was critical. A little bit too low down and the bow would be sucked further down—the aerodynamic controls would not hold it up—and then the plane would do a "water loop",[3] caused by the center of pressure on the hull moving ahead of the center of gravity. But why did it move ahead when the pilot was trying to keep the bow up? Much more complex were the hull forces that resulted in porpoising when one landed with the bow too high. But why? No one knew.

Gray was giving the problem a great deal of thought. To start with, elementary aerodynamics taught us all the importance of the location of the plane's center of gravity. It had to be within design limits and stay there no matter how the plane was loaded, or control would be lost. With light planes and even with most twin-engine transports, the C.G. stayed within limits no matter where the passengers sat and no matter how the cargo was loaded. But now, with our much bigger planes and with the extremely critical angle of trim on seaplanes, the C.G. had to be computed and the plane loaded for precise C.G. location before any takeoff or landing. The Boeing Company had furnished us with circular slide rules as C.G. calculators for the B-314. Gray promptly designed for Boeing and for us a much simpler, smaller and easier to use slip-stick slide rule.

It would be more than two years before we or the designers began to learn much about seaplane hulls, and by then seaplanes were on the way out. Gray had also designed and proposed an averaging device to go on the octants so we could read the average of ten sights by visual inspection, thus eliminating troublesome addition and division. This device was built into bubble octants subsequently, but Loran and now Inertial Navigation have made bubble octants all but obsolete.

May 20, 1939 rolled around and we were scheduled for the second B-314 Atlantic crossing on the 12th anniversary of Lindbergh's flight. I was going out with Captain Mike LaPorte who had been checked out on the trip before by Gray. This was to be the first flight to carry the mail. It also carried Army, Navy, Coast Guard and CAA personnel. The mail would be mostly first-flight covers, bags and bags of them.

We ferried the plane up from Baltimore, and left the same day from Port Washington, amid a crowd of celebrities, including the Postmaster General and Mr. Trippe. We went straight to Horta arriving there in about 13 and a half hours. We all went ashore at Horta with many sacks containing two kinds of mail. The first was mail cancelled in New York for delivery in the Azores, stamped there to show delivery and resacked to be taken back to New York for collectors. The second mail was for mailing in the Azores, to be cancelled and stamped with a cachet showing "First Transatlantic Air Mail—Azores to New York". I think the cachet stamps were provided by Pan Am except, of course, the cachets put on by the U.S. Post Office for first flights from the U.S.A. to a foreign country. Now, however, we had to take over the local post office to provide the manpower to affix stamps and cachets. There were thousands of letters to be mailed for collectors from Horta to the U.S.A. as well as from Horta to Lisbon, to Marseilles and to Southampton, which was our itinerary. We worked in a frenzy as we had to get back on board and get to Lisbon the same day.

It was a smooth takeoff in the ocean between Horta and Pico although there was a little crew tension for we were not yet familiar with the plane in open ocean operations. It was only about seven hours to Lisbon and there we spent the night. This time at the Avis in Lisbon, perhaps the best and certainly the fanciest hotel in the world. It had been the Avis family palace and was now, as a hotel, the home of Calouste Gulbenkian. The few rooms were all palatial suites and the huge bathrooms had gilt fixtures and enormous bathtubs sunk in the floor or raised on beautifully tiled platforms upon which you climbed to get into the tub. It was all super-plush. The Avis bar had plaques on the walls commemorating the great Portuguese navigators and explorers such as Prince Henry the Navigator, Vasco da Gama and Magellan. Shortly after the first passenger flight, a new plaque appeared starting with Harold Gray, followed by the names of his crew and then of the passengers. Today, 1978, the Avis has been torn down and the plaques have vanished.

At dinner, the table next to the crew was occupied by an elderly gentleman with a large white beard. Suddenly the flight engineer looked up and, seeing our neighbor, exclaimed, "Good Heavens! That's Uncle Joe". He got up and went over to speak to his uncle who was, of course, Mr. Gulbenkian, said to be the richest man in the world.

Gulbenkian, an Armenian from Constantinople known as "Mr. Five Percent" because that was his regular commission, first arranged for a British-German-Turkish petroleum company to seek oil in Mesopotamia before World War I. Later he was referred to as a wily oil wheeler-dealer who often was in the middle of oil negotiations though he never produced a barrel of oil in his life.

The next day we flew to Marseilles and again helped with the post office to cancel and stamp the huge amount of mail. We found, however, that Marignane was now fully manned and equipped and we no longer had to keep a crew member on watch all night. We dined at a top restaurant in Marseilles and naturally ordered their famed bouillabaisse. It was quite a shock—a watery mixture of greens which would have been classified as inedible weeds at home, and fish such as octopus, eels, squid and other Mediterranean underwater creatures that are not normally eaten elsewhere.

The following day we flew to Southampton, then back to Marseilles; and then to Lisbon with only an overnight at each stop. From Lisbon we flew to Horta, stopping only to refuel and on to Bermuda, arriving 17 hours later. The last day, May 27th, we returned to Baltimore via Port Washington, completing the round trip to England via Lisbon and Marseilles with 80 hours of flying in seven days. Before leaving San Francisco I had completed senior pilot exams in Semaphore, Blinker and Spanish and, in Baltimore, on June 1st, I was promoted to First Officer Ocean.

In June I was back on Bermuda flights in the S-42, *Betsy*, flying with LaPorte again and then with Blackmore, Gray and Ford. I flew five trips in all.

The Bermuda trip with Gray was fascinating as always. We talked about the weather on the Bermuda route, which is along an area where fronts are born and deep lows appear on them in a matter of hours. It is impossible to forecast them, and the weather people in the U.S.A. had no way of knowing that storms were forming. After World War II, weather observation boats were stationed in such areas all over the world and the one between New York and Bermuda was called *Weather Ship Hotel*.[4] It would have been nice to have had one when the service began. Gray told me he flew for seven hours out of Bermuda once, and found he was only halfway to New York—normally the flight to New York took seven hours—and returned to Bermuda. The weather on most of this route was normally overcast, especially in winter. The navigation was therefore mostly dead reckoning using multiple drift sights. These often worked out to show unbelievably high winds at low altitudes even though the surface appeared smooth and calm. Again, Gray told me that on one trip the wind had been over 40 knots, swinging through all 360 degrees of the compass. No such winds had appeared at any point on the forecast. It kept the navigator on his toes. Sailors who have gone in the Bermuda Races tell of some horrifying experiences with the winds en route, but these races are held only every other year and only in the good-weather summer months.

In July (1939) I went out on my third mid-Atlantic trip with Captain Bill Winston, earlier referred to as "the pilot who taught Lindbergh's instructor how to fly". When he was a young man, he was not much liked, so, one day he decided to improve his personality and be popular. He did so overnight. He had an inexhaustible fund of very funny stories, could do enough sleight-of-hand tricks to qualify as a professional magician, could play any card game well, and could play the piano quite well, anything from jazz to Beethoven.

By now we were staying at the Estoril Palacio Hotel at Estoril, a seaside resort outside of Lisbon. We would go up to the casino next door to the hotel and play roulette after dinner. Sometimes we would go swimming on the beach in the morning, but we would have to rent a bathing suit top as one would be arrested for appearing topless—either man or woman.

I was assigned next on July 26th, to a ferry flight with LaPorte to bring a third B-314 from San Francisco to Baltimore. We took domestic airlines to the coast, Pennsylvania Central to Cleveland connecting with United at 12:40 A.M. which got us into San Francisco at 2:41 P.M. the day after we left Baltimore. It was fun to see the west coast again, and the new Pan Am base on Treasure Island where the World's Fair was just opening. We ferried the new Clipper back via San Diego and New Orleans.

In the summer of 1939, a North Atlantic run to England was started, to parallel the mid-Atlantic which went to Marseilles. On August 4th I went out with LaPorte from Baltimore/Port Washington with the first stop at Shediac, a little town in New Bruns-

PAN AMERICAN AIRWAYS SYSTEM

TRANS-ATLANTIC FLIGHT

NEW YORK TO SOUTHAMPTON

AUGUST 5, 1939

CREW LIST

CAPTAIN A. E. LA PORTE
Commander
HORACE BROCK
First Officer
J. NORMAN GENTRY
Junior Flight Officer
WILLARD B. BIGGERS
Junior Flight Officer
CAPTAIN AUDREY D. DURST
Junior Flight Officer
GARRETT T. MACEWAN
Engineer Officer
STEPHEN H. KITCHELL
Assistant Engineer Officer
ADDISON W. BEIDEMAN
Radio Officer
HARRY L. DRAKE
Assistant Radio Officer
JOSEPH RAVIOL
Steward
ALDERT A. TUINMAN
Steward

PASSENGER LIST

COL. A. M. HITCH
MISS ROSA PACKARD LAIRD
MRS. FRANK ANDERLINE
MISS SOPHIE SHOUMATOFF
MR. C. M. HOSKINS
MR. HARRY F. McLEAN
MISS JENNIE GOUGHAN
MR. OWEN J. KEENAN
MRS. RICHARD WALLACE GOODE
MR. W. R. HEROD
MRS. L. H. McCOURTIE
MR. WENDELL H. M. McCOURTIE, JR.
MR. FRANCIS OGILVY
MR. LEO JACOBSON
LORD CHARLES CAVENDISH
MR. HOWARD ERIC
MRS. MARGUERITE ERIC
MR. JAMES PAUL MILLS
MR. PEMERTON BILLINGS
MR. CYRUS EATON
MR. WALTER STARK
MR. HENRY O'NEIL
MRS. GEORGE L. RIHL

During the first years of transatlantic flights, we always issued passenger lists to all passengers.

wick, Canada, about 15 miles northeast of Moncton on North-umberland Strait which separates New Brunswick from Prince Edward Island. It was only about four and a half hours from New York and only about three hours from the next stop at Botwood, but the stop at Shediac was required by the Canadians to exchange transatlantic mail to and from Canada. We took on fuel and went ashore for lunch. We had lobsters, there was nothing else.

There was only one business in town, a lobster cannery; and there were only two occupations, catching lobsters and canning them. The catch was dropped daily into lobster "cars" which hung under long floats in front of the cannery. In the early morning a whistle blew and the whole town, all who were not out in boats, women, children and the elderly, trouped down to the cannery and spent the rest of the day boiling the lobsters, opening the shells and removing, canning and packing the meat. They were the best!

Botwood was on the north coast of Newfoundland and was an old coaling station for steamers on their way into the St. Lawrence basin. Here we made a quick stop to top off our tanks: it was our departure point for the North Atlantic crossing to Foynes which would take 11 to 12 hours going over and 16 to 17 coming back. Botwood served no purpose except the temporary one of a sea-plane terminus for the North Atlantic which would vanish with the advent of landplanes and the opening of the great airport then being built at Gander Lake.

Navigation would be tricky in these northern latitudes and much more so on the North Atlantic than on the North Pacific because the north magnetic pole is closer to the North Atlantic, and com-passes do not work very well near the magnetic pole. They just seem to wander back and forth, and the directional gyros of those days drifted off a few degrees every minute. Besides, we would be on instruments most of the time without celestial sights or surface drift sights. With more than usual concentration on navigation and with slowly improving radio bearings, we had no real problems on the North Atlantic and soon we made the expected landfall at the mouth of the River Shannon. Foynes hadn't changed and we had a pleasant overnight at the Dunraven Arms.

The next day we flew over to Southampton, conscious of the strong westerly winds which would take us over in two and a half hours while it would take four hours to come back from Southampton to Foynes.

War was in the air. We had three days at Southampton before we started back. I remember air raid shelters being dug all over the parks and the store windows full of gas masks. The return trip to New York and Baltimore was uneventful and we found no realization in the United States that war in Europe might break out at any moment.

The trip back over the North Atlantic was uneventful except that, on the last leg down from Botwood to New York, a great wind blew up from the northwest. There was no sign of it on our weather map, but the sea got very rough. We went down to about 100 feet to look at the sea, flying generally to the southwest. Soon we had a drift of about 45 degrees meaning a wind of over 100 knots. Huge seas built up in the Bay of Fundy and as the gale increased, it blew the waves flat. The surface became totally covered with foam. Soon, as Cape Cod came up on the horizon, the wind abated and the mainland had no sign of a gale.

I was scheduled on another flight to Bermuda on August 19th-20th; then I was to leave on the 25th for another North Atlantic with Captain LaPorte. This time we spent the night at Shediac. I remember lobsters for lunch, dinner and breakfast. Lobsters and nothing else. Very good!

On the 27th, with a short stop at Botwood, we were off on the great circle to Foynes again, but this time the radio was crackling with general alerts to all shipping. The radio operator would copy all of these and hand them up to the cockpit. Most were from the British Admiralty directing all British ships on the North Atlantic to head for the nearest neutral port. I remember many ships were being ordered into Cork on the south coast of Ireland. Again we spent the night at the Dunraven Arms and the next day went to Southampton where the river Test was alive with speedboats from British Power Boats Ltd. and with more Imperial Airways seaplanes at their moorings than we had ever seen before.

On the water we broke out little Stars and Stripes and Union Jacks and put them in sockets just installed outboard of the cockpit windows, port and starboard respectively. A launch took us from the Pan Am mooring to a dock in Southampton from which we took a taxi to the Polygon Hotel where the crew was to stay on this trip.

That night, August 28th, the blackout was in force. Opaque black curtains covered every window in the city, and a brief excursion into the street found the city entirely dark. Not a glimmer of light anywhere. No street or traffic lights, and all cars were moving slowly without lights.

We had two days of layover in Southampton. When we awoke on the morning of the 30th and pulled back the black curtains, to our astonishment the wide harbor was bare of anything afloat with the sole exception of the Pan Am Clipper which rode at its mooring all alone in the normally jammed harbor. A big U.S. flag had been painted on both sides of the hull and on the top of the wing of all the Clippers, which made our solitary flying boat very conspicuous.

We left for Foynes that morning and there we stayed awaiting further orders from home. Germany invaded Poland the next day and both England and France declared war on Germany two days later. I do not remember any radio broadcasts—perhaps there was a radio blackout—but I do remember walking to Limerick to get a paper and to find out what was happening. It was six or seven miles and we had intended to walk back, but took a bus instead.

Shortly we were dispatched from neutral Ireland back home. The airwaves were singularly silent on the way. We were all speculating wildly what would happen. At Southampton everyone had expected immediate German bombing of Portsmouth and London, but nothing happened and the "phony war" dragged on into the next year.

On September 9th I went to Bermuda with Captain Blackmore, and on the 15th I was off across the North Atlantic again with Captain Lorber. This time we would only go to Foynes and would be met there by Imperial Airways (converted to BOAC—British

Overseas Airways Co.—on April 1, 1940). The Neutrality Act limited us to neutral territory, Ireland and Portugal, although an occasional secret Pan Am flight went on to Poole in England.

It was getting late in the year for the North Atlantic. We had inflatable rubber de-icer boots on the leading edges of the wings, indeed these had first been installed on the S-42 which flew the North Atlantic survey flights in June and July of 1937. We were not too comfortable with them as there were disquieting stories of North Atlantic wing ice forming so fast and so thick that before one could turn on the de-icers they would be so covered they could not work. We longed for thermal de-icing, but this was yet to come. At this time there was a problem with water runoff from thermal de-icers which froze over the ailerons. We did have de-icer fluid for the propellers. Before this, ice forming on the propellers, breaking off and hitting the sides of the fuselage would sound like machine gun fire inside the plane.

All American planes had carburetor heat to melt carburetor ice. Yet, it was the lack of such heat on the Imperial Airways Short-S-23 Empire *Cavalier*, our opposite number on the Bermuda run, which once caused all four engines to stop; and it went down between Bermuda and Port Washington. Here is the story as I obtained it from passenger Max Talbot's notebooks.

On Jan. 21, 1939, a month before I transferred from the Pacific to the Atlantic, the *Cavalier*, a Short-S-23 Empire British Flying Boat, operating between Bermuda and New York for Imperial Airways, came down on the ocean about halfway between New York and Bermuda at 1:25 P.M. EST. It was flying at 5,000 feet and all four engines quit in rapid succession so the captain had to make a "dead stick" landing. The hull split open on hitting a swell, inrushing water swept the captain and first officer back into the cabin and the plane sank in 15 to 20 minutes. There were 13 on board, four male crew and nine passengers. Four or five were women. Apparently the passengers had never put on life jackets because the newspapers and other accounts said the steward got some life preservers from the cabin before it sank and he and the first officer formed a ring of the passengers and life jackets to keep each other afloat. In the ten hours they were in the water, the steward and two passengers let go, floated off and drowned.

The radio operator had sent out an SOS on the descent at 1:25 P.M. It was picked up by the *Esso Baytown*, a Standard Oil tanker going from Boston to Houston, by the automatic radio alarm system which all one-radio-operator ships carried to cover the distress frequency when the operator was asleep. The *Esso Baytown* immediately proceeded to the SOS position arriving there about 10:30 that night. The captain turned on every possible light and observed other ships nearby also lit up. Searchlights revealed nothing, but a life boat was lowered at 10:45. The ten heads were invisible at night in the water, and a bad sea was kicking up. The survivors could see the *Esso Baytown* nearest to them and Captain M. R. Alderson of the *Cavalier* and the radio operator left the ring in charge of the first officer and swam over to the *Esso Baytown* where their shouts were heard. The survivors were promptly picked up. A company periodical of the Standard Oil Company called the rescue "the most brilliant rescue in the annals of the sea" and it may well have been.

The accident filled the front and even the second pages of the New York and Boston newspapers, and attracted an enormous amount of publicity which may or may not have helped our Bermuda business.

We considered carburetor ice a major hazard on the Bermuda route and monitored the carburetor air temperature gauges continuously in flight.[5]

The buildup of ice on the wings which could destroy their lift and weigh the plane down, was a different problem. What we knew was mostly learned from the U.S. domestic airlines, some of which had a great deal of experience. We suspected that the North Atlantic might well furnish the worst conditions in the world. Few experiences are more intimidating than looking out the cockpit window and watching ice build up on the leading edges, when you are in the middle of the ocean. *Betsy* on the Bermuda run, often was quite heavily encrusted with ice in winter, especially on the struts which supported the vertical fins and rudders on the tail.

Sometimes a strut would be missing on arrival—broken off by ice and the resulting vibration.

When Foynes became our Eastern terminus, we found a place that rented bicycles and we spent our three day layover touring Clare and Limerick counties. The landscape there was literally dotted with castles—almost all burned and ruined wrecks. We did not know our history and no one knew which were burned by Cromwell's men and which had gone in the "Great Trouble". A few were inhabited, and we would cycle up to the door, often over a portcullis into an inner courtyard, and bang a bell usually hanging somewhere. An American would appear and, hearing the name Pan American, would ask us in. He would be an Irish-American who had prospered in New York, probably in the city government, and had come home in his rich old age to the "ould sod", and bought himself a castle. The castle would be livable but only just. His usual request would be to bring him back some Kodak films.

The stories told about the Trouble were pretty grim—stories of Englishmen buried to their necks in the beach at low tide, etc. Near every old and destroyed mansion would be a good sized mound where silver and art objects were said to be buried. These mounds were so sacred that no one ever dared touch them. The countryside was unbelievably poor. The Irish Free State constabulary, a famous organization on which the Canadian Royal Mounted Police and Colonel Thayer's Pennsylvania State Police (the first U.S. state police) were modelled, would tell of finding whole families starved to death as they made their periodic rounds in winter. To stay warm the whole family lived in the one room of their thatched stone house with any livestock, cows, pigs, chickens, and anything else alive. The smell was awful. The town street was often deep in fresh manure so an automobile could not navigate it and the passengers would have to get out and push. But when the sun shone, which it seldom did, the scene was indescribably beautiful. The green countryside was like no other green. Truly, Ireland is the Emerald Isle.

Although the war was on in Europe, the Western world was

quiet except for Poland; and the North Atlantic still looked normal
—what we saw of it. I was not to see it again for several years. On
October 3rd I had my 13th Bermuda trip, with Gib Blackmore,
and I left with him on a mid-Atlantic on the 12th.

The North Atlantic route was intended to close between September and the following June because the harbors at Shediac and
Botwood would be frozen over. Foynes stayed open, of course,
because Ireland was bathed by the Gulf Stream. Now both flights
a week would go to Lisbon via the Azores, but one of these would
go on up to Foynes. The war had stopped flights to Marseilles and
Southampton.

The sea was friendly outside of Horta and we were gaining
knowledge and confidence with the swells. We had three days at
Lisbon now, at the Estoril Palacio. I remember a live pigeon shoot
at the local country club which I watched. The stand was on a level
spot like a golf tee, looking down over the entrance to the Tagus
below. The live pigeons were thrown up by a concealed trap un-
derneath the stand and popped out of a hole in front of the shooter.
Their tail feathers had been pulled out so they flew away, down-
hill, in a most erratic manner and were very hard to hit. Most were
missed and, no doubt, grew back their feathers if they survived
long enough.

We played roulette every night and were now developing our
own systems. A "guaranteed" way to win would occupy much of
the conversation. It was fun because the chips were five escudos
each for the smallest, with which we played. As I remember, the
escudo was worth about a nickel then. The largest chips were con-
tos, a thousand escudos, and worth about $50.00 each. One night
some newly arrived American businessmen were at the table next
to ours in the Estoril dining room. Their conversation raised the
question as to what to do after dinner. "We could play roulette
next door", one of them said. "What's that?", said another. His
three companions explained it to him and he remarked, "We
ought to be able to take them at that". Later on we were at the
casino playing our carefully husbanded five escudo chips and we
saw the men enter. They bought pockets full of conto chips. The

man who had asked about the play selected a table and watched a long time without venturing a single chip. Finally, when he had it figured out, he started to play, and he won and won and won. His companions stopped to take his piles of chips back to the cashier. The croupier would signal for more chips and they would appear from time to time. When he was tired, they all went home. The bank wasn't broken as far as we could see, but nearly. We left too, and followed them back to the hotel, curiously as I remember, for we were all sure they would be held up and relieved of their winnings and never reach the hotel with them. But they did.

We were home on the 18th and two days later I had a check flight with Captain Sullivan on which a CAA official rode along and gave me a 5W rating on my license, which was the highest rating obtainable—for the biggest and heaviest planes, land and water.

On November 4th I went out to Lisbon again, but this time with Captain Ford. I had known Bob Ford as one of the young first pilots at Trinidad when I was there nearly four years before. Everybody, except the brass, liked him very much and thought highly of him. He was a very good pilot, bright and outspoken and often spokesman for the pilot group with their complaints to the operations office. The trip was fun but uneventful and we were back on the 13th.

The next trip, leaving on December 2nd, would be with Captain Sullivan. He had been with Captain Musick on the Pacific surveys and then was chief pilot at the beginning of the Atlantic Division. He had been a Navy CPO, a chief bo'sun's mate, I believe, and may well have been the toughest one the Navy ever had. It was an experience to do anything with him. If you got anywhere near him, he would punch you jovially on the upper arm and nothing in that arm, not even the fingers, would work for several days thereafter. Any doctor would have put it in a cast, if not in a sling at least; but, of course, no one would give a sign that anything had happened.

It was a routine flight over and back until we left Horta for Bermuda. About halfway over, it became overcast. We were fairly sure of our latitude but our only method of obtaining distance, i.e., longitude, was by a double drift sight which did not give a very accurate wind calculation, and consequently not a very accurate ground speed. Shades of Columbus! We knew the G.M.T, but we needed a little more. We flew and flew and flew. Our ETA (estimated time of arrival) came and went. I checked the navigation work with great care. Not a sign of Bermuda. We had four hours of reserve fuel. When we were three and a half hours into the reserve, the whole crew was on the flight deck with every eye focused on the horizon ahead. There was total silence in the cockpit except for the smooth engine noise.

Suddenly a ship appeared dead ahead on our track. Frantically the radio officer sought contact. Nothing doing. Perhaps a tramp with the one radio officer asleep. As we rapidly overhauled it and then passed overhead, Sully asked each of the crew if they wanted to land alongside the ship or thought we ought to. A unanimous "no". The flight engineer, almost the most important man on the crew at this juncture, rechecked all his figures and promised Sully at least 30 minutes more flying. Five minutes later a murmur arose from all on the flight deck. Of course, Sully saw the lighter green water before anyone else. Because of the stiff headwind at all altitudes, we had been down on the deck at perhaps 200 feet or less for some hours; the wind was less there, and we had to be right on the islands to see them. We landed in the Great Sound and taxied in.

On December 9th I was scheduled out on my 10th transatlantic trip in nine months, again to Lisbon on December 23, 1939, with Captain Winston. This was ordinarily a trip to look forward to, even though I would be away for Christmas; but this time was different for I was in love. I had met my girl, Hope, as a blind date with Eno de Buys one evening the previous October. Eno also had his girl, Judy, whom he was later to marry. We all gathered at the Belvedere Bar in Baltimore and stayed there for dinner.

After dinner Hope and I won a rhumba contest in the ballroom. The focal point in my life then was just moving to New York to paint in her Greenwich Village studio under an extremely good painter, a Japanese named Inukai. I had to go to New York, when I could, and stay at the Hotel Weylin, also famous for its bar, to see her. She would be home for Christmas, for she was a Baltimorean, but I would not. At any rate I was back on January 15th and right off to New York. I secured a vacation in February and our engagement was announced on her birthday. We planned to be married in May, God and Pan Am willing.

I was scheduled out on another trip with Captain Pat Nolan on March 5th. Nolan was from the Western Division and, as far as I knew, he had absolutely no boat experience except for his checkout on the B-314. The trip over was all right as far as Horta, but there we spent five days waiting for the swells to abate enough to take off. In Lisbon we took off on the start of the return on March 18th but returned to Lisbon as Horta remained too rough to land. On the 20th, we flew to Horta and landed with no great problem, although taxiing in over the big swells to the harbor must have been something new to Pat. We were now about five days behind schedule for our passengers.

The same day two more Clippers came into Horta. One was the westbound behind us, and the other was an eastbound with Captain Gray. So we had three Clippers, the entire Atlantic fleet, in Horta at the same time and the accommodations were bulging.

The next morning, by virtue of our having been the first arrival, we were to be the first to take off. Gray was to be third, and, when I saw the sea, I could not help thinking he was wise to watch someone else try it first. We all three taxied out of the harbor in a row. Outside there was much more than a three-foot swell. Pat showed no concern of any kind; but, after all, the chief pilot was behind him and looking at the same sea. When the flight engineer said "OK for takeoff", meaning the temperatures were all okay, Pat turned to me and said, "What do you think?", and I replied promptly, "Nothing to it. You'll make it on the third bounce".

Pat pushed the throttles all the way forward, and I held them there with my left hand for it was going to be very rough, and we made a third bounce. But then there was a loud crack, like a pistol shot, and I pulled back the throttles as Pat tried to reach them, although it was all he could do to handle the flight controls. Right behind Pat the navigator said quietly, "Captain, the window seems to have broken". When we had slowed down, we turned around and not only was the window by the navigator's station broken but the whole flight deck seemed to be just a little out of line with the rest of the hull. We slowly taxied in to the harbor followed by the other two.

Once at our mooring the flight engineer quickly found that the port seawing was loose. The forward and main attachment point had broken loose and only the fairing held the sponson on. We went back to the hotel, but our passengers, not in the least daunted, started to complain that we were taking longer than Columbus to get across the Atlantic. While the flight engineers were frenziedly trying to decide what to do, one passenger cabled President Roosevelt to get them back to the U.S.A. Most were refugees anxious to get to the States just as quickly as possible.

The next day the *Conti di Savoia* was diverted into Horta and took off all of our passengers except a man and his wife. Although Mussolini had not yet joined Hitler in the war, our two remaining passengers, who were Jewish, were not about to trust Mussolini's fascism any more than Hitler's.

The flight engineers had found a machine shop and the wreck of an old Ford Model T. They radioed Baltimore who telegraphed Boeing in Seattle to ask if they could replace the special aluminum alloy "aircraft bolts" (very special and about $50.00 apiece) with ones they would machine out of a Model T drive shaft. The answer came back quickly, "Go ahead". Much later we were to learn that Henry Ford specified such high quality steel alloy for his stressed parts like the drive shaft, that the engineers at Boeing had no qualms about the strength of the bolts. With any other automobile manufacturer or with a modern Ford, they would not have approved. The CAA also approved the repair by radio, and we were safely back in Port Washington with our two passengers on March 27th, before the *Conti di Savoia* docked.

That was my last trip on the Atlantic as first officer. On April 1st I was transferred to Miami as a reserve captain, to report there on April 9th.

CHAPTER V

———————————————— ‹›— ————————————————

Pan American Airways, Eastern Division, Rio de Janeiro, Brazil and Miami, Florida

APRIL 1940 – JULY 1942

RIO DE JANEIRO

AT Miami I reported to Mr. Critchley, the operations manager, at Coconut Grove and was given some time off to find a place to live. I was also advised I would be promoted to captain and transferred to Rio in the middle of June. I was due a vacation and was promised 30 days from May 15th to June 14th, during which time I expected to get married. Captain Fatt was still chief pilot, and he assigned me immediately to a week of instrument flight training and practice in a Stinson and in a Commodore. On April 22nd and 23rd Captain Fatt himself checked me out in an S-38, an amphibian used on water and land; then I spent a week on solo practice flights off Dinner Key and at the 36th Street Airport.

May 1st I was assigned to a Rio trip with Captain Craig. All this time I was in frantic communication with Mr. Critchley trying to get my belongings out of Baltimore by May 20th and to pin down my proposed transfer to Rio. My flight with Craig went smoothly to Port of Spain, Belém, Recife, Rio and back to Miami arriving on the 10th. Then finally I went on leave and headed for Baltimore. Hope and I were married on Saturday, May 25th, after a hectic round of parties in Baltimore and Philadelphia.

I was back in Miami on June 10th, but now with Hope; and we stayed at the Hotel Good in Miami Beach as we knew we were soon going to Rio. On the 15th I was checked out by Fatt on the S-43, land and water.

Rio was a Pan Am pilot base for six crews who lived there and covered the west coast of South America up to Trinidad and down to Buenos Aires. On June 19th I was off for Rio with Captain Shorty Clark, taking Hope with me "subject to payload"; but she was off-loaded at Port of Spain, Trinidad, where we changed equipment from an S-42 to a smaller S-43. On the return I made the landing at Recife and bumped the bow while docking at the barge we used there for refuelling. The dent was barely visible and needed no repairs; but Shorty Clark was distraught. He had never even scratched the paint on any airplane in his more than 20 years of flying. Some 30 years later, meeting Shorty in New York, he reminded me of this mishap, and I remembered too—I never forgot—although it was the only time I ever scratched the paint on a plane. I picked up Hope at the Queens Park Hotel in Trinidad where she had been staying waiting for onward space with me. We finally got off for Rio with Captain Bob Gibson in an S-43 on July 7th.

Few airline pilots are bachelors and their wives are very much a part of their lives. Hope was an ideal companion; she was candid and critical, she loved to paint and sketch and with her training she saw things with the eye of an artist. Her presence made all the difference.

"I must admit", she wrote in her diary, "that it is with a slightly jaded eye that I view Trinidad. I've seen so many places like it, only better, in the East; and even the Britishers here seem frowsier than their brothers in the Orient. Perhaps it is because I'm less credulous and impressionable at twenty-two than I was at eighteen.

"The trip down, touching at the larger islands of the West Indies, I liked enormously despite the tediousness of sitting for hours in a plane. It was also a very good lesson in not judging one's fellow passengers too quickly—a very good lesson indeed. The best moments were the arrival at San Juan at sunset, the terrace there above the sea, the beaches and the coral reefs with the even lines of waves

Pan Am passenger terminal, Pearl Harbor

Diamond Head from Waikiki

Dick Campbell

Long dock to
lagoon, Midway

Brock and
Leffingwell

Approaching Wake

PAA Hotel at Wake Island

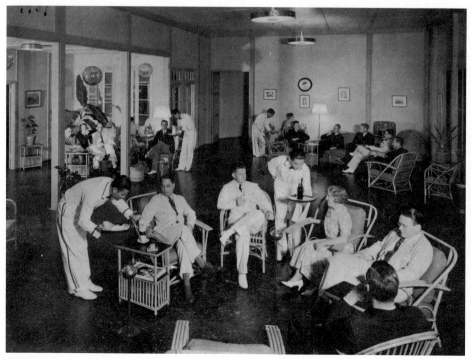

Hotel lounge

Hotel, Guam

Base, Guam

PAN AM TERMINAL, MACAO

Cavite, Manila

Waterspout

Junks on Pearl River

River life, Canton

Coolies, Hong Kong

Cash Street, Hong Kong

New York World-Telegram

Local Forecast:—Thundershowers late today or early tonight followed by clearing and cooler; moderate temperature tomorrow.

NEW YORK, FRIDAY, JULY 29, 1938.

VOL. 71.—NO. 24.—IN TWO SECTIONS—SECTION ONE. Entered as second-class matter, Post Office, New York, N. Y.

**** ***

7TH SPORTS

Complete Tables
Bid and Asked Prices

PRICE THREE CENTS

PACIFIC CLIPPER MISSING WITH 15

WEATHER.
(U. S. Weather Bureau Forecast.)
Mostly cloudy tonight and tomorrow; probably showers tomorrow; not much change in temperature; light variable winds. Temperatures today:—Highest, 82, at 10:30 a.m.; lowest, 71, at 6 a.m.

Financial News on Page 11

NOON
LATEST NEWS AND
WIREPHOTOS

The Evening Star

WITH SUNDAY MORNING EDITION

86th YEAR. No. 34,423. Entered as second class matter post office, Washington, D. C. WASHINGTON, D. C., SATURDAY, JULY 30, 1938.—TWENTY-EIGHT PAGES.

(A) Means Associated Press. THREE CENTS.

OIL PATCH FOUND ON COURSE OF CLIPPER

Registered United States Patent Office

THE SUN

WEATHER FORECAST

Generally fair today; slightly cooler. Yesterday's Temperatures: Max. 94; Min. 71.
(Details on Page 18)

BALTIMORE, SATURDAY, JULY 30, 1938

Vol. 203-B

PAID CIRCULATION JUNE
MORNING, 143,641
EVENING, 132,263 305,180 | SUNDAY 211,881

Entered as second-class matter at Baltimore Postoffice. Copyright, 1938, The A. S. Abell Company, Publishers of The Sun.

British House Of
Commons Cheers
U. S. Aid For Jews—Page 9

18 Pages   2 Cents

SHIP FAILS TO FIND CLIPPER

THE WEATHER

Generally fair today and tomor- row; slightly cooler today.

The Only Newspaper in Maryland with Associated Press, Universal Service, Associated Press, Interna- tional News Service and United Press.

THE BALTIMORE NEWS-POST

AN INDEPENDENT NEWSPAPER

The Largest Daily Circulation in the Entire South

VOL.CXXXIII.—NO.73. C

Entered as second-class matter at Baltimore Postoffice. Copyright, 1938, by Hearst Consolidated Publications Inc.

SATURDAY, JULY 30, 1938

PRICE 2 CENTS

COMPLETE MARKETS

14 NAVY VESSELS JOIN HUNT FOR MISSING HAWAII CLIPPER

Giant Clipper, 15 Aboard, Missing, Unreported Over Pacific Ocean

Dial 3-3431 Calls The Times-Dispatch — Three Cents

:3

15 Aboard Plane Long Overdue At Manila Base; U.S. Transport At Scene

Wide World—Times Wide World
M. A. Walker, first officer

(A. P. Wir
CAPT. LEO TERLETZKY

Gigantic Hunt Pressed As No Word Is Heard From Hawaiian Clipper

PHILA INQUIRER

Army and Navy Seek Clipper Missing With 15 On Guam-Manila Flight

Baby giant panda at our house

Dean Sage Jr. and panda

Boeing B-314

Boeing B-314: 1. Bow hatch 2. Forward compartment 3. Cockpit 4. Captain 5. First Officer (far side) 6. Radio loop 7. Radio Officer (far side)
8. Radio equipment 9. Navigation Officer 10. Charts 11. Flight Engineering Officer 12. Extra crew 13. 1500 HP Wright Cyclone engine
14. Space in nacelle for in-flight engine repairs accessible through wing to control deck 15. Landing light 16. Wing span 162 ft. 17. Wing tip light
18. Cargo hold 19. Crew sleeping quarters in wing center section 20. Luggage holds 21. Radio antenna 22. Forward passenger compartment
23. Spiral stairway to control deck 24. Men's room 25. Galley 26. 27. 28. Passenger compartments 29. 30. 31. Same with berths made up
32. Ladies' lounge 33. Rear passenger compartment 34. Cargo hold 35. Step (for planing on water)

Bermuda ferry, Captain Winston and Goyette

Darrell's Island, Bermuda

stretching for miles below, the turquoise and blue of the water—to be able to paint from the sky, that would be something.

"Port of Spain, a negative town at best. The Savannah and Royal Botanical Garden would raise it a little above average. Otherwise there is nothing. The beach at Maqueripe is pleasant but anticlimactic as is so much of Trinidad. Ahead lie the mountains of Venezuela, on either side rise dramatic promontories and at your feet the beach, a quite shoddy piece of land. The best time here is at sunset as it is anywhere in the world where it is possible to witness the retreat of light. Thank God we are not sent here to live. I don't actually dislike the place but it seems so very limited.

"We celebrated the 4th of July, 1940 in true fashion with Dottie and Bob Fordyce and Hugh Gordon at the Trinidad Country Club with much quaffing of the cup. Such good tennis as we had one afternoon and such fun to sit and draw Horace hour after hour. And all the dreadful movies we went to to pass the time! The vegetables from Cannings, the frozen cubes of consommé, Gordon, our waiter, who reminded me hysterically of Bobby Homans, the zombies who glided in and out of our rooms, the trouble with the laundry, and above and beyond all the constancy of Pan American personnel. Dear God! But I'll be glad when we'll have a place of our own and cease to be victims of hotel lobbies and bars. But on the whole my 17 Trinidad days were worthwhile, very decidedly. The memory of Queen's Park and Room 302 will be ever green. I forgot to mention the famous night when there were two blackouts within 15 minutes followed quickly by a ten second earthquake! A restful evening indeed.

"The time that I liked Trinidad the most was the morning we left. The mountains loomed up tremendous against the blue of early dawn and the flowering trees never looked lovelier. But then it is always like that when leaving the now familiar for the unknown.

"At six we were headed for Georgetown, then Paramaribo, Cayenne and finally we landed at Belém at sunset, after an hour crossing the Amazon. It was a dreary day over brown waters and matted jungles broken only by those three stops to refuel. Crossing the equator, wrapped in a heavy coat due to the cold of the altitude, was a strange contrast to my other crossing of it in '35 on the *Tjinegara* in the Dutch East Indies. No Neptune certificate for this trip!"

The Grande Hotel in Belém (Pará), on the equator, was clean and the food wasn't bad. There was only warm beer to drink, good meat with baked plaintains and always *flan* (caramel custard) for dessert. Breakfast before dawn consisted of papayas, mangoes, toast with guava jelly and Brazilian coffee, almost thick enough for your spoon to stand up in.

The beds had no springs, just wooden slats, and the mattresses, if any, were less than half an inch thick, stuffed with something even a bug couldn't live in. But it was very hot and one had to lie under a mosquito net. Shortly after falling asleep, I was awakened by screams from Hope who had just felt something run across her face. It was probably a rat so we sat up the rest of the night. The next day our schedule would get us to Recife by nightfall, and the third day we would be in Rio, having stopped at Maceió, Bahia, Ilhéus and Caravelas before coming around the point opposite the Sugar Loaf and entering Guanabara Bay with the lovely city of Rio on the south side and the Corcovado behind it. The Corcovado is a colossal statue of Christ on top of a small mountain behind Rio. It is lighted at night and quite a sight to passengers approaching by air from any direction. We landed on the water off Santos Dumont Airport, a very short strip built out into the bay from downtown Rio, where we had a seaplane ramp and a hangar.

Rio at last! It was to be our first home. I was allowed one day off and then out again the next day, leaving Hope alone in her new world without a single friend or a language she could communicate in.

These were Hope's first impressions: "Well, now the trip down is over and we are in Rio at last. It was interesting, yes, but terribly tiring and uncomfortable. The night we spent at Pará I shall never forget nor will Horace what with the great black "crab" that advanced on me in the night and those trolleys that crashed beneath the window every eight minutes. A ghastly night. Recife was a welcome contrast with its good beds and general cleanliness.

"Coming into Rio from the air is a dramatic sight indeed. The gaunt brown skeleton hills and mountains preceeding our arrival from the north were an awesome sight. No evidence of roads or houses. I think the wildness of Brazil is the strongest example of man's inability to subjugate nature I've ever seen. True, Rio has been utilized and made a brilliant example of how cities can look but the side by side contrast with the wildness of surrounding country is extraordinary.

"We were exhausted from the trip so after a few drinks and a rather disappointing meal of rubbery chickens we went to bed. I must say I like hard beds but even I find the Brazilian mattress a little wearing. And so ended our first day in Rio, July 9th, 1940.

"Wednesday morning we rushed around leaving cards at the embassy and went to Pan American and a 'quick' visit to the post office. Very few Portuguese speak any English and I have a feeling the language must be mastered. Gods! What a language it is.

"Horace left at 4:30 the next morning to be gone six days. I hope I'll get used to it someday.

"He got off all right and I spent the morning looking for an apartment very unsuccessfully. I finally resorted to the beach which was very fine indeed, and there Hugh Gordon and Fuji, Jimmy Walker's[1] wife, took me over to a group of Pan Am people. The water is just right but the undertow is terrific. I've never felt a worse one. They say that people are pulled out all the time.

"That afternoon Fuji took me to see an apartment which seemed pretty attractive. It is hard to know what to choose, but there is no rush.

"Such a discouraging day and I have a feeling it will be much, much worse. None of our furniture, etc., has been shipped and Mr. Lorber, the transportation agent, is anything but encouraging. I wish with all my heart I could disappear into the bowels of a studio and not emerge again except to be with Horace when he is here. What awful escapists my generation are! If only one could peer into the future—Will we be here six months or a year and will we like it? I do think Rio is very pleasing to the eye and that always helps. But, please God, no babies here unless things turn out very differently from what I expect".

We found a quite lovely apartment in a brand new building diagonally behind the Copacabana Palace Hotel on Copacabana Avenue. That meant we were one block from the famous beach along which ran the Avenida Atlantica. The latter was built up with a line of high-rise apartments on the land side but nothing on the beach. A sidewalk ran along the beach inlaid with a mosaic of little black and white squares in varying patterns.

The surf at Copacabana was incredible. It was constant, built up by the never varying southeast trades. One had to shout to be heard above the crash of the surf. All windows facing the beach had to be kept shut because the spray covered the windows up to the 10th floor. Incoming swells broke sharply off the beach, quickly rising to 20 or more feet before crashing on top of you. Beyond the line of breakers a small rowboat or two patrolled as a beach patrol, but no lifeguards were visible on the beach. Occasionally a red flag would be flown meaning "No Swimming" when the undertow made it impossible to swim back to the beach.

Hope took to the surf like a porpoise, diving out through the terrifying surf with some of the other pilots like Jimmy Walker who was equally at home in the sea. I was not. Practically living on the beach during the daylight hours on our days off, we talked of Brazil.

The President of Brazil at this time was Getulio Vargas, a most appealing man, at least to foreigners. He had run for president in 1930, been defeated and led a revolt, marching up the road from São Paulo to Rio (the only road in Brazil) at the head of a ragged band of ruffians. As all dictators know, he knew the history of Napoleon's return from Elba and copied it. When the approaching army of the government marched down the road to meet and seize him, he stopped his pitiful little force and advanced alone to face the army. The army cheered, turned around and marched back to Rio behind him.

So now Vargas was President and determined to make a cohesive country out of the welter of races and tribes despite the lack of any communications in the fifth largest country in the world. Brazil was divided into twenty-seven states each with a governor. The largest, Amazonas, was very recalcitrant. The Indians north of the Amazon simply killed anyone who bothered them. Three armed government expeditions into the area had never been heard from again. Vargas asked for volunteers for a fourth. There were plenty and they set off into the jungles unarmed. The Indians were so impressed at their persistence and courage that they put away their blowguns and bows and arrows, sat down to talk and pledged allegiance to the government at Rio.[2]

Back in Rio we now had an apartment but no furniture. All our wedding presents were left in storage in Baltimore. I had shipped down a couple of beds and tables from Baltimore, but it would be much longer than a month before anything got to Rio by sea. We were an inexpensive transfer for Pan Am. There was no such thing as a department store in Rio. We did acquire a double bed, and I designed and commissioned a local cabinetmaker to build us an armoire to hold our clothes, as there were no closets. We also picked up a chest of drawers and were then in business.

On August 1, 1940 I took out my first flight with an S-43 from Rio to Trinidad and back with overnights at Recife and Belém. I was to fly this route 23 times until transferred back to Miami the following June.

The first DC-3As had arrived at Miami in 1940 and pilots were checked out as quickly as possible for local runs, with DC-3As soon to be sent to Rio. Havana had an airport, and at Nassau Sir Harry Oakes was planning to build one. The following year I would see him at the site supervising the work in person. These were to be the first landplane routes from Miami—Miami to Havana and Miami to Nassau. The DC-3As to be based in Rio would fly to Buenos Aires and from Rio north through Barreiras to Belém.

I was to be checked out in Rio on the DC-3A, so I spent most of my spare time, between S-43 flights, in the maintenance shops. Paul de Kuzmik was the *Chefe de Manutencao* as well as a member of an old Hungarian family. I had to pass an oral exam given by him. He tended to treat the pilots a bit superciliously, not quite like peasants and perhaps a little less so than he treated ground personnel. No doubt I was a bit supercilious myself or perhaps did not show adequate respect, because he finally broke off his examination, and, with no little show of annoyance, he said: "Captain Brock, do you know what a torsional dynamic balancer and what a compensated cam are?" I replied with a smile, recognizing the put down, "No Sir, I've never heard of them". Before I went to bed that night I knew. Four days later I was officially qualified on the mechanical properties of DC-3A planes. It was not long before I became a close friend of Mr. de Kuzmik as did Hope.

DC-3As were soon to be introduced on a "cutoff" route from Belém direct to Rio. The operations manager, Fritz Blotner, had surveyed a direct route from Rio to Belém some years before, going on foot, led by Indians from unknown tribes, crossing the barren, windswept plain where he located a midpoint refuelling stop at Barreiras about 300 miles NNE of where Brasília was to be built some years later. Leaving the plain, he entered the impenetrable Amazon forest where for days he never saw the sun through the 200 foot high canopy of jungle trees. From the air, as we flew over it we would never see the ground nor the streams and rivers which ran through the forest.

Pan Am was switching from seaplanes to landplanes which would be much less expensive to operate provided someone else would pay for the airports. The Pan Am Airport Development Program, under Sam Pryor and Bob Cummings, got under way in 1940.

It was in November 1940 that the contract was signed between the U.S. government and Pan Am to build airports all over Central and South America. These were first to be a defensive ring around the Panama Canal; but later, at Trippe's suggestion to Churchill, and Churchill's to Roosevelt, they became thought of as an offensive chain too, to move supplies first to the beleaguered Allies on the Mediterranean and shortly thereafter to the Russians via Teheran and to the Far East via India.

Prior to the formal contract, President Roosevelt had instructed Trippe to proceed with airport construction in June 1940, in secret and using special funds provided by the President. General Marshall told the President that: "The immediate conclusion of the PAA contract is now more essential to our national defense than any other matter".

ADP built forty-nine airports throughout the Caribbean Islands, Central America and South America. Sam Pryor ran the organization which by 1942 employed about 125,000 laborers, 1,500 engineers and managers and 500 executives. The entire program cost the U.S. government $90,000,000.00. The Pan Am fee agreed to in the contract with the government was $1.00.

After completing new ground school courses in DC-3 As at Rio, I was checked out in December by Captain Ben Jones. Although I was route checked over the cutoff, I never flew this route as there were too few of us to run the water route (S-43) up the coast. This was slowly being taken over by Panair do Brazil who got our S-43s as we switched to landplanes in 1941–42.

Business Week on September 7, 1940, announced the cutoff service, cutting the Miami—Rio service from five to three and one-half days and referred to "The great new airdrome in the interior of Brazil". On my check flight on November 4, 1940 into Barreiras, the field was hard to find, marked only by a windsock on a pole. There was not even a fence, but then there were no cows. There were no trees, the grass had been chopped off with machetes, the ground was reasonably flat and larger rocks had been removed, but that was all at the "great new airdrome". The only building was a shed covering several gas drums.

From December 1940 through January 1941 I continued my twice monthly schedule along the coast to Belém—a four day round trip every other week. In November I flew a total of 116 hours—only nine days off with Hope. In December I flew 112 hours. I was called out Christmas Eve to fly to Bahia and back on Christmas Day. It was a lonely first Christmas for my lovely new bride.

A few days before Christmas I was advised that some packages had arrived for us and were being held at Customs. Through a Panair do Brasil official I found a Customs broker who spoke a little English. I was told it would take four to six weeks to clear the shipment. I grabbed the broker and we got a taxi to the main Customs office. On the way I rehearsed with my new friend, the broker, a little speech. On arrival I demanded an interview with the Chief of Customs. I made a very great and loud fuss. Finally, we were admitted to the head man. He was an older man, dressed neatly and meticulously all in black; and was seated behind a very large desk in a very large, ornate room. He smiled and I spoke, showing all the deference I could, and becoming more and more impassioned as I tried, three-quarters in English, one-quarter in Portuguese to explain: 1) I was a Pan Am pilot; 2) I had brought a brand new, 22-year-old and very pretty wife with me to Rio; 3) we were overwhelmed by the beauty of Brazil, verily, Rio was the home of the Gods; 4) my new young wife would be sad at Christmas with all the presents from her family and mine tied up in Customs. I stopped. The official said a few incomprehensible words to the Customs broker who bowed and went out followed by me expressing profound thanks from my wife and myself to His Very Distinguished Honor. Outside, I said to the broker, "Well?" "I'll have your things delivered to you this evening". "Any duty?" "No". "Should I give the Chief anything?" "Certainly not, and your stuff won't even be opened. I've never seen this happen before".

I had written home: "We have had three cooks now—we hope this one stays. The maid says she drinks. She says the maid does. The maid is leaving. She is wonderful, but doesn't like to wait on the table and only wants to sew. No one talks anything but Portuguese except the janitor who can speak half French, half Portuguese".

Various distinguished people went through Rio when we were there. Greta Keller, the then famous German torch singer; Paul Draper, perhaps the greatest dancer of his kind the world has ever seen, came and danced; and Yehudi Menuhin came and played in the State Theatre, resting between pieces with his violin tucked

under his chin but with both hands hanging by his side and per-
spiration running down his face in rivers. One violin string popped
from the heat. It was December, and there was no air-conditioning
in Rio with the sole exception of the small bar in the Copacabana
Palace Hotel, known as the "ice box".

By December 1940 Hope and I were very conscious of the war,
and thought we should be in it; but we were unaware of the sharp
feelings in the diplomatic colony. Mundino Di Robillant was the
local manager of LATI, the Italian International Airline and was
our good friend, as was his kind American wife. So was Nicky
Horthy, the son of Hungary's dictator, Admiral Horthy. To the
British and other Allied diplomatic personnel they were enemies.
Di Robillant was later thrown out of Brazil after he was found to
be an Axis spy.

U-boats roamed the Atlantic and tankers were sunk daily: Brazil
had no oil wells and so little gasoline. Most cars and buses burned
charcoal in a small gas producer called a "gasogenio" mounted on
the back end of the vehicle. Others burned alcohol or mixtures of
alcohol and some hydrocarbon fuel, and the exhausts stank badly.

By September it had become hot and December was unbearable.
The heat would hang especially heavily on the city whose main
drag, the Avenida Rio Branco, was thick with a choking fog of
auto fumes, mostly from buses.

On one occasion Bob Gibson kindly lent us his car—he may
have been the only pilot who had one in Brazil as there was a pro-
hibitive duty on them—and we drove up into the mountains for a
cool weekend. The road up to Petropolis was lovely. Trees were
in bloom. The telephone poles, newly stuck in the ground and
strung with wires, were all sprouting branches. Petropolis was the
summer capitol to which the government moved in September.
We went through it climbing to the next higher town of Therezopolis, about 100 miles from Rio.

We stayed at a small pensao run by a Czech, which was delightful. The lovely jacaranda, mahogany and immortelle trees had given
way to pines. The pensao had horses and bridle paths, a tennis court
and swimming pool, and little cottages for rooms, each with a fire

burning cheerfully every night. It was very cool at night and made one feel like a million dollars. After martinis and dinner we heard the sounds of soldiers drilling back in the woods. Commands were barked out in German. We went to look and there, in a clearing, men were drilling with wooden rifles in goose step. The Germans were thought by some to be preparing to take over all Latin America, any day now in 1940; and perhaps only the Pan Am ADP deterred them from doing so. The Latin Republics were totally isolated from the weak Army and Navy forces which were all we had. We had heard of and now we saw, the secret underground drilling every night. It was eerie.

The air route from Rio to Buenos Aires stopped at São Paulo, the mushrooming industrial and business center of Brazil where high-rise office buildings were going up overnight; next at Porto Alegre, near Santos, the principal coffee port, and then at Montevideo before turning NW up to Buenos Aires. Leaving Montevideo we would circle low over the superstructure of the *Graf Spee* which stuck out of the water where she had been scuttled the year before.

The *Graf Spee* had been raiding the South Atlantic since the outbreak of the War. She took refuge in Montevideo after the action on December 13, 1939 when engaged by two British cruisers in pursuit. The *Spee* had eleven inch guns; the British cruisers eight inch and six inch. Hitler ordered the *Spee*'s commander, Captain Langsdorff, to refuse internment in Montevideo and to fight his way out, scuttling the ship as a last resort. Langsdorff transferred 700 of his crew to a German merchant ship in the harbor and sailed out to sea at 6:15 on the 17th. At 8:45 he scuttled her within sight of the waiting British cruisers. Two days later Captain Langsdorff shot himself.

"Our first bow to Rio society", Hope wrote in her diary, "took place at our embassy at a cocktail party a week or so after we first arrived. I shall always remember the feeling I had, poised on the threshold, literally knowing that before me were a crowd of total strangers some of whom would probably be my friends before many months passed.

"Ware Adams was the first person we met, as, being Second Secretary, he was introducing people to Ambassador and Mrs. Caffery. Then we were handed over to Randy Harrison and introduced generally. I liked Anne Adams the first time I saw her and we soon became close friends".

I had arranged my schedule to have a week off after Christmas in Buenos Aires, and I went down on a DC-3A route check on New Year's Eve with Hope.

"January 1, 1941", continues her diary, "found us in Buenos Aires. Rio was hotter than Hell the week after Christmas with a choking wind from the north. And so on the morning of the 31st when the plane took off and Rio was left far behind, I was very, very happy indeed. Ev Bierer flew us down and after one bumpy stop at Porto Alegre we finally winged over the Río de La Plata (muddier than the Mississippi) and the broad city of B.A. to land about fifteen miles out of town.

"From the time we stepped onto the bus until we left, I liked Buenos Aires. The countryside was green, scattered with cows, horses, sheep and pigs and the city was large, clean and stimulating. The buildings are beautiful and the small parks restful in their greenness.

"We went to the Plaza Hotel, the first good hotel I've encountered in S.A., and probably the only one. We were given a large, cool room on the 6th floor and it was really the most welcome of places. That evening after a bath and rest we met E.B. (Capt. Bierer) in the Plaza Bar and had a couple of rounds of champagne cocktails. About nine-thirty we rolled into the grill and had our first Argentine beef and, incidentally, the best food I've ever tasted. Horace summoned up a bottle of Lanson '28 and we were very, very content. Before midnight we went into the big dining room where everyone was dressed, and welcomed the New Year with whistles, confetti, balls and more champagne. Bierer flirted right and left but, sad to relate, failed to find a 'late date'. We broke up around three, being exhausted from the trip and the excitement of it all.

"New Year's Day found us with terrible hangovers, not unexpectedly, but happy. We staggered to La Cabana, the famous beef restaurant, which is in some seemingly distant part of town, and were served enormous slabs of meat that had been passed through the fire once or twice. Despite its rawness, it was good, although I can't say the same for the 'fungi' (mushrooms) that we had with it. They tasted like raw fish. A pitcher of wine and fruit completed the meal. We then took a taxi and drove out the Avenida Alveolar, a lovely drive very much like Constitution Avenue in Washington. After a little delay we located the American Embassy and left our cards. Having made our grand jaunt of the day, we went back to our room and took a nap. E.B. came over for a drink and then we dined with him at a place called Maxime's which was very pleasant. It was very cool and breezy that evening when we walked down the Diagonal and up Florida to the hotel. We saw lighted advertisements and window displays that shifted automatically. It would seem that B.A. is one up on New York!

"Thursday, January 2nd.—After a long sleep we consumed marvelous scrambled eggs and bacon, coffee and croissants—such breakfasts! Then we spent the most interesting morning on the part of Florida near the hotel. Our first stop was at Comte's, a very fine furniture and objets d'art store. Horace lost his heart to a painting of Figan's (Argentine artist) of Indians slouched over on horses against the night under the moon. I didn't like it, and a couple of days later when we returned Horace didn't like it either. I did like a beautiful cigarette box with a sewn leather top, but it was too expensive.

"Across the street we wandered into the Galleria Muller where we unearthed a lovely painting by Mariette Lydis, a modern Austrian painter who has had an enormous success abroad. It was of a girl in a hat and made a lasting impression. The eyes, the gamine look; it had a certain *je ne sais quoi* that intrigued. The atmosphere was marvellous—unlike any other I've ever seen—a little reminiscent of El Greco but much less sinister and more feminine. We bought the *Chapeau Fruits* and so started our collection. (Price $210.00.)

"The 3rd we lunched with Ambassador and Mrs. Norman Ar-

mour at the embassy residence which is the loveliest one I've ever
seen, both from outside and within. The Armours were charming
and gave us a delightful lunch. Our friend, Mrs. Warren Delano
Robbins was present and John Gunther. He is a big man with mousy
blond hair, blue eyes and a hearty laugh. He looks like a travelling
salesman at best but, naturally, is extremely interesting to talk to.
Right now he is writing *Inside Latin America* and says he likes Mexico the best, comparing it to China's place in the Orient. I shall be
very interested to read, eventually, what he makes of Brazil. One
can't help but feel that, travelling as fast as he does, he must have
only a superficial knowledge of the countries, but perhaps not. He
said Colombia was the most consciously civilized of all the New
World countries.

"We restauranted around and found the grill at the Plaza to be
the best and Los Patitos next. On Sunday we drove out to Avenida
Alveolar and back through the Rose Garden which is lovely and
then to the races at Palermo in the afternoon. That was very amusing and I must say that I have never seen such a beautiful race track.
It makes Pimlico look like a Victorian relic, which it is in a way.
The thing that baffled us was the immensity of the three tracks
(one within another). It looked like at least a three-mile run on the
outside one. The horses were nice looking animals and we didn't
lose very many pesos, so it was a highly successful outing.

"The highlight of our stay was lunch Tuesday with Mrs. James
Miller, Brazilian wife of the head of the United Press of S.A. 'Ro-
salina' is an extraordinary personality. Slick, short, dark hair, Pa-
risienne à la 20's, with large dark eyes and piquant features matched
with great vivaciousness; she is someone to meet and know. Mr.
and Mrs. Armour were there; also the Mayor of Buenos Aires and
his wife, who is charming; the Brazilian Ambassador to the Argentine, and a rich Spaniard were the guests besides ourselves. I had
the luck of sitting next to Mr. Armour at lunch and we had a
lovely time discussing the Green Spring Valley and its inmates! He
had been an usher for Anne and Sally's father[3] at his wedding,
which gave us a lot in common. When the conversation moved on
to the war, he said that everything hangs on the way the Balkans

act in the next few weeks. It seems too bad that he wasn't sent to London instead of Harry Hopkins, but who knows.

"Back to Rio on Wednesday, January 8th with John Gunther as a fellow passenger. He arrived at the Pan Am passenger terminal at 6:20 muttering about his hangover and one hour's sleep. We chatted while waiting for the plane, and once on board he passed into the realm of slumberland only to come to at Porto Alegre where he was welcomed by a teeming bevy of Brazilian journalists. It really was funny to watch. He rushed into the men's room to escape but was pulled out very quickly. In Rio his reception was quieter. We got through the customs quickly and, after gathering our enormous mail, taxied home. Thus ended our 'Eight Days'.

"February 4th. Rio again, the same as ever, only a little different. One is never conscious of the passage of time here. One month is like another. How nice the seasons are—how distinct each one is with its own personality and attractions.

"We gave a dinner for John Gunther before he headed home, which went off quite well. The Graves and Sieberts attended and John Gunther was in good form. The only outstanding remark I remember him making that evening was that Rio is the most wide open town where women are concerned he's ever seen! He illustrated it by saying that there was one whole section of the city for sailors, another for richer folk, etc., and concluded with the now famous remark, 'And, of course, there is always the Copacabana Hotel!' I don't guess having to lock his door every night was very hard on him".

We lived well in our apartment. Hope used the bedroom as a studio and painted portraits—very good ones—of many of our friends and their daughters. They were always enamored of the results and would ask to keep them, and Hope would give them to the sitters.

The food was good, usually *frangos* (chickens), occasionally a *peru* (turkey), and excellent fish. We also had steaks but not in a class with those obtainable in Buenos Aires. With every meal except breakfast, we had *vinho tinto* or *branco* (red or white). The local wines were cheap and really excellent, as were those in the Argentine and Chile, but they were rarely seen in the U.S.A. and no good when found there. Perhaps they didn't bottle much wine and the long trip across the equator would ruin any exported. We also grew fond of exotic tropical fruits like mangos, sapodillas, love apples, pomegranates, persimmons and the ubiquitous papayas.

I took to growing orchids on the narrow porch outside the living room of our apartment, all cattleyas. There were no insect sprays then in Brazil, but I dusted them occasionally with tobacco dust obtained free from a local cigar factory, as did the pro growers. We also acquired a miniature, short-haired dachshund which we named Samba and which had to be carried in town when the side-walks grew so hot they would burn the feet of a dog not equipped with shoes.

The first schedules I flew out of Rio were all six-day trips to the north to Port of Spain. Later, with the opening of the cutoff route with the landplane DC-3As, via Barreiras to Belém, I flew only four-day trips along the coast with the S-43s, to Belém. This was a local route, entirely within Brazil, to be turned over to the national airline, Panair do Brazil, as soon as their pilots were qualified on the S-43s which would be turned over to them. Consequently, I often had a Brazilian captain as co-pilot to check out on the equip-ment and the route. Few of them spoke English and I spoke little Portuguese, but we got along, sometimes in French.

The route I flew up the coast, leaving Rio northbound, stopped at Vitória, Caravelas, Ilhéus, Salvador (Bahia) the city of mostly churches, Aracajú, Maceió, Recife where once I overnighted dur-ing Carnaval (like Mardi Gras in New Orleans), Natal which soon came to be our jumping-off point for Africa, Fortaleza and Belém, the end of my route. After an overnight there, I came back making the same stops in reverse. All were water landings in rivers with refuelling from barges.

The top, northeast corner of Brazil, Natal to Fortaleza, was very, very poor. The people were destitute and starving. About the only export was carnoba wax from palm nuts and the only market was the floor wax companies in the U.S.

In March my mother came down on the *Uruguay* to see us. The

Moore-McCormack Line ran the only steamer service from New York to Rio and the passage took 30 days. She spent two weeks at the Copacabana Palace and sailed back on the same steamer on its northbound trip. Her second day out I left on my coastal schedule in an S-43 and I detoured out to sea to look for her, found her—it took a bit of navigating—and had my Brazilian radio operator send her a message to identify myself. Of course, it was quite illegal to use our airway channels for any purpose other than airway information or emergencies, so it was a somewhat circumspect message. I just hoped the operations manager would never hear about it.

As the spring (or rather fall, in Rio) wore on in 1941, we began to realize that I would soon be transferred back to Miami. Finally the orders came through and I was to leave Rio on June 7th, report to Miami on the 9th and leave for a month's vacation on the 11th. We packed frantically, for we had collected quite a bit of stuff by now in Rio.

The pace was accelerating towards U.S. involvement in the war. Four of the Moore-McCormack boats had been taken over for service to England. The docks at Rio were piled high with stuff awaiting shipment to the U.S.A., and little but war supplies moved. I wrote my mother asking her to use any drag she could to get our things home. Mother got action, as usual, and through Rodman Griscom—son of the founder of Moore-McCormack, who promptly saw the current president—our things were shipped.

Pan Am had ordered and taken delivery in 1940 of the first commercial transports with pressurized cabins. These were the large, four-engine Boeing S-307s called Stratoliners. They operated at about 20,000 feet with the cabin pressures held to 8,000. They were large with four engines, and the cabins were divided into compartments. They had just been put into operation on the Miami—Buenos Aires route, stopping only at San Juan, Port of Spain, Belém, Rio and Buenos Aires. I returned to Belém from my last S-43 trip on June 2nd; and on June 7th we had space to Miami on an S-307 in which we rode in a compartment with Mrs. Armour who had boarded at B.A. I was never again to fly a "Baby Clipper", the twin-engine S-43 amphibian. I missed them.

Now let us return to Hope again:

"I should mention the state of the world in 1940. Dunkirk had fallen on our wedding day, May 25th, and the threat of Hitler to England had become imminent. The Battle of Britain had taken place soon after our arrival in Rio, and the strain reflected by our English friends was very apparent, particularly Bobby and Margie Isaacson. Bobby was Commercial Attaché in the British Embassy and they became our best friends.[4]

"The best way I can describe the atmosphere was the standing joke that Hitler could take Brazil by telephone. It sounds amusing but if you lived there you weren't overcome by the humor of the remark as the south of Brazil was largely populated by Germans and Japanese. The Brazilians themselves had no proper military defenses, and, yes, a telephone call wouldn't have been too far off the mark.

"Our embassy was under a lot of strain as Roosevelt was desperately trying to beef up our posture in South America and set up air bases, etc. Brazil was very important. Jefferson Caffery and his good wife, Gertrude, was an able and hard-working Ambassador. Ware Adams was Second Secretary and Randy Harrison, urbane and Mephistophelean in appearance, was First. Elim O'Shaugnessy, surely one of the world's most attractive and outrageously behaved younger members of the State Department was Third Secretary. When we first arrived, he'd been banished to Natal by the Ambassador for having been involved with a prominent Brasilian's wife. On his return we became fast friends, and I must confess that even my mother-in-law felt his charm on her visit to us that winter. Eddie Graves, our Naval Attaché, and his attractive wife, Betty, also became good friends, as did the Sieberts. Colonel Siebert later became head of Army G2. Then there was Tom White, Air Attaché, cool and brilliant, and his pleasant English wife. Tom was later Chief of Staff of the Air Corps.

"Then there were the Americans who lived there working for American companies. Carl and Helen Kincaid were very good to us and had me up to their house in Therezopolis once when Horace was on a flight. It was in the cool mountains above a boiling Rio summer. He represented Anderson Clayton, the great cotton merchants. Mr. Clayton, my old friend Julie Clayton's father, who was to become Under Secretary of State, wrote the Kincaids about us. They were very kind indeed, especially to a young married couple. I also recall a Carl Sylvester who was an attractive older man and head of Electric Bond and Share which I mistook for chair and couldn't get it out of my mind that he didn't preside over the manufacture of electric chairs!

"The State Department kept sending down V.I.P.s to Rio to show the Brasileiros how much we loved them. And one and all were poorly briefed and totally insensitive to the nuances in dealing with the people of the country. There is no color line; and Indians, Negroes and Portuguese blended together through the centuries to make the current Brasilian.

"A steady stream of refugees made their way there from Poland, Belgium, France and other places via Lisbon which was the big clearinghouse for escaping Europeans. It wasn't too difficult to emigrate to Brazil, and it was much less expensive than the Argentine or the United States. We met many of them and found them courageous and cheerful considering their total uprooting. Our very special friends were André and Helena Tarnowski. He was a member of one of the top twelve families of Poland and had been decorated at the age of sixteen in World War I for having killed two hundred Russians. He grew up to be a most attractive, bright minded man who was on the Davis Cup Team, was the Vickers agent in Poland and the owner of vast palaces. His wife, Helena, was the daughter of Count Larich of Austria. Horace's cousin, Tony Biddle,[5] was Ambassador to Poland when the Germans invaded and helped smuggle André out of Poland to Budapest in the back of a truck. Somehow he rejoined Helena and their two daughters, and they made their way hitch-hike fashion across Europe to Lisbon from where they got to Rio. We have many memories of his dining with us in our apartment and his appreciating so very much more than any other guest the candlelight and the Bernkasteler Doktor! His mother, the old Countess Tarnowska, had led the procession of Poles, as head of the Red Cross, to plead with the Russians during World War II. (Five years after we left Brazil he was killed by a lorry as he was leaving the golf club at Gavea where he had just won the Club Championship. What an ironic way to go two years after such a heroic life in Poland. Some years later, Helena married a Prince Yurievich, another war casualty and fascinating person.)[6]

"I had known Jack Kennedy slightly at Harvard and in London when his father was ambassador, so it was a pleasant surprise when he turned up in Rio sometime early in '41. Jack's greatest attribute was his ability to listen and learn. I have a picture of him sitting on the beach with his head cocked to one side listening to Henry Lage fill him in on Vargas and Brazil in general. We drove up to Petropolis one day with Paul Draper, the tap dancer, to lunch with God only knows whom. I pull a total blank on our hosts, but not the hairpin turns, driving up and down, and the wit and charm of both Jack and Paul. The latter was performing at the Copacabana and used his great style and talent to the accompaniment of Bach, Brahms and Beethoven. Unusual and still memorable. Jack had just published his first book, *While England Slept*, and was enjoying success and a little recognition.

"We had arrived in Rio in June and when Christmas approached we decided to give a party near Christmas Eve to pay back everyone who had been kind to us and to generate a little Christmas Spirit which was hard with the thermometer standing at 95 degrees and the palm trees swaying overhead. The United States was not yet at war, and in my innocence I thought it would be all right to invite one and all.

"Well, one and all accepted and a constant stream of activity around the eggnog bowl indicated a successful party until the arrival of our Hungarian and Italian friends. The English, French and other assorted Allied sympathizers quietly put down their drinks and simply disappeared. Luckily, there were enough Americans to shore up a crumbling situation. I learned my lesson: when in doubt, don't!

"The year we were there passed all too quickly and pleasantly. Golf at Gavea which certainly is one of the world's loveliest golf courses with its blossoming trees and mountain holes above the sea; sailing on Guanabara Bay under Sugar Loaf; marvelous swimming on Copacabana Beach with the huge waves to dive through to get out in the clear, calm waters of the South Atlantic; low-stake gambling at the casinos with European refugees trying to make a killing; weekends up in the mountains at Petropolis and Therezopolis in the welcome cool air after the dreadful heat of Rio in its summer months.

"It was gay, always interesting and yet very lonely when Horace was out on trips for days at a time. But people were kind and I was included in all sorts of parties and activities.

"There was one hairy experience which illustrates the years 1940–41 in Brazil. Eddie Graves, our Naval Attaché, and his wife, Betsy, asked me up to Therezopolis over a hot weekend as Horace was away flying. We had a cabin at the Pensao Piñeros and one night when we were playing bridge after dinner we heard a knocking on the door. Eddie went to open it and we heard him talking quietly to some man outside. Eventually he returned to the table with a grim face but volunteered no information. Three days later when we were back in Rio he told me the man who'd come to the door was a German who wanted a passport to the United States. He continued to say that he knew Mrs. Brock was a guest of the Graves' and he knew her husband was the captain of a PAA plane up over the coast and he could have it sabotaged at any time. How Eddie resolved the situation I was never fully told other than 'it had been dealt with'.

"And so we watched the world from the sunny beaches of Rio drift slowly but inevitably into the blackness of German domination in Europe and Japanese in the Pacific. I must admit I was relieved when we got our orders to return to the United States as it was obvious we'd be drawn in and soon. And if Hitler took Brazil by telephone, I'd just as soon be on our own ground at home!"

MIAMI

In May 1941 I got my orders transferring me back to Miami, to leave Rio on June 7th and with vacation until July 21st. Now our first concern was to find a place to live, but Hugh Gordon, my great friend and fellow captain, had offered to lease us his new house in Miami Shores. He had recently married a lovely girl from Charleston named Mimi. They had just built a house on the bay near his father's when he was transferred to Rio, so the house was brand new and it was very attractive.

We spent my vacation mostly in Baltimore with Hope's parents while Hope was a bridesmaid at Betty Iglehart's wedding, and in New York where we bought some furniture with money saved in Rio. We also bought a Cadillac in Baltimore, a dealer's demonstrator, for $1,600.00. It was a black, two-seat convertible with red leather upholstery—quite the most glamorous car we ever expected to or ever did own. We drove it to Miami.

Back on duty, my first trip was a route check to Nassau in the morning and to Havana in the afternoon in a DC-3A. From there on I was to fly DC-3As almost exclusively for the next year as the ADP airports were appearing everywhere. Seaplanes were on their way out. For the nine months I had the perfect schedule—like some domestic flight schedules, no doubt, but never before enjoyed in Pan Am. I went to Havana and back in the morning, had lunch at home and again to Havana and back in the afternoon. It took about one and a half hours each way, so that was six hours a day with lunch at home. In August I flew 96 hours.

The end of July, between Havana schedules, I was checked out by Bob Fatt on the S-42 and got my CAA rating on it. We had a Cessna for instrument practice and checks by our first professional instructors, Patterson and Conrad. In September I was checked out on night landings in the DC-3A by Captain Ben Jones. Night flying was soon to start for the first time in the Eastern Division, as the new airports were being equipped with lights. By November we had a Stinson Trainer at Miami and another instrument instructor, McGahey. That month I was appointed a DC-3A flight check pilot which got me an increase of $25.00 a month. The basic captain's salary had also been raised from $500.00 to $600.00 a month.

In October we caught a real hurricane, and I had to take a DC-3 of Pan Africa to Atlanta as all planes at Miami were being moved north. This meant leaving Hope alone on the edge of Biscayne Bay; but, fortunately, Hugh Gordon had built near his parents, an old Atlanta family; and I knew they would look out for her. It was quite an experience for my young bride, all alone, with over 100 mph winds which made a deafening roar while she watched coconuts and then whole palm trees fly through the air horizontally.

I wrote to my mother:

"We have just weathered a hurricane. At the last minute I was sent away—I had to take a plane away from here for fear the hurricane would destroy it. I was very mad as it was not one of our planes but one awaiting here to be ferried across the Atlantic to the British. Anyway I was ordered to take it to Atlanta. They called me on the phone Saturday night just as I got home from Havana. We worked all that night boarding up the windows of the house. Sunday morning at 10:00 I had to leave for Atlanta with the plane but without Hope, leaving her all alone. But we arranged for Mr. and Mrs. Gordon, Sr., to stay in our house that night with her. So I spent the night in Atlanta, Ga., calling up every two hours till the wires went out. The storm hit about 5:00 A.M. on Monday morning and blew about 100 miles an hour past our little house here, blowing down the two oaks in front—it blew them right out of the ground. I was able to get out of Atlanta about noon Monday and got back that night. I had not been allowed to take Hope with me, of course, although I tried. I was refused permission on the grounds that the planes belonged to the government and that it was a strict rule that only official crews could be on them—yet a Mr. John Steele (PAA official) in charge of the ferrying of these planes to Africa, was using one to joyride his family a few days ago.

"The storm did not last long so the water did not rise which might have swamped our house. The center passed by only about 25 miles from here, so I guess we were lucky, only to lose two trees. They have been put back but I doubt if they live. Every hibiscus bush and bougainvillea vine that we have was stripped of every leaf and all the palm trees are burned brown by the driving salt spray of the storm—so things do not look so beautiful for the time being. We have been putting fertilizer around today in the hope of restoring some life into the plants".

Well before we entered the War, U-boats (German submarines) infested the Caribbean. They refuelled from bases on the east coast of Mexico. They sank tankers taking oil from Venezuela to our allies. Their attacks were causing an appalling toll of shipping on the Atlantic. After Pearl Harbor, the U.S. activated bases in Greenland and soon after in Iceland. Down in the Caribbean there was little defense against the subs. Navy dirigibles appeared along the coast, but they were of no use in spotting subs or attacking them. The subs just submerged whenever they saw a blimp. Naval patrol planes with depth charges were few, then, and far away, unable to get to a sub, spotted on the surface, in time to sink it.

The northbound tankers kept offshore from Miami Beach to avail themselves of the northbound Gulf Stream while the southbound ones kept very close inshore, out of the stream. It was the loaded northbound ones which were torpedoed regularly, and we could see the burning ships off Miami Beach every night and the columns of black smoke during the day. The crews could often row ashore and survived. The tankers held crude oil, not explosives. We soon experienced the blobs of oil all over the beaches, so rags and a bottle of kerosene went along with a bathing suit.

We often sighted enemy subs on the surface, and once I saw one with a crew relaxing in the sun on the deck, drying their laundry on wash lines. We reported all sightings to the Navy, but there was not much they could do until ADP built the bases at which they based PBYs.

On Sunday, December 7th, right after lunch at one thirty, I had gone outside to work on the place and Hope had just turned on the radio to listen to the New York Philharmonic concert, when the broadcast was interrupted with the news of the Japanese attack on Pearl Harbor. Shortly thereafter we were officially at war and the telegram arrived ordering me to active duty with the Air Corps followed, almost immediately, with orders assigning me to detached duty with Pan Am. The Washington office had worked fast —otherwise the Company would have been shut down as almost all the pilots were reserve officers in either the Army or the Navy. I remember the shock of the news and wondering what was happening in the Pacific Division. Much later I found out what had happened.

On December 7, 1941, when the Japs attacked Pearl Harbor, four Clippers were out on the line; one coming in to Pearl Harbor from San Francisco, one at Wake, one at Aukland and one at Hong Kong.

Captain Harry L. Turner was coming in from San Francisco in a B-314 with a full load of passengers. Just 40 minutes from Pearl Harbor he got word of the Japanese attack. Turner was 40 minutes behind schedule, and it was all his fault. He had asked dispatch at Treasure Island to delay the departure for a few minutes so he could go and hear the first few notes of his daughter's first piano recital in Oakland. From Oakland the traffic was unusually heavy and slow. The predeparture briefing at Treasure Island was long, due to the political atmosphere in the Pacific. Turner's ultimate destination was Singapore. He departed just 40 minutes late and made no effort to catch up in flight so as to save fuel. With the news, Captain Turner immediately diverted to Hilo and got there in four hours, staying in the clouds as much as possible on the way. The crew was a little nervous about what the Japs or the citizens of Hilo, who had never seen a Clipper, might do. Turner dragged the harbor, landed, picked up a mooring, went ashore with all the passengers in a Navy launch and went to the hotel. There he telephoned the station manager at Pearl, got him on the phone and was hearing the battleships exploding outside the window when the phone went dead.

Remembering an old dodge from barnstorming days for painting an easily removable sign on the side of a plane, he obtained five gallons of buttermilk and some lampblack and the crew painted over the entire Clipper. Then they pulled and pushed it into some bushes on shore.

Next day, filling the Clipper with all the gasoline he could obtain, Turner and the crew took off to return to San Francisco; but none of the passengers elected to return to California. Perhaps they thought about what the Japs might be doing to California next. Arriving safely at Treasure Island they were met by quite a crowd, as they were the first people to come in from the Hawaiian Islands.

Captain Ford, down at Auckland, left to go west when it became obvious that he could never get back across the Pacific. He returned to San Francisco westbound, first going to New Caledonia to pick Pan Am personnel, then to Australia, Ceylon, Saudi Arabia, North Africa, across the Atlantic and to the U.S.A.

Captain Ralph, caught in Hong Kong with the S-42B, saw it repeatedly hit by the Japs, catch fire and burn to the water. He picked up rides westbound and met up with Captain Gray in Calcutta, returning home with him.

Captain Hamilton was out of Wake westbound for Guam, was called back and was there when the Japs struck. The Clipper was riddled with 97 bullet holes but still got off with 70 people, leaving six dead behind and one who didn't make it and was captured by the Japs.

After Pearl Harbor the Pan Am Pacific Division became, in effect, part of the Navy Air Transport Service. Captain Turner flew Admiral Nimitz to Hawaii to replace Kimmel, and then flew him around the Pacific in Martins and PBYs on survey trips. Pan Am pilots promptly were qualified on the Navy flying boats and flew regularly as part of NATS.

Nothing so dramatic as the above happened to us flying out of Miami and, throughout the winter of 1941-42 I was home most of the nights with Havana and Nassau trips interspersed with giving check flights on DC-3As. We were far from the Battle of Midway, and the press censorship kept us from ever hearing about it. We had no way of knowing about the great events which were happening and building up in the Pacific.

In March I flew to Rio, changing equipment on various legs from a DC-3A to a B-307 to an S-42. Including all the local check flights I logged 102 hours in March, 100 in April and 100 in June. In June I flew a DC-3A to Rio twice. It was with great nostalgia that I visited Rio again. An instrument letdown into Guanabara Bay was always dramatic. One went down through the clouds knowing that Corcovado, the five Dedo de Dios, Mount Gavea and other unnamed peaks were close by, and broke out into the clear with mountains all around sticking up into the clouds. The landplane approach from the north, i.e., from Bello Horizonte, was even more thrilling than the seaplane approach which was always below the clouds along the coast and turning into the narrow entrance next to Sugar Loaf.

As of July 1, 1942 I was transferred to the Atlantic Division again, now based at North Beach, a seaplane facility at LaGuardia Field to which headquarters had moved from Baltimore. Now I would be qualifying as a Master Ocean Pilot. For Hope it was just another move. We decided to live in New York without a car, so we sold the Cadillac in New York. My gas coupons had been insufficient to permit even driving to work at the 36th Street Airport, and I had bought a very small two-seated runabout which I sold in Miami. Hope found a very nice apartment at 30 Sutton Place, which would be our home for the next year and a half.

CHAPTER VI

<>

Pan American Airways, Atlantic Division, Transatlantic during the War

JULY 1942 – JANUARY 1944

I ARRIVED back on the Atlantic to be checked out on the big flying boats, and ground school began again. I had passed my senior pilot exams in July, 1940; now, two years later, I faced new sets of exams to qualify as a Master Ocean Pilot. I began with Radiotelephone Procedures, Phraseology and Equipment Operation, and Signalling by Aldis Lamp. By September I had passed 13 tough exams in ocean navigation followed by 11 more completing the ground school for Master Pilot. I would be promoted to Master Ocean Pilot when I first went out in command on a revenue producing flight.

In between times I qualified as a "War Production Job Instructor". A government course in this type of instruction technique was being given in almost all industries as part of a "Training Within Industry" program; the purpose being to train anyone in a matter of weeks where before it took months or even years of apprenticeship. It was vital to us in making more skilled airplane mechanics available.

In the summer of 1942, the Atlantic Division was flying across the mid- and South Atlantic to Lisbon and sometimes from Lisbon up to Foynes, but it was not flying across the North Atlantic. There were three general routes: 1) direct from New York to Bermuda, Horta, Lisbon and back; 2) an "O" route to Lisbon as before but returning via the South Atlantic, going from Lisbon to Bolama,

175

Fisherman's Lake in Liberia and then across to Natal on the Brazilian coast and back up to New York via Belém, Port of Spain, Bermuda and New York. This "O" route could be operated clockwise or counterclockwise; and 3) a "U" schedule which, both over and return, was via the South Atlantic, avoiding the mid-Atlantic both ways. There were two reasons for the various routes, to take military supplies to Fisherman's Lake for transshipment to Pan Africa and to avoid the swells at Horta.

Now in the Atlantic I would be flying Boeing B-314s. Only twelve B-314 flying boats were ever built. Of these Pan Am had six based at North Beach (adjacent to LaGuardia Field) for the Atlantic, three on the Pacific and three were transferred to the British. The B-314 in passenger configuration had about 32 berths for passengers and two for the crew.

As far as I know, no Pan Am flight was ever cancelled. The schedule always went through with its top priority loads. Our passengers to Lisbon were diplomatic couriers often with their pouches handcuffed to their wrists, foreign correspondents and very important government people in a hurry. Pan Am provided the U.S. and her allies the only means of transportation between the U.S.A. and Europe except for the very slow and very risky convoys, proceeding at eight knots. Return trips from Lisbon frequently brought English schoolchildren travelling unaccompanied to American friends who would keep them "for the duration".

I went out on my first trip, a familiarization one, with Captain Lodeesen to Lisbon. It was out via Africa and back through the Azores. The stops on route were Bermuda, San Juan, Port of Spain, Belém and Natal. The landing at Natal was in a narrow bay in from the coast protected by a sandbar and was always very tricky. There was a strong current, and the wind, the Southeast Trades, blew hard at all times and was nearly 90 degrees to the area in which we had to land. As I remember, it seemed like 20 to 25 knots with gusts up to 35 to 40 knots. Landing crosswind was tricky enough, but making the buoy was worse. Much of the town lived on fishing and the boats were all lateen rigged.

We could see the advantages of the lateen rig—the sail is attached to a boom which is hoisted about halfway up the mast so that about one-third is forward and two-thirds aft of the mast. In very gusty conditions, the boats would keel over spilling the wind quickly and would not be knocked flat by even the most violent gust.

From Natal we flew at night to Fisherman's Lake in Liberia, which was the shortest crossing of the South Atlantic, only 1,876 nautical miles (2,150 statute miles). The Clippers were the only planes in the world that could fly this distance non-stop with a good load. Fighters and light bombers, being ferried across by Pan Am Ferries, used the ADP airports at Natal and Roberts Field, Monrovia, the capital of Liberia, very near Fisherman's Lake; and they had to stop at Ascension Island, a tiny speck in the mid-South Atlantic belonging to Great Britain, where an airstrip had been built.

We spent the night at Fisherman's Lake where Pan Am had built a camp, several buildings up on posts on one side of a large, cleared area where we played softball during the daylight spent there. A huge baobab tree at one side shaded the home plate and any spectators. Liberia is on the Gulf of Guinea (the old Slave, Ivory and Gold Coasts), and it is one of the hottest and most unhealthy places in the world. Malaria was endemic. The natives all carried amoebic and enteric dysentery. It was called the "white man's graveyard" until Pan Am set up its bases there.

We were under strict medical discipline. We took our prescribed anti-malarial drug, Atabrine and, later chloroquine, daily for the required time before, during and after each trip. We had booster inoculations for typhoid, paratyphoid, typhus, tetanus and cholera every six months, yellow fever shots every two years and smallpox vaccinations every year. In West Africa we had to wear long sleeves, socks and shoes always after dark. Our quarters at Fisherman's Lake were power sprayed with insecticide twice a day. We always slept under mosquito nets. No standing water was allowed anywhere. Every post that supported buildings was equipped with a barrier to prevent anything from climbing up from the ground such as insects. We paid no attention to crocodiles, although at night, walking the path from the mess hall to our quarters, we would often hear one hiss.

Mosquitoes and malaria disappeared in a few weeks after the Pan Am health experts moved into a place where 70% to 80% of the people, black and white, normally had malaria at any time. It was a health miracle the world had only seen before in Panama. We understood that the success was due to the rigid quarantine of the Pan Am bases. The female anopheles mosquito, which alone carries malaria and only bites after dark, can only fly three miles. No natives were allowed to live within three miles of the base, and those working there could only go home when they quit. No crew member ever got malaria.

Dysentery, the other endemic disease normally suffered by everyone in West Africa (usually the less dangerous amoebic variety) was controlled by examination and treatment of the cooks and waiters—and everyone touching the food wore clean, white, cotton gloves when working. These were fresh, clean and sterile for each meal. Almost no one got dysentery.

The food at our African bases was mostly flown in. There was bread made locally, and two kinds of butter, one brought from Denmark, a dark, yellow liquid at local temperatures and most unattractive; and an American Army variety treated so as not to melt, hard at almost any temperature although spreadable, and about the consistency of candle wax. But we had peanut butter which everyone loved. Of local food we had plentiful and delicious alligator pears, sometimes called butter pears, and gazelle meat. I'm sure no one knew what kind of gazelle, just all kinds of small deer which were quite good to eat.

Stopping in Liberia, I began to hear firsthand stories about Pan Am's African operation. Flying only landplanes, they operated out of Roberts Field near Monrovia, while, with our flying boats at Fisherman's Lake, we transferred cargo to them. All of the cargo we off-loaded at Fisherman's Lake was moved to Roberts Field by truck. The story of PAA–Africa is worth telling. It is one of the least appreciated achievements of the War.[1]

Pan American Airways–Africa

On August 19, 1941, the *New York Times* reported that President Roosevelt announced that American civilians would ferry U.S. warplanes from this country to British forces in the Near East and that it had arranged for Pan American Airways to ferry the aircraft and to operate a supplementary air transport service to carry spare parts and to return the ferry pilots.

The military situation facing the British in Egypt was deteriorating fast. They found themselves no longer able to supply the Desert Armies by sea across the Mediterranean. Britain was forced to turn to a primitive air route across Africa, set up by Imperial Airways in 1936, an airway so precarious that an estimated 20% of the planes attempting to fly it crashed en route. Britain lacked the materials, men and aircraft to operate the route. Churchill pleaded with Roosevelt for help.

The U.S.A. was very anti-interventionist. In 1939, Congress passed a Neutrality Act which prohibited American ships from entering the War Zone. The first Lend-Lease Act only provided money. Britain had to come and get what they so desperately needed. Roosevelt turned to Pan American as his "Chosen Instrument" not only to aid the British but to protect the U.S.A. A second Lend-Lease Act permitted delivery to the British but the Neutrality Acts still did not permit going into the War Zone. Only by some official but rather questionable interpretations of the Acts was Roosevelt able to authorize the Pan American Airways operation.

The trans-Africa air route was strategically vital for more reasons than to support Montgomery and the Desert Armies against Rommel and the Afrika Korps who were stopped only temporarily while Hitler diverted all supplies to his coming attack on Russia. It was also vital to India and the Far East and remained so even after we got into the War. It became vital to the support of Stilwell and Chiang. The Africa route brought the supplies which went over the Hump.

With the Germans in possession of Crete, Malta neutralized by

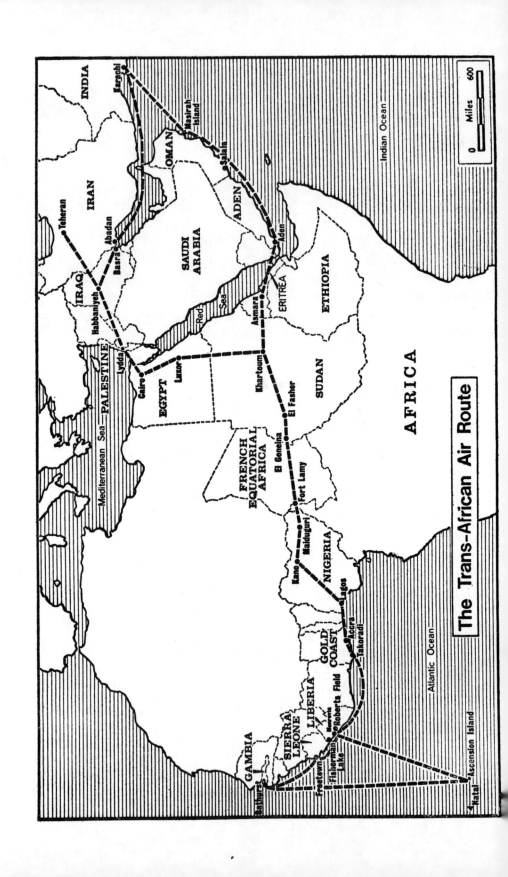

The Trans-African Air Route

aerial bombardment, German and Italian aircraft taking fearful toll of British Navy ships and able to bomb any supply ships in the Mediterranean from Italy, Sicily, Greece, Crete and Libya, the Middle East became 12,000 miles away from England around the Cape through waters infested by German submarines. Our Navy chiefs believed that if the Germans got complete control of the Mediterranean, isolating the Middle East, the War would be over.

The Africa route went through British controlled territories, starting in Takoradi in the west across to Khartoum in the east. Britain was a belligerent and Congress prohibited virtually any dealings with a belligerent including its colonies. The Latin Americans were just as fiercely determined as the United States citizens to avoid any possible entanglement with the Allies or the Axis. When the first Lend-Lease plane, with R.A.F. markings, ferried by a Pan Am Air Ferries crew, landed at Natal, the plane was seized and the crew put in jail. Thereafter the planes were marked as Pan Am planes. Pan American and Pan American alone, a commercial company with the technical competence, foreign contacts and the diplomatic skill, could carry out what Roosevelt and Churchill saw had to be done.

During these days when the U.S. was still at peace, Trippe had been busy. In Portugal he had gotten concessions to land at Macao in China and at Bolama (Portuguese Guinea) in Africa, and begun negotiations for operating rights in Liberia and at Léopoldville in the Belgian Congo.

The British felt very strongly that the air routes of the world were the exclusive province of Imperial Airways. They distrusted Trippe's postwar plans and feared Pan American might displace Imperial on the air routes of the world after the War. In opposing Pan Am's entry into Africa, in every way they could, it sometimes appeared that they valued Britain's future peacetime commercial supremacy in the air over winning the War.

Trippe, given the African assignment by President Roosevelt, moved with incredible speed, not waiting for CAB and other formalities which were not completed until December. On July 1, 1941 the top executives were advised of the project by confidential memorandum. Gledhill was put in charge. Kraigher was brought from Brownsville to be operations manager. Yeomans was made assistant manager. Shoemaker was made traffic manager. Some 150 key personnel with special expertise gained in constructing the Pacific island bases and the ADP airports were assigned to the African project. Gledhill and Kraigher left the same month, to survey the African route. By August materials were being collected. In one large Sears Roebuck store a man walked in and bought out the entire stock of saws, hammers, drills and hand tools. Another got some steam shovels and graders from Mayor LaGuardia that the city didn't need. Data from all sources was collected overnight on the terrific heat and humidity of the West African coast.

Kraigher had to get pilots. Gledhill told him to pick them up on the street. He refused. Priester could spare six and gave him Kristofferson, Goyette, Glen, Maxwell, Buschmann, and another. Then Mrs. Archibald, head of the Washington office, got General Arnold to release about 200 of his best Army pilots, 20 at a time, and Kraigher picked out what he needed.

The first ship to carry the new venture to Africa sailed from New York on October 9th, 1941 with 195 PAA–Africans and was joined by three destroyers off Cape Hatteras and a cruiser later on. She arrived safely at Accra which became headquarters and unloaded her entire supply of materials to construct the airports. A second fully chartered ship left on December 3rd and was in the mid-South Atlantic when war was declared, but made it safely. So did a third ship which crossed at the very peak of the submarine warfare. The passages, zigzagging and blacked out, each took about 21 days. Some of the supply ships were torpedoed later.

Transport to coastal bases and interior points on rivers moved by barge, but some roads had to be built to desert bases. At El Fasher fuel had to be brought from Khartoum by camelback. Runways had to be improved and built. Pan Am found a local clay called laterite and invented a way to build good runways by using it with asphalt. Within a few months some 269 buildings were built and 243 existing ones were rebuilt. Power plants, lights, radio stations, sewage disposal, barracks, repair shops, warehouses and other facilities were constructed or installed and all the time the airlift was operating. Gledhill was there, once averaging 2,500 miles a day for 30 consecutive days. Kraigher and the young construction men rarely slept. There were no days off. No Sundays or holidays.

The worst problem, of course, was the anopheles gambiae. Five or more men would come down with malaria every day. Dr. Saunders, the Chief Medical Officer, was swamped. Dr. L. T. Coggeshell, an authority on tropical diseases, was promptly sent out and the medical department greatly expanded. Almost all who worked at the fields along the coast had malaria. Within a month of arrival 40% of the personnel at Accra were stricken. Quinine or Atabrine was consumed daily by all as part of dinner. Quarters were sprayed hourly and this had been done since the beginning.

All work on construction stopped to dig drainage ditches. Eighteen miles of ditches were dug in one day and finally a total of 45 miles, just around the camp at Accra. Oil covered the ditch waters and any standing water. Natives were not allowed to live within a circle about a quarter mile beyond the camp. Soon the PAA–Africa camp was safe but the city was not.

Relations with the Britishers who were in Africa were very good. The latter welcomed the Americans on arrival and they often dined together in each others' mess. The English were very friendly, kind and helpful. But it was not so with British officials who tried their best to limit the scope of Pan Am's operation to military transport and to prevent Pan Am from getting any commercial rights to operate in Africa or through the Middle East after the War or even during it. Trippe naturally sought such rights and obtained such exclusive ones in the Azores, Bolama and Liberia. Air Marshal Tedder, head of the R.A.F. in Egypt, did all he could to denigrate Pan Am to the point of being reprimanded by the Air Ministry in London. The very hard feelings between Pan Am and BOAC who felt threatened, as indeed they were, may have had some bearing, later, on our government's decision to turn over the Pan Am operation to ATC.

Voigt Gilmore, keeping a report for Pan Am in New York, wrote that a British journalist "must have been strangling on his old school tie" in grudgingly admitting a PAA-Africa achievement.

Almost as soon as the African operation started it was extended
to meet urgent Russian and Chinese needs. For Russia it went from
Cairo through Lydda in Palestine and Habbaniyeh near Bagdad, to
Teheran where the planes were turned over to the Russians. For
the Chinese theater, it went from Khartoum through Asmara,
Aden and along the south coast of Arabia to Karachi where PAA–
Africa ended. Sometimes Pan Am went on to New Delhi and
Calcutta where it met with CNAC (Chinese National Airways
Corporation, owned jointly by the Chinese government and Pan
Am) which operated twice a day to Rangoon, Kunming, Chengtu
and Chungking.

El Alamein was the critical battle of the War for England. Towards the end of 1941 the British were pushed back to Egypt. By
November they were getting supplies and parts across Africa on
the old and defunct BOAC African route now operated by PAA–
Africa including 24 B-24 bombers sent on the personal orders of
President Roosevelt. So, by November 18th, General Auchinleck,
commanding the British Eighth Army, took the offensive and
drove Rommel back to the border of Tripoli. But early in 1942
Rommel was supplied with planes by Hitler and drove the British
back again into Egypt being stopped at El Alamein just short of
the Nile. On the evening of July 2nd, waiting for Rommel's final
attack in the morning, the Eighth Army ran out of anti-tank shell
fuses. Without them they had no hope. At the same time, at Lagos
on the west coast, 3,000 miles away, a ship was unloading the
needed fuses. At PAA–Africa's headquarters in Accra, everyone
was aroused in the middle of the night and put to work. As each
plane came in, it was unloaded on the double and sent right up to
Lagos to be reloaded with fuses. The first DC-3s arrived at Lagos
at 6 A.M. on July 3 and arrived at Cairo full of fuses at 4 P.M. on
July 4.

During the operation, one DC-3 ran out of fuel in a storm and
crash landed near Ft. Lamy. Next day two Americans were flown
in with money and tools. One hundred natives were hired and
cleared a runway during the day. A second DC-3 followed, landed,

picked up the fuses and got them to Cairo 36 hours after the first
one went down. Fifteen tons of fuses were delivered to the Eighth
Army in this one operation.

Rommel was stopped in this second battle of El Alamein. Goering couldn't believe that British shells flown from America had
stopped the German tanks. "Nothing but latrine rumors", he told
Rommel. "The Americans only make razor blades and refrigerators". Rommel politely asked if his army could be issued similar
razor blades.

Air warfare over the desert had peculiar problems, especially
sand, twenty pounds of which could collect in an airplane in less
than an hour and even a small quantity of which, getting into an
engine, would ground the plane. Engine sand filters were a desperate necessity. PAA–Africa flew six tons of sand filters to the
British at this time. It also ferried 1,455 new aircraft to the front
lines in seven months of 1942. These planes were delivered by Pan
Am Air Ferries pilots who were flown back to West Africa on the
PAA–Africa transports.

After Pearl Harbor American aircraft production got into full
swing and by April of 1942, Accra operated around the clock with
planes landing and taking off every fifteen minutes. The North
Atlantic route to England had to be shut down by winter weather.
The loss of Wake and Midway left no possible air route across the
Pacific. The first heavy bombers sent to MacArthur in the Philippines went from Sacramento via Miami, Natal and the African
route.

The English historian, Guedalla, wrote that "Victory in Egypt
came by the Takoradi route", that is by the trans-Africa route rebuilt and operated by PAA–Africa. He could equally as truthfully
have said by Juan Terry Trippe.

In early 1942 the War was on with a vengeance for America.
The swift advance of the Japanese into Burma threatened India.
On April 6th, PAA–Africa Captain Sherman was ordered to take
charge of three transports to fly to Dum Dum Airport, Calcutta,
pick up 30,000 gallons of aviation gasoline and some USAF men
and fly them to Dinjan about 600 miles to the north and they did

so. The three unarmed PAA-Africa transports had been scarcely equipped to fly over the highest mountains in the world and under Japanese attack. The weather was violent with the monsoons just starting. Ice formation on the wings was normal. They had no de-icing equipment. But the clouds hid them from the Japs. They had no communications with anyone and no navaids. When they returned all Air Force people had left Dum Dum.

The evacuation of Burma, in which PAA-Africa participated, was from Myitkyina. Pan Am pilots involved were, in addition to Captain Sherman who was in charge, Captains Sam Belieff, George Lanning, "Fuzz" Furr and Hubbard Euwing and possibly some others. The evacuation was a very well run, business-like operation.

But PAA–Africa was coming to an end. It only lasted 16 months. On December 15th, 1942 all its property and material were turned over to the Army Air Transport Command. Trippe had been using all his wiles to hang onto the African route for his postwar airline, but the military, quite probably thinking also of the coming invasion of North Africa, were determined to take it over and were backed to the full by the President and Secretary of State. Most PAA–Africa employees were commissioned in the ATC, some went home. Kraigher was commissioned as a full Colonel.

My second familiarization trip was on August 21st with Captain Joe Hart, the same schedule via Africa on the eastbound to Lisbon and back across the mid-Atlantic via Horta and Bermuda. I went out on my first trip in command on October 4, 1942 via Bermuda and Horta eastbound to Lisbon, and returning via Africa. We went straight through to Lisbon, overnighted there and started back the next day, stopping and spending the night at Bolama.

Bolama at this time was the principal city of Portuguese Guinea and we had a skeleton base there as part of our Portuguese operating rights. Today the independent country of Guinea-Bissau has a capital, Bissau, and includes Bolama. The latter was then a tropical town with virtually no sign of life. As far as we could tell no one was ever occupied in any way; but there was a good smooth landing area in a river on the edge of which the town was built. It was a singularly unhealthy looking place, and the hotel could hardly be called a hotel. We were glad to leave at dawn the next morning.

Air Ferries and Pan Africa were now operating full blast, and we began to use the B-314s in cargo configuration to move supplies to West Africa where Pan Africa would move them on to Cairo for Montgomery and through to Teheran where the Russians would get them. Stalin was in bad trouble at Leningrad and Stalingrad, and the U.S. kept two routes open to help him—the North Atlantic sea route to Murmansk and the air route across the South Atlantic and Africa, to Teheran. Armies no longer moved "on their stomachs" as Napoleon said, but depended desperately on a supply of ammunition and weapons.

The B-314 had an approved takeoff weight of 84,000 pounds, but we used a wartime gross of 90,000 pounds. No one paid much attention to figures in loading, and the only time I remember checking every item on board because of great difficulty in taking off at Port of Spain, the total gross weight was well over 100,000 pounds. The fighters and bombers being ferried to our allies via Ascension Island could take nothing but the fuel to get across. Supplies were therefore brought down via the ADP airports to Natal where a base was built from which the Clippers (B-314s) could shuttle supplies stockpiled there, across to Fisherman's Lake.

On October 20, 1942 I took out my first shuttle schedule. We stopped at Miami, Port of Spain, Belém and Natal. The stops were only for fuel and we had a day of rest at Natal. Then we flew five round trip shuttles between Natal and Fisherman's Lake with a day off at the Natal base between each one; then a week's rest at Natal, two more shuttles and home via Port of Spain and Miami, arriving November 22nd after a one month trip. My flight time in October was 192 hours followed by 121 hours in November. December was a light month followed by 170 hours in January and so on. In March 1943 I flew 205 hours. I remember one regular schedule of over 200 hours in 20 days. There were times when we never seemed to be out of the plane. In addition to the captain there were four pilots on every flight, one of them exclusively devoted to navigation. There were always two pilots on duty, the others standing relief as flight engineers or drowsing.

The base at Natal was outside of town. We had a mess hall, a large lounge with a paperback library, barracks and a large field for athletics. The base housed and handled several hundred people, mostly Pan Am and Air Ferry crews. We played softball mornings and afternoons. It was very hot, and there were no frills like a pool.

I remember a dog chasing some animal coming toward me, and the animal, seeking refuge, leapt in the air and clamped itself on my shoulder. I stopped dead, unable to see what it was, and very gingerly reached up a hand expecting I might lose a couple of fingers. Instead, I was able to get it on my hand, chattering away, and saw my first coati. It was a brown furry animal, much larger than a squirrel with a ringed tail just like a raccoon.

Another time at lunch in the mess hall, a Brasileiro waiter was not wearing gloves—the freshly washed cotton gloves *always* prescribed. The doctor, a very young, slight, Harvard M.D. stationed here who must have reprimanded the man before, got up, went over and stood in front of him and just looked at him. The man looked back somewhat insolently. The young doctor hit him, knocking him off his feet, and went back to his lunch. The room froze. The station superintendent was unable to speak. Hitting a native was something one *never* did, and this prohibition was well drilled into everyone. It was just as prohibited as an officer striking an enlisted man. We were only guests in Brazil and not wanted besides. This was, in effect, an American Army base with personnel wearing Pan Am uniforms as a cloak. But nothing happened. The man got up and got his gloves, and I doubt if anyone ever forgot or failed to wear them again.

Such was the magic of a doctor in this remote place where few had ever seen one or been treated and cured of any disease, ailment or complaint. He was worshipped, and that is an understatement. It was more likely that the gloveless local would disappear than that anyone would mention the incident to a Brazilian government official.

One day during a rest period at Natal, my crew and others were scheduled for a ditching drill at sea. The Southeast Trades blow hard off Natal and the sea is rough. We went out in an Army Air-Sea Rescue Boat—a converted PT boat. We left our seaplane base in the boat, expecting a pleasant 40 kt. ride, but once over the bar, we could only go about 10 or 15 kts. The skipper estimated the swells at about 17 feet. About a mile offshore, in plain view of the coast, we hove to and got our instructions.

We were to go overboard with life jackets on but not inflated until in the water, get to, get on and inflate a life raft which would be thrown overboard from the PT, and then paddle it to shore (the wind would help blow it that way). We were to fly the kite antenna, contact our radio station with the Mae West portable radio, try the emergency food packets, sea dye and all other equipment and supplies and, hopefully, not require a test of the shark repellent.

"All ready?" we were asked. No reply. Finally I said, "Not me". I was quite sure that I could not have lasted long. "You show us, Lloyd", I said to Lloyd Osborne, a fellow captain and friend who had been captain of the Yale swimming team and a noted intercollegiate water polo player. "OK", said Lloyd, "but I'll be damned if I'll wear a life jacket".

Lloyd went over the side followed by four or five others out of our test group of some 15 crew members. The skipper then threw a life jacket to Lloyd which he put on and inflated promptly. The big problem was keeping the swimmer in sight; but few of us realized how quickly a swimmer, that is a human head, disappears completely in a rough sea. The bridge on the Air-Sea Rescue Boat was quite high up—perhaps on purpose—and the skipper knew his stuff. He could keep track of everyone and everything in the water. But the men in the water quickly vanished from each other and had to try and find the ten-man life raft. Anyway, coached by Osborne and the skipper on the bridge, all the men got together and into the raft. They landed on the shore safely through the surf, but were never able to fly the kite (a model invented by Mr. Leuteritz) carefully "engineered" to carry a copper antenna wire. The Mae West could not raise the shore station maybe two miles away.

It was supposed to have a range of 50 or 60 miles without the special Pan Am kite and many hundreds of miles with it. Only one man tried the food rations and was very ill. The doctor later said that the chocolate bar was poisonous. They also tried a new method of obtaining drinkable water from seawater. Special chemicals were mixed with seawater which was then squeezed out of a special bag. The result was quite undrinkable due to the taste, but might have preserved life in desperate circumstances.

I remember another time that we tested Army flares for night landings. We carried four of them on B-314s. Only one or two of a dozen tested dropped and lit. Most did not drop but hung up when we pulled the cockpit release. We were running tests to determine the best height and place to drop a flare so as to make a 180 degree turn and land under the light before it went out. The test was a total failure, but later, improved flares and release mechanisms, procured by Pan Am, worked well.

The German submarine menace on the Atlantic was at its peak in the summer of 1942 and was not broken until mid-1944. Convoys were just beginning to be used; and huge convoys were built up off Port of Spain, blacked out at night, always radio silent, and were kept as secret as possible, especially as to departure time. There was no shore leave for any crew, the Clipper had blackout curtains which were always drawn, and no passenger was ever permitted to look out, either going into or out of Trinidad.

The harbor off Port of Spain, in the Gulf of Paria, was a spectacular sight when we went through there. It was the collecting point for ships bound for Europe and North Africa. There they were made up into convoys and set off when the escorts arrived. Many hundreds of ships would be at anchor, covering the water as far as you could see, fully manned and ready to get under way at any time. We had to land and take off among this huge fleet, often at night.

At night the ships were only shadows but our launch had put out 1,500 feet of floating lights and patrolled the area to keep small boats away from it. There was no problem with landing. Taking off at night was a different situation. There would always be a dead calm, flat glassy water, temperature over 80 degrees F., and we would be heavily overloaded. The Operating Manual called for maximum time of 30 secs. at takeoff power. To Hell with that. The co-pilot called off the time—"30 seconds, 45, 60, 90 secs."; the last float light went by; it was pitch black ahead; we just prayed with the entire crew jammed together on the flight deck peering out for what might lie ahead. Fortunately, there were miles of water as we normally took off SW away from Trinidad. After about a minute and a half—no one ever aborted a takeoff and it was better not to look at the cylinder head temperatures—we would get off and start a very gentle climbing turn to the left to cross Trinidad through the central valley. Then a British searchlight would go on from somewhere near the airport at Piarco, pointed directly at the cockpit. It was totally blinding. So we flew really by sound, the old "seat of the pants", till we could screen the windshield and recover our sight enough to see the flight instruments.

One of our worst fatal accidents occurred with Captain Sullivan on the Tagus River in Lisbon, on February 22, 1943. Just after sunset, still twilight, while turning to land in front of Cabo Ruivo, a wing touched the water and the B-314 *Yankee Clipper* crashed. Sullivan survived but 19 of 27 passengers and five of nine crew members were killed or drowned. The fourth pilot officer, Johnny Burns, rescued and later married one of the passengers, Jane Froman who was a star popular singer at the time. She was paralyzed by injuries in the crash but came back to sing again on the stage in a wheelchair, to tumultuous applause.

By March, 1943 I had flown 15 round trip shuttles from Brazil to Africa. On the return to North Beach via Bermuda on January 26th, we had a mechanical failure on No. 4 engine. A control quadrant, that is to say a bracket which supported the control cables to No. 4 engine broke off which made the cockpit controls to that engine inoperable. I could not operate the throttle, propeller controls nor anything else which operated by cables to that nacelle. But the B-314 had a very thick wing with a catwalk from the flight deck out to the nacelles in each wing. The flight engineer therefore had access to each nacelle in which he could almost stand up to work on the rear of the engine in flight. The flight engineer, whom we shall call Mike, was unable to repair the broken cable quadrant, so it was necessary to set all engine controls manually in the nacelle. I told Mike he would have to go out to the nacelle and shut down the engine completely on our approach to Bermuda, for a three-engine landing. We were en route from San Juan to North Beach, refuelling at Bermuda instead of Miami.

It was about midnight and the launch had put out lights in the Great Sound near Darrell's Island. On the downwind leg I sent Mike out to shut down No. 4, which he did quickly; and, as I turned on final, he returned to the flight engineer's station and sat there speechless, clutching the table. I called to him—no answer. The radio operator, who was only about two feet away, turned around and tried to get his attention, but Mike was frozen with fear. As I levelled off in our landing area, Mike started to yell: "Look out! We're going to crash!" As we landed smoothly and I cut No. 1 to taxi in to Darrell's Island on the inboards, getting hold of himself, Mike yelled to me: "Well, skipper, I guess we made it". I said nothing but reported to the operation manager the next day when we arrived at North Beach that I thought Mike was temperamentally unsuited for any type of flight duty. But he continued as a satisfactory flight engineer for the next four years.

In 1948, when I was back on the Atlantic Division as division manager, Mike cracked again. Coming into London Airport for an instrument letdown in bad weather, one engine lost all power. The captain called for feathering the bad engine which involved propeller controls located only at the flight engineer's station. Mike feathered the wrong engine so two engines were now out. As the captain tried to restart the good engine, Mike lost his head and went wild, pushing various feathering and other buttons and turning fluid cutoff valves. First one, then two and then all three alternators burned out from overloads as Mike forgot all the procedures he knew. All the flight instruments, which were electrical, went off. The radios went out. Heathrow approach control called an alert detouring all traffic in the air around London to other airports.

The Clipper broke out of the clouds and landed. Mike returned to New York as a deadhead on another flight. The union gave him no seniority in the mechanics rank so we couldn't put him back on ground duty as there was no vacancy. Of course he had far more company seniority than most of the mechanics. The union filed a grievance. It came up before a full board of adjustment—the final appeal court on grievances. I took myself to the hearing, asked to testify and then spoke directly to Mike who had flown with me many times. After a warm greeting I said, "Mike, you know and I know you're scared of flying. You must give it up. I will do my best to get you another job of some kind in the maintenance department". The board turned down the grievance. I was sad but I thought one had to be tough, and only when very sure of one's judgment.

In May 1943 coming back from Fisherman's Lake, we had on board President Tubman of Liberia on his way to see President Roosevelt in Washington. We flew into Baltimore. It was dark and Tubman was met by Major General Benjamin O. Davis in full Army dress uniform, the only black general in the U.S. Army at this time. Waiving all customs and other formalities, Tubman was spirited through the airport and driven to Washington to stay at Blair House. There was no publicity as Baltimore was a Southern city in its attitude toward blacks. We then took our remaining passengers to New York.

Back in the Pacific Division where Pan Am was now entirely a Naval Air Transport Service, where the war was almost entirely an exclusive Japanese-American affair, a lot was going on. We would only hear a little from an occasional Pan Am friend who might be temporarily in the east.

Sometime in May, 1943, Captain J. H. Hamilton was bringing back a Navy PB2Y3 from Funafuti (Ellice Islands) to Honolulu via Canton when a propeller governor motor failed and then the engine caught fire between Canton and Honolulu. The fire was put out but only with the disconnection of the electrical system which also fed another engine so only two engines were left operating. With only two engines Hamilton had to land and did in 20-foot seas. Huge swells are far apart so he bounced off one and landed in the trough before the next.

Within minutes 16 of the 19 persons on board were violently seasick. Hamilton sent in his position and a request for a new prop motor and some cement to stop leaks. Then he went to work, bailing and plugging hull leaks as best he could, filling rivet holes with pencils and cracks with shellac and rags. About four hours later Captain Biggers (all pilots referred to herein were Pan Am) flew over from Palmyra in a Martin, circled and sized up the situation as OK. A Navy plane with parts and supplies and a Navy destroyer both were then en route. So Biggers went on to Honolulu on his schedule.

Night was spent in total darkness, radio silence and bailing. Next morning, the two flight engineers being too sick even to stand, First Officer Saulsberry climbed out on the nacelle and removed the faulty prop motor. About 9 A.M. Captain Harry Beyer arrived overhead from Palmyra where he had been grounded with a faulty propeller and advised Hamilton that another plane was now en route with Captain G. F. Maxwell with the parts and a maintenance crew. Maxwell arrived soon and landed in the huge swells so Beyer returned to Palmyra, as he was southbound.

Almost immediately all personnel on Maxwell's plane were too seasick to move, so Saulsberry stayed on the nacelle and installed the new governor motor. Soon a Navy patrol plane arrived and landed, but then took off and left, seeing that nothing more was needed. Finally everything was ready to go, seasick crew notwithstanding. Hamilton started three engines, but the fourth would not start.

The destroyer arrived. One of Hamilton's Navy passengers was en route to Honolulu to take command of a new destroyer. He wondered if this one might be his. It was. At Captain Hamilton's request, the destroyer skipper sent over a gasoline driven bilge pump and a crew to stand watch the second night, taking Hamilton, his crew and passengers aboard the destroyer.

The next morning it took the crew no time at all to get No. 4

and then the other three engines started and checked out. Captain Hamilton took off safely and went on to Honolulu only 42 hours late.

On the other side of the world, back on the Atlantic, although I was based in New York, I was flying mostly between Natal, Brazil and Fisherman's Lake, Liberia. We flew only at night with radio silence. The only weather report before departure was a coded "A", meaning satisfactory weather, and "B", meaning unsatisfactory. No one ever got a report of weather "B". The South Atlantic was full of German subs, and there were reports of shooting at the Clippers; but I never saw anything on the surface as any ships would be blacked out, of course. I do remember seeing some flashes nearby in the air once or twice, but I was inclined to think them shooting stars or hallucinations rather than anti-aircraft fire from a sub. But some of the ferried fighters going through Ascension were fired on.

We landed at Fisherman's Lake before dawn, down a row of float lights, and left the same day after dark. The African coast was unfriendly as most countries were French colonies reporting to Vichy, France, and so operated as German bases. Admiral Darlan refused to surrender the French fleet to the Allies after the landings at Algiers, Oran and Casablanca on November 7–8, 1942.

Natal was about six degrees south of the equator and Fisherman's Lake was about seven degrees north, so our route took us through the intertropical front which moves slightly north and south seasonally, but we almost always had to cross through it. It is a line of violent thunderstorms. The CBs would build up after sunset and we would see the line of lightning to our north gradually getting closer until we had to cross through to get to Fisherman's Lake. The intensity peaked just before midnight and the storm died shortly after, so it was usually clear when we landed at Fisherman's Lake. But not infrequently, just before we landed and just after the launch had put out the float lights, a thunderstorm would occur with squall gusts up to 60 mph and sweep all the lights ashore so we would come in and land without them in the tropical darkness with our wing landing lights.

The Pan Am terminal on the edge of Fisherman's Lake had a zoo near it. The natives apparently captured young animals, with incredible skill and no fear of the mothers, and kept them penned up or tied to stakes to amuse the crews, passengers and themselves. They loved animals and they caught various cat cubs, panthers, cougars, leopards and various gazelle fawns. How they were caught we never knew. If they looked too sad, I think the natives would let them go and get new ones. Not all specimens were caught or welcome. One day as I was turning in the log and filling out forms on arrival, one of the crew noticed a snake over our heads in the rafters of the building. The natives quickly got it down and killed it—a black mamba, Africa's deadliest snake.

One night the intertropical front appeared to remain close by, north of our track, getting closer and closer. I kept going further and further south of our desired track to avoid a really vicious-looking line of thunderstorms. Toward midnight the lightning was so steady that we could read without difficulty in the cockpit. If we could keep clear for another two hours, the CBs would quickly clear and the stars would come out again. But we were getting too far south. Soon I had to turn to a straight line to Fisherman's Lake. I went down to about 400 feet just below the cloud base where a wall of water, continuously punctured by lightning, had to be crossed at right angles to get to the other side. Flying below the cloud base was the preferred technique at that time and with those particular planes. I put up the blind-flying curtain, turned all the cockpit lights on to full brightness and with my co-pilot also on the controls, headed straight for the wall. Seeing nothing outside, we were all pretty tense expecting something very rough. It was really scary. We flew and flew and flew without even a bump. Finally I had the blind-flying curtain taken down, and we all looked outside. Not a cloud in sight! A full canopy of stars overhead.

The return trip from Lisbon usually involved a somewhat dramatic departure. It was always at night so at least the flight to Horta would be in the dark. At dinner in the Estoril Palacio, at a table for five in a corner near the crew table, sat a German said to be the head of the Gestapo in North Africa. He would enter the dining room in the middle of his four guards and sit with his back to the corner of the wall, effectively screened by his bodyguards. My crew would discuss the group quite loudly; and even though they certainly understood English, they only spoke in German. We were at war with them and they were enemies, but the conversation at my table consisted mostly of speculation on how one could shoot the Gestapo man and how good his screen was. It was good. No one could ever find a spot in the room from which he might be shot.

After dinner the crew station wagon would take the captain and the first officer down dark streets to the rear of a blacked-out building, part of the British Embassy. A small back door would open and we would pop inside into total darkness. The door would close, a light would go on, and we would go up an elevator to a large, well-lit room, the meteorology office. Weather maps were being prepared every hour for the North Atlantic and Europe from coded reports. Then we would get a weather briefing, be given our recognition code sheet and draw up the flight plan. The sheet was just a list of challenge and response signals. The challenges would be directed at us by ships if we flew over them. They were a one-letter challenge sent by searchlight or signal lamp, and answered by our Aldis lamp from the cockpit. They were changed every four hours and a new list was issued every day.

"The Portuguese capital was a neutral and international port. In its cosmopolitan hotels, narrow back streets and noisy cafes, there pullulated agents and double agents of all sorts and all nations". So it is described in *The Murder of Admiral Darlan*. One time at the Estoril Palacio Hotel the table next to us was occupied by a distinguished looking Frenchman whom the headwaiter said was Admiral Darlan, but there is no record of his ever having been in Lisbon. It was just before his assassination in North Africa on Christmas Eve 1942.

One night we had a very strong west wind increasing at altitude, so our flight plan called for low level flight, a couple of hundred feet. Somewhere west of Lisbon I saw a flash from the surface, perhaps a long and two shorts (D). Scrambling for the Aldis lamp, getting it out of its case and plugging it in, for I had never had to use it on a transatlantic crossing and knew of no one who had, we had long since passed the challenge before ready to respond. More flashes were seen, hard to read and almost impossible to respond to in time as we were so low and speeding by. Soon flashes appeared right and left but much above us. Obviously anti-aircraft bursts. We gave up on the Aldis lamp and concentrated on the sea below. There were hundreds of dark shapes—ships—and we were flying right down the middle. It was a huge convoy rimmed by destroyer escorts. Nothing hit us. Soon we were past it flying smoothly through the silent night.

In about May 1943 we started flying shuttles from Lisbon to Foynes and back to Lisbon as an extension of our Atlantic service to Lisbon. France was now occupied by Germany and had war-planes patrolling far out to sea to enforce the blockade of England. We flew to Foynes only at night and only in bad weather, keeping on instruments at all times.

The British maintained irregular direct service from England to Lisbon, flown by KLM planes and crews which had escaped to England and operated as a unit. I remember being in Lisbon when a KLM plane was carrying Leslie Howard from London to Lisbon. It did not arrive, presumably shot down over France and later so confirmed. I left the next night for Foynes, keeping well to the west of Brest.

Coming back from Lisbon to New York through Horta on one flight we picked up a rescued crew from a freighter torpedoed on the Murmansk run. The sailors had been left at Horta by the res-cuing warship for return to the U.S.A. and were a tough lot. We talked and I found that most had never been to sea before, and had enlisted just for the money—they got a big bonus for this run.

The first half of June 1943 I spent at North Beach giving training and first officer checkouts to newly transferred co-pilots on the

B-314. The ice was out of Shediac (New Brunswick) and Botwood (Newfoundland) by now. The sub menace on the Atlantic was coming under control, and we resumed service across the North Atlantic to Foynes. I went out in command for the first time on the North Atlantic on June 17th.

Leaving Newfoundland and heading out on the great circle course to Ireland, we were astonished to see the sea almost covered with icebergs, thousands of them, all small ones. These were streaming down from the Arctic through the Hudson and Davis Straits, but it was very late this year for we were taught to expect the break up of the Arctic ice before June and, after all, the *Titanic* went down in April. These must have been the tail ends of the floe and melting fast for none were there on our return.

When I was home again, I had a vacation for the month of July. Then, after one Bermuda trip, I made alternate Bermuda and North Atlantic trips. I particularly remember having Douglas Fairbanks, Sr. and Lady Ashley as passengers on one trip and showing them the town of Foynes. He was very attractive and so was she. I also remember another passenger who was noticeably tipsy. On disembarking at Foynes, this passenger was passed out in his upper berth, and the two stewards were unable to get him out. I told the two flight engineers to lend a hand, and they were able to turn him over to the station manager. Our poor station manager was instructed to look after him. He had no papers, passport or ticket which could be found, and there was some question, according to the stewards, whether indeed he wanted to go to Ireland. He had proclaimed loudly that he didn't, but I thought it more courteous to leave him there than bring him back to wake up in Canada or the U.S.A.

During 1943 Mr. Priester promoted an idea for a new rank of "Command-Master Pilot", to be a retired Master Ocean Pilot in command of the crew. I bitterly opposed the idea and still think it was a poor one. While the reasons for the position were persuasive, they were specious. I suppose the cost of an extra crew member defeated the proposal, but in my opinion, nothing could be more dangerous than divided authority in the cockpit. Emergencies in flight require fast, trained reactions. There is no time for agreement or discussion. One man, the senior operator of the controls, the licensed, qualified flying "captain" must be the one to decide what to do and his decision will take into account his personal knowledge of his own abilities or lack of them. A further unmentionable consideration was that many very senior men knew less than their more thoroughly trained juniors.

Early in December 1943 I took a trip across the mid-Atlantic to Lisbon, which was to be my last sight of the Azores. My Atlantic days were drawing to a close. From Lisbon I flew our passengers on a shuttle up to Foynes; but, coming back on instruments all the way for the war was not yet over, I found Lisbon closed in, zero-zero, not having opened up as forecast. I elected to go to Port Lyautey in French Morocco which I had never seen but to which Captain Winston had just diverted ahead of me. In fact I had never heard of Port Lyautey before but operations could think of no other alternate nor could I. At least the French forces there were now under Allied command and the weather was reported clear. There may have been other alternates suitable for landplanes but we were a giant seaplane with nowhere else to go. Our ETA was just after midnight, and we didn't have enough fuel to last until daylight.

Circling the area several times, I could discern no sign of Bill Winston nor any sign of a marked landing area among the few lights showing. So, having dragged what seemed to be a smooth water area with landing lights on and seeing no obstructions, I came in and landed. Coming to a rest I was surprised to find we were in a quite narrow slip with one wing overhanging a low seawall.

A French Navy crew secured the Clipper, refuelled us and, when daylight came and word that Lisbon weather was OK, we took off and flew back there in about four hours. It had been a little over 11 hours from Foynes to Lyautey.

After a day's rest in Lisbon, I left to return via the South Atlantic, but this time we stopped at Dakar, now an Allied Navy base, and passed up the miserable town of Bolama, a once indispensable Portuguese link in the start of Pan Am's transatlantic airline.

One time I was sent to Washington to a conference on aerial navigation called by the Chief of the Hydrographic Office of the Navy. This is the office where all hydrographic charts and publications originate. Representatives of the Coast Guard, the Air Force, the CAA, navigation instructor Charly Lunn (head of Pan Am's navigation school in Miami) and myself were present. The chief hydrographer, presiding, was an admiral in full-dress uniform and so impressive that even Charly, an ex-Merchant Marine officer, didn't dare speak to him unless spoken to first. I was not impressed. I spoke up, reminding him of the disaster of the first edition of H.O.214 (so full of mechanical errors that a sight solution using this table might put you anywhere in the world but where you were) and complimenting him on the revised H.O.214 which now was standard for celestial navigation. Then I lit into my pet peeve, the U.S. Nautical Almanac. Why didn't he put out an Air Almanac? Couldn't he copy the English one? I had to get my Almanacs in London. The admiral was most polite, making no comment. No one else said anything. Within months the Hydrographic Office produced a new Nautical Almanac in its present form using all the features of special interest to air navigators and a big improvement on the English Air Almanac.

In time I realized that only the enormous prestige of Pan Am and especially of a Pan Am Master Ocean Pilot, plus the desire of the Navy Department to be the best in the world, produced this crash program regardless of the budget in the Navy Hydrographic Office.

In New York at the end of December 1944, I found my old friend from Rio, Captain Jimmy Walker, who had replaced Bob Fatt as chief pilot in Miami and who was being promoted to operation manager of the new "Latin American Division" (LAD), a consolidation of the former Eastern (Miami) and Western (Brownsville) Divisions.

There was a pilots' meeting in New York and Walker was there. Representatives of all the three divisions were complaining violently and contemptuously about minor, unimportant grievances, and I was among them. Tired of all the griping, I spoke up at the close of the meeting at which Walker was present and said I really thought we were all pretty lucky to be with Pan Am. I guess everyone else thought so too and, for a moment, forgot their gripes. All agreed and Jimmy Walker offered me the job of chief pilot in the new division. I accepted, thinking all the while of one more move for Hope—back to Miami again but now with Johnny, our first child just born in February.

Now, it so happened I had one more schedule before the end of the year, merely a maintenance flight to check a B-314. It came on a very cold and very windy day, and the area where we took off and landed between Riker's Island and the Whitestone Bridge looked very unpleasant. The B-314, when taxied 90 degrees to the wind, buried the downwind sponson and assumed a frightening list with the wing tip under the water. Furthermore, our practice was not to take off until the engine temperatures reached a recommended minimum value. That day, another B-314 was ahead of me on the same mission, a maintenance flight with three takeoffs and landings.

The route from the hangar to the takeoff area was upwind, along a little, narrow channel to Riker's Island, then around it crosswind, to the takeoff area. Arriving at the takeoff area, the engine temps would be too cold, so the other plane would begin the takeoff at part throttle until they were warmed up by which time they would be too close to the Whitestone Bridge to take off so they would cut the engines, make a 180 as slowly as possible and go back to takeoff position by which time the temps would be too cold again. Meanwhile, it seemed like hours went by while I maneuvered well out of the takeoff area waiting for it to be clear.

Finally, the other plane got off, followed by me, made their three landings, and went in. All systems were checked OK by the inspectors and flight engineers on board and we were tired, bored, very cold and anxious to get home. The weather was worsening. It was getting dark and the wind was now around 40.

I came in and landed in the narrow channel from the hangar to Riker's Island. It would have been much too short in any wind but a gale. However, it saved that long taxi downwind, back from the Whitestone. I drifted astern back to the waiting ground crew which attached the cradle under the hull and pulled the ship back up into the hangar. I went home.

It was only some 30 years later that I heard from Captain Gulbransen what had happened in the Pan Am offices which were upstairs in the building which is now the LaGuardia marine terminal. Gulbransen was coming in the front entrance when the B-314 passed overhead just clearing the roof by a few feet and a solitary skycap by the door looked up, greeted him and muttered, "There's a guy that won't be flying for Pan American any more".

Although it was long after 5:00 P.M., normal closing time for the offices, the lights were on upstairs and Gulbransen went up to Chief Pilot Harold Gray's office. As he started to enter, the division manager, John Leslie, came running down the hall, pushed by him and, entering Gray's office said: "Get rid of that man". Blandly, Gray looked up and said, "I can't. He has just been made chief pilot of LAD".

There was considerable pressure to get the Latin American Division set up as quickly as possible, and I was told to report in Miami on January 17, 1944. Leaving Hope in New York with baby Johnny and a nurse, I went to Miami where I found a lovely, small, new house with a patio, a screened porch and a lawn running down to the bay surrounded by coconut trees. It was on one of the little oval islands on the Venetian Causeway. The woman from whom I bought it had furnished it with an incredible number of pots and pans and dozens and dozens of every kind of linen items still in their unopened boxes, besides adequate furniture from Burdines department store. When Hope arrived I was out on a trip. She took one look at our new house, our first owned home, and set up an auction on the lawn of everything in it except a baby grand piano which she knew I wanted. The auctioneer had no trouble selling everything. The aluminum pots and pans were instantly bid on for fabulous prices as the War had caused an acute shortage of metals, especially aluminum which was virtually non-existent commercially. We made a lot of money and, of course, our own things arrived before too long from New York.

CHAPTER VII

————————————————⟨⟩————————————————

Pan American Airways, Chief Pilot,
Latin American Division, Miami, Florida

CAPTAIN Jimmy Walker was the first of the younger pilots to be made chief pilot and he was a fortunate selection. The old-timers were tough, independent men, mostly Navy CPOs or Army NCOs who respected only seniority. The most senior expected to be chief pilot and always had been. None was about to take orders from a junior man with far less experience. But Jimmy Walker was a very good pilot and a most engaging personality. As junior officer, I had made many trips on the Pacific and the first one across the Atlantic with Jimmy, then a junior officer also. He had gone to both the Army and Navy training schools, graduating from Pensacola. How or why he transferred from the Army to the Navy I never knew. He was an exceptionally smooth pilot and a pleasure to fly with in the cockpit.

As chief pilot, Jimmy Walker gained the respect and confidence of the men much senior to himself. He had been on both the oceans and they had not. He promptly instituted some far-reaching changes which set world standards in airline flying. First, he required and enforced a cockpit checklist before every takeoff and landing. George Kraigher at Brownsville had originated the procedure but it was an oral, feel and check. The captain memorized the checklist and recited it out loud, touching each control or adjustment. For example, before landing he would call out "gear down and latched" touching the gear handle and the small locking lever so as physically to check their positions even though he had just told the co-pilot "gear down" and the co-pilot had called out "down and locked, green lights on". The order and wording of the check were invariable. The Walker system was a written list of checks and responses. The pilot would read each item and the co-pilot would give the correct response while both checked the item visually. After Walker, no pilot ever landed an amphibian on land with gear up or on water with gear down as had happened before.

Walker set up a training section with what we called "professional instructors", the chief of whom was John Patterson. These were not airline pilots and were paid less. Previously airline pilots were checked only by especially picked "check pilots". It was quite an undertaking for Walker to persuade the old-timers, each of whom had over 10,000 hours and a few over 20,000, to be "checked" by some 2,000 hour commercial pilot. The instructors started out as "instrument instructors" and flights in the training section were called "refresher courses", which everyone needed as we got little practice on instruments on the Latin American routes.

The flight surgeons "sold" the pilots on physicals (not as exams to pass or fail and be grounded, but as health checks to spot any incipient trouble, cure it and keep them flying). The flight instructors in the same way became highly thought of and every line pilot came away from an assignment in the training school knowing he was a better pilot than before.

Now Jimmy Walker had been moved up to operations manager of the new Latin American Division and had made me his chief pilot. In considering the job ahead of me, I was determined to have the best pilot group in any division. Along with most of the pilots senior to me, I was a real snob in the flying profession, believing the Pan Am pilots were an elite group. Certainly the vast amount of training we got made all other pilots, military and civilian, seem less knowledgeable and competent.

I was determined to get rid of any pilot that did not meet my standards. It would be easier said than done. Up to this time, no captain had ever been fired as far as I knew. Jimmy Walker, when he was chief pilot, may have gotten rid of one or two. In time I eliminated nearly 30 by various means as will appear.

Now I was happily settled in with Hope and Johnny on San Marino Island, and I was about to start on my new job. The first thing to greet me was a petition to my boss, the new operations manager, signed by almost all the pilots in the old Western Division asking for my removal. It was not hard to find out that the petition was the work of Jimmy Maxwell, who had been chief pilot of the Western Division and had taken it for granted he would be the chief of the combined Western and Eastern Divisions. Walker ignored it and Maxwell.

I required four assistant chief pilots and immediately appointed the same four that had been assistants to Jimmy Walker. They were my contemporaries, no old-timers. Very shortly I appreciated Walker's skill and judgment in selecting men, for these four were among the best pilots in the company with administrative skills and leadership to boot. They were:

CYRIL GOYETTE — ex-Army, was Administrative Assistant, my alter ego in all matters. He had come back from Pan Africa, perhaps the toughest flying then being done anywhere in the world, except across the hump in China which came later.

BEN JONES — ex-Navy, was Assistant Training–Landplanes. He was a product of Kraigher at Brownsville. He was very calm, meticulous, and permitted not the slightest deviation from accepted procedures, regulations on cockpit management and flight techniques. Anyone who was qualified on a DC-3 by Ben Jones fitted a mold and there could be no better landplane pilot. There would be no flying cowboys as the Eastern Airline pilots were called; no show-offs like Eastern's Dick Merrill who sought publicity backed by the company as advertising; no smiling Jack from the comic strips; and no personalities or prima donnas in the flight group checked by Ben Jones, or any of the rest of us.

JOHNNY NOLAN — ex-Navy, was Assistant in Charge of all Flying Boat operations. I came to consider him the best flying boat pilot in the Company, past or present.

DICK VINAL — ex-Navy, was Assistant–Engineering. He was a first-rate aeronautical engineer, at least the equal of any in Chief Engineer Priester's office in New York.

Jimmy Walker retained his pilot status while operations manager and occasionally took special flights, but he did not fly regular schedules.

I considered each of my four assistants a better pilot than I was and that was just what I wanted. Before long all four had taken some mild objections to me and spoke to Walker. Walker ignored them but gave me my first lesson in how to get things done and still get along. I think it may have had to do with silly admonitions of mine regarding uniforms, deportment and such matters as appearance.

In time I realized that my four assistants thought exactly as I did, so it was the greatest pleasure to work with them. I just did not believe in being "fair" to any pilot. I still don't. The usual concept of "fairness" to any individual, giving them the benefit of the doubt, seemed to me to disregard the idea of "fairness" to the passengers who had to entrust their lives to the pilot. I was determined that no pilot of whom I had any doubts would fly in command in my division. To Hell with proof. If I didn't trust him, he wouldn't qualify—fair or unfair. Too bad if he was to remain co-pilot the rest of his life—I wouldn't "check him out", i.e., promote him to captain.

It happened that in a huge postwar expansion of Pan American, the LAD became the training section for the Company and most of the captains flying in the postwar era were qualified by me. By the end of my second year as chief pilot, there were about 600 pilots and 350 flight engineers and radio operators in LAD; and I was responsible for their training, competence and morale. My chief pilot's office had four secretaries and a male office assistant.

As I have mentioned before, a major requirement for a captain, in my opinion, was command time, preferably acquired in the Army or Navy. Solo air time in command of military or naval planes was a screening process that quickly weeded out both cowards and brave-but-reckless pilots. Of course, the old-timers had survived an era which most pilots did not, and there could be no question about their courage or air wisdom. The "combination men" were another matter. These were men carried as co-pilots who were qualified as mechanics and radio operators and who had acquired private or commercial pilots' licenses when Civil Air Regulations (CAR) required the carriage of a licensed co-pilot in scheduled air services. Naturally, they all, rated as flight mechanics, wanted to be captains.

The word quickly got around that the combination men had no chance of ever being checked out by me. In the ocean divisions they moved up the ladder to first officer and at least one got checked out in the Atlantic when the DC-4s came into service. He had been an engineering officer on the first transpacific flight and had a great deal of experience. I knew him well and trusted him completely; so, although I might have made an exception for him, I didn't have to because he was transferred to LAD as a captain, and I put him in charge of training on the DC-4s and then in charge of all cargo operations. He was exceptionally well qualified on the mechanical systems and a very good instructor for transition to the big landplanes; but he was a rough pilot who could never have qualified on aerobatics or formation flying, required of an Army or Navy command pilot.

There were quite a number of these "combination men" who had acquired thousands of hours in their logbooks but with almost no command time. In short, they had no experience in which crucial decisions in flight were up to them and no one else. I recall the case of one such pilot who was made chief pilot of the Pacific Division by Harold Gray and who was sent on a trip in the Atlantic with Waldo Lynch on one of the first jet schedules with the Boeing 707s. While Captain Lynch was in the cabin, this man completely lost control of the plane. Let Lynch tell what happened on February 4, 1959:

"The flight left Paris for NY about 1800 Paris time. I decided to stop in London and Gander because Keflavik had been out of communication for about 72 hours. I wasn't worried about KEF weather because they had an excellent GCA but was concerned about runway ice. We were about one and a half hours short of Gander when I went back to the toilet. Evidently Sam was distracted looking at a map, when the automatic pilot was disconnected. I don't know how the aircraft got on its back and into the dive, but I managed to get up there, cut the power and wrestle it under control. We went from 35,000 feet to about 6,000 feet. I put 6.5 Gs on it getting it leveled; and, although the wings and fuselage were wrinkled a bit, they are probably still flying somewhere. All the fairing came off, one outboard aileron torque tube broke and the horizontal stabilizer had to be replaced. It was badly bent but stayed in place—Thank God!"

When I was last in the Atlantic Division, I had received new orders transferring me from the Army (2nd Lt. Air Corps Reserve) to the Navy with rank of Lt. Commander, USNR, on detached duty with Pan Am. The only requirement was to complete a course in Naval Regulations, which I did.

Due to the mushrooming need for pilots for civilian, military and quasi-military operations, all sorts of schools grew up such as the Boeing School, Parks Air College and Embry Riddle at Miami. We began getting pilots from these civilian or military contract schools and to me they were all suspect. Nevertheless, a few turned out to be among our very best.

Civil Air Regulations were now becoming stricter and stricter, and for the first time CAA flight inspectors were being assigned to Pan Am flights. Both CAA flight and maintenance inspectors were rarely up to Pan Am standards. In many cases they were castoffs from the airlines—men fired for incompetence or ignorance. With their newfound power as government inspectors they were hard to get along with.

Few if any regulations applied to the non-scheduled airlines. These were operated by all sorts of sometimes doubtful persons, but their flights were limited in number to two or three schedules a week between points served daily by certificated, scheduled airlines like Pan Am or Eastern.

One day a new inspector appeared on our line and announced he was going to see how we checked a pilot. At this stage in the development of the Civil Air Regulations, a pilot had to be checked out on each type of equipment he flew and rechecked every six months. Also, he had to be qualified on every route which he flew and rechecked on each such route every six months. Such qualifications and checks were performed by the chief pilot, assistant chief pilots and by specially designated check pilots.

On this occasion I took up an Inspector Yandell as an observer while I gave a six month check to one of the captains routinely scheduled for it on a DC-3A. Yandell was loudmouthed, critical of everything, abusive and very objectionable. The captain ran through stalls, engine failures, engine fire drills, missed approaches and go-around procedures with one engine failing just as the runway gave out. The captain did a very creditable job, and, standing on the ramp by the plane afterward, I gave him an "A" on all items. But then, Yandell, perhaps he was scared, began yelling that he'd show me who was running the airline and he drew back his fist, whereupon I seized him around his arms and, when he cooled off, I let him go.

Then I went straight to my office and wrote the head of the CAA regional office describing Yandell's conduct. I never saw Yandell again. To a scheduled airline, a CAA inspector was onmipotent. The Civil Aeronautics Act prescribed procedures "satisfactory to the Administrator". Those words came to mean that the CAA issued "Operating Specifications" to which the airline had to adhere. Every pilot had to be listed on the "specs", so did every plane, airport, check pilot, checklist, instrument approach procedure, weather minimum and many other details. Operations not in accordance with "specs" could subject the airline to heavy penalties and even cancellation of its operating certificate.

John Shannon, as the operations head of Panagra in Lima, disregarded the CAA and tried to argue and get tough with them after

Panagra had initiated night flying. The CAA simply removed the night authority from their operating specs and they went back to daylight only. What was needed to restore night approval was not clearly specified but it was apparent that the removal of Shannon was what the CAA desired. He was made vice-president–traffic and sales.

My first crisis as chief pilot came in the Brownsville Section. Night flying south from Brownsville throughout Central America had recently begun where the flight crew consisted only of a captain, first officer and radio operator. Now we proposed to remove the radio operators and change to radiotelephone throughout all of LAD except in Brazil where the country's law required one. My assistant in charge of the western section, Maxwell, wrote my boss, Walker, that they needed the radio operator "and wouldn't fly without them, and that the operation wasn't safe anyway because the DC-3As could not go above 11,000 feet on one engine and the terrain was over 11,000 feet going into Mexico City". Walker bucked the memo down to me saying: "Do something!"

Of course the specifications gave its full load, one-engine ceiling as well over 11,000 feet but it would do no good to argue with a group who were among the best and most experienced DC-3 pilots in the world. Upon reflection, I circularized the division that, in the interests of efficiency, I had set up a new procedure where all six-month checks would be done in the Miami training section to standardize the procedures.

I scheduled all the pilots from Brownsville for six-month checks in Miami as fast as they came in from their schedules. Then I called in John Patterson, head of the Flight Training Section and told him to see, personally, that every Brownsville pilot on his check would be required to climb up to 10,000 feet under the hood, do an orientation problem to the SE leg of the Miami Range, at which point the instructor was to cut one engine and tell the captain to climb to 13,000 feet.

"Furthermore, John", I said, "I want you to make certain that every Brownsville pilot is shown the lead-shot ballast bags with which the trainers are now loaded and that he is told and shown that the gross weight will be 24,200 pounds" (the maximum allowed). The Brownsville pilots looked with contempt on the sea level, flying boat, fairweather operation of the Eastern Division; and now, to add insult to injury, the new chief pilot was having their flying checked by professional instructors who were not and never had been airline pilots. Before anyone caught on to the fact, they had all climbed to 13,000 feet on one engine. The switch to radiophone and removal of the flight radio operators went through without a hitch as scheduled.

To do my job properly as I conceived it, I set out to fly with every captain in the division and keep myself route qualified on all routes. The routes involved the east coast of South America to Buenos Aires, the Brazil cutoff, the north coast of South America, the route from Brownsville to Panama via all the countries of Central America, routes to almost all the Caribbean Islands, and a non-stop route from New Orleans to Panama. My work involved supervising scheduling and pilot records so no pilot would ever take out a schedule if not up-to-date on his physical exams (two a year), equipment qualification, route qualification and instrument letdown procedures (link trainer). I normally worked every day, six and one-half days a week, and many nights due to night flying checks and training.

Hope saw little of me but was busy enough with little Johnny, a nurse and an occasional maid. Social life was quite hectic at the Bath Club. Miami Beach proper had been taken over almost entirely by the U.S. Navy which operated all sorts of officer training schools in the various hotels. There were now no tourists. The Bath Club at the north end of the beach was a gathering place. We knew many young Navy officers including close friends.

My brother, Alexander, went through there on his way to Assam in Naval Intelligence, attached to General Stilwell, where he spent much of the War behind the Jap lines. School and college friendships were renewed and new ones made such as Sonny and Milo Gray, George and Alice Aldrich, Bus and Nancy Hovey, Monty and Betty Ritchie, Pierre and Lilias Johnson, Bobby and Addie Whitney, Jimmy and Lilias Knott and many, many others ending with Jack Kennedy now back from his tour of duty in the Pacific. John Hersey, who had written about Jack's PT boat exploits for the *New Yorker*, sent him the galley proofs of the article; and Jack gave them to Hope to read for comment.

Many other old friends were part of the Miami scene, particularly, my fellow Pan Am pilot, Doug Moody, who became engaged to Emily Alsop at Boca Raton and married her there. I was the best man. There was also Suzi Brewster, the all-time *Vogue* cover girl and a top professional model, who was quite enchanting. Hope did a portrait of her in a purple dress with a green parasol. She eventually married another Pan Am pilot, George Duff, who was also a close friend of ours. Other beauties crossed our paths occasionally since Pan Am pilots seemed to have a special attraction for them and vice versa. The name of only one, Babs Beckwith, comes to mind today. She was also a famous cover girl.

At this time I viewed airline flying as a special branch of commercial flying, the top branch of the profession. It required, in addition to skill, courage and aggressiveness, a much greater degree of excellent judgment than was required in military or private flying. A military pilot might be expendable, an airline pilot with his passengers was not. The purpose of each flight was to arrive at destination *safely* and on schedule. A late arrival due to mechanical repairs or a detour around very bad weather could be excused. Failure to go through to destination could not, unless there were extra-special circumstances. It was obvious that the safest pilot was one who stayed on the ground if in any doubt at all about the condition of the plane or weather for the flight. That was correct for a private pilot but not for an airline pilot whose passengers expected to be delivered on time no matter what. In Pan Am the captain was expected to know as much about the mechanical parts of the plane as any maintenance man. He was a licensed airplane mechanic too, and he was expected to know more about the weather than most meteorologists. Of course, such expertise in the cockpit is no longer possible because of the greatly increased complexity of transport planes, but it was true on Pan Am planes during the time of which I write.

One day from the window of my office which overlooked the passenger terminal and the ramp in front of it at the Miami 36th Street Airport, I saw a commotion there centered on a DC-3 which had not left yet for Havana. Cyril Goyette, assistant chief pilot–personnel, had gone down to investigate the departure delay and was looking at the elevators of the plane which were fabric covered. On his preflight inspection of the plane, the captain said the fabric was rotten and to demonstrate it had poked holes in it with a sharp tool of some kind. I looked to the south and huge cumulonimbus clouds were building up in the distance over the Keys, which was not unusual for the time of year even though it was still morning. I knew (or thought I did) why the captain cancelled and I was sure Goyette did too.

The chief inspector had come over from the hangar next door to the terminal and said the fabric was OK. Then he fetched a fabric testing machine and pieces of fabric were cut out and tested much stronger than the approved minimum strength. Goyette fired the captain on the spot. I took him off the schedule and the payroll the same day. The passengers got another DC-3 and another captain.

The captain filed a grievance and the system industrial relations grievance board came down from New York and reinstated the captain. I called a meeting of all my assistants and we discussed the matter and it was pointed out that a pilot (or any other person) must never, never, never be fired on the spot—in the heat of passion. Pan Am pilots had finally and somewhat reluctantly joined the Airline Pilots' Association and signed a contract with the Company. We learned that a grievance committee (half ALPA, half PAA in this case) would never back up any disciplinary action unless it could be shown that it was deserved, fair and deliberately and dispassionately applied. Any grievance on a disciplinary action would be upheld if the slightest taint of prejudice, anger or haste could be shown.

Now, what was I to do with the captain? I called him in and said: "I'm sorry you had so much trouble, but you've caused me a lot too. You are still in trouble with me, but if you'll do what I ask, all will be forgotten. I want you to come down to the hangar floor with me and apologize to the chief inspector. Now wait", I said as he showed signs of talking, "you have hurt him badly, professionally and publicly. And don't forget your life and mine can depend on him. I want you to say you're sorry and now think you were wrong". He got up. "OK, let's go". He apologized and then I knew I had a good man. He just needed a little more experience with tropical thunderstorms which I saw that he got with our best check pilot. He turned out to be a good pilot and he stayed with Pan Am until his retirement.

As I have said, I thought the most dangerous pilot was a scared one. I wanted pilots who were not afraid of anything *because* they had confidence in their ability to handle it. Part of my job at this level of training was to see that they got this confidence. Once I took a pilot on a trip to Mérida who was to check out as captain. From Havana to Cozumel, the route was always covered with mushrooming CBs at the time we flew by. It was very rough. The prospective captain was a big and powerful guy, seemingly afraid of nothing. He was at the controls and dodging CBs, but it appeared it might be impossible to dodge them all. He looked at me from time to time presumably to see if he was doing what I wanted him to do—hopefully, perhaps, to turn back. At one point I said, as nonchalantly as I could, "Let's fly 250 degrees". That course would be directly toward the center of the biggest, blackest and greenest CB ahead of us. Captain X hesitated. I waited silently. Finally he turned to 250 degrees and I leaned over to say: "All right. Let's go down to 600 feet". We went through a battering of rain and hail, the cloud occasionally glowing with a lightning flash, but we were quickly out in the clear with the blue Cuban sky overhead. The captain mopped his brow and I relaxed knowing that here was another pilot I could forget about. He was good and now fearless.

As time went on, I found out that my assistants and I all felt the same way and it made the job much easier. They also felt, though we never said so, that there would never be any question of being fair to a doubtful pilot. He had to be very good or we'd get rid of him. But times were changing. Now that we were in the War, the

Army took over more and more of the operations previously conducted by Pan Am.

It was a losing battle to maintain standards but we did what we could. It was not too hard to refuse to qualify a man on flight check who was not yet a captain. It was very hard to get rid of a pilot checked out as a captain and who could fly competently. As an example there was one captain who was an ex-prizefighter and a good pilot; but odd stories came to my attention, indirectly, of violent scenes in his house, beating up his wife and upsetting his neighbors. The most disturbing stories were from co-pilots who weren't about to criticize a captain—nor would I allow it. From them I heard stories of erratic conduct in the cockpit. One day I called him and asked him to come and see me in my office. He replied: "I'll bring my lawyer". He was rumored to be flying trips to New York for one of the many non-scheduled, fly-by-night operators in Miami. I checked his schedules with us and found he was scheduled and had been flying his full 85 hours each month with us. I checked with the local CAA office and confirmed that a CAR applicable to us limited monthly flying to 85 hours.

The pilot duly appeared with his lawyer. I said, "Bill, I'd like you to resign". He said nothing. His lawyer said nothing. I continued. "Bill, I hear you've been taking flights to New York for the non-scheds and that you may be exceeding the 85 hour limit, for which you might even lose your ticket". Bill got up, saying nothing, followed by his lawyer who still had not uttered a word. Both shook hands with me politely as they left. Two days later I received his resignation in the mail.

Some 30 years later I ran into Johnny Nolan who had been my assistant in Miami in charge of all the seaplane flying. We got to talking, for the first time, about getting rid of doubtful pilots— that is pilots we hadn't trusted but had lacked clear evidence for grounding. He said to me: "Horace, you know, one time, long after you left, I was chief pilot in London of a group of crews based there. One day a captain gave me a very bad ride, but the pressure was on and I figured, what the Hell, the co-pilots are pretty good and his can keep him out of trouble. So I passed him. He was scheduled out the next day and I happened to be at the airport and saw, to my horror, the one and only co-pilot about whom I had doubts, going out with him. Both were killed that day on a bad weather approach into Berlin. At least there were no passengers".

I felt very strongly that the pilots should be able to take care of *any* emergency that could occur in flight, so I attempted on a much broader scale than usual, to simulate all the emergencies one could think of. Of course, an explosion in the baggage compartment which blew up the plane could hardly be simulated, but dense smoke from a baggage compartment fire could be. In fact we had such an occurrence on a flight shortly after leaving Miami for Havana and the captain successfully landed at Homestead and evacuated the passengers before a major fire broke out. Investigation disclosed that the suitcase of a German passenger—who denied ownership of it—was filled with bottles of 100% hydrogen peroxide, a supersecret condition of a common chemical at that time. He was arrested on the spot.

I remember wondering if some of the pilots were relying so much on their instruments that they might panic if they were without them. What would one do if his most important instrument, his air speed indicator, failed and that of the co-pilot's too? In our DC-3 training and checks we required that the pilot cross the fence into the airport (i.e., just before landing) at 90 mph. The DC-3 landed at almost 70 mph at maximum landing gross weight. What if he had no air speed indicator? I took to giving captain checks with a roll of adhesive tape in my pocket and as the pilot turned on final I would tear off two pieces and put one each over his and my airspeed indicators. The pilot would break out into a sweat as he faced an overshoot if too fast, a stall if too slow, and had none of the sounds of air rushing by which he had used in open cockpits in primary training at Pensacola or Randolph. No one had any trouble but most were made very nervous. Only one refused and tore the adhesive off, twice, looking as if he'd kill me if I tried again. He happened to be ex-Army and a very good pilot, so I had no worries although I would have preferred to see him accept the challenge.

In December, 1944 Hope's father died unexpectedly in Balti-more. I simply could not be out of touch and remained in Miami. It was at a time when we had no nurse for baby Johnny; however, I was able to get a Puerto Rican woman as a baby-sitter but only in the morning. So, I went to the office then and came home for the afternoon, but I was always on call. I very much regretted being unable to attend the funeral of Mr. Distler as he was a man of very great charm who had been extremely kind to me.

When I knew Hope was finally coming home, I had little Johnny scrubbed and brushed to the nines, and his suit was especially washed and pressed. I took him to the station with me, and as we sat in the car watching the train pull in, he got so excited that he wee-weed profusely all over himself and the car. Before I had a chance to say anything, no doubt because he expected something not nice to be said, he started to yell—loud enough to attract the attention of local policemen. So Hope detrained, carrying her own bag, and thus found us in the car.

October 1945 came and another child was due to be born, which raised unusual problems as there was a considerable shortage of doctors due to the war. Many an obstetrician or gynecologist found himself in a base hospital on a Pacific island where there was little opportunity to practice his specialty but a lot to learn about surgery and wounds. But Hope secured Dr. Wilson, a really delightful old gentleman, retired, who had resumed his practice of obstetrics only because he was so desperately needed.

As the time came due, Hope had a room at the St. Francis Hos-pital which the Duchess of Windsor had just occupied when she went there for some dental surgery. Horace Wood Brock was born on October 7th, but soon developed impetigo—a very serious skin rash for young infants. The maternity ward and the nursery at the St. Francis were closed down. Hope and little Woody came home but there were no pediatricians. Finally we got Dr. Quinlan, a young doctor just back from the Pacific, and he was able to cure Woody. We had been very worried.

We gave few parties but we did give a big one after little Woody's christening. All my assistant chief pilots were there—

Goyette, Vinal, Jones and Nolan and their wives. Also Lt. Harry Harrison, an old Philadelphia friend from the Navy Opaloca base nearby; Emily Moody's sister and her husband; the Moodys, of course, as Doug was Woody's godfather; and many others now forgotten. We consumed gallons of the current drink—frozen daiquiris with ice crushed in the new Waring mixer.

Disregarding the Central American routes, the most hazardous operation in the Latin American Division was flying into and out of Rio's Santos Dumont Airport. This was a landfill in Guanabara Bay with one paved runway, the full length of the fill, 800 meters (about 2,500 feet) long and pointed directly at Sugar Loaf, a short distance from the end of the runway. Upwind was always toward Sugar Loaf necessitating a sharp left climbing turn, begun almost as soon as you cleared the field. The city was to the right so the turn had to be to the left over the bay. All pilots took extra care checking the magnetos on engine test before taking off.

Now I went down to Rio to check each of the captains. On every check, as the captain cleared the field, headed for Sugar Loaf, throttled back and began his steep climbing turn, I pulled the throttle for the left engine, on the inside of the turn, all the way back to idle. The captain would blanch and continue a carefully coordinated turn, as if his life depended on it, which it did—and mine too. Failure of the inside engine on a steep, slow turn would cause a stall, loss of control and a crash into the bay. Again, only one pilot refused and firmly pushed the throttle forward again and held it there. He was a friend, a Pensacola graduate and so very good that I had made him local chief pilot of the group based in Rio.

I knew, however, that all the Rio group now slept better knowing that they could handle, courtesy of that madman, Captain Brock, what they had always dreaded—a left engine failure on takeoff from Santos Dumont Airport.

On a trip to Rio I remember finding Mr. Priester, the greatly respected and somewhat feared chief engineer, riding with me as a passenger. I went back to chat with him saying I didn't know he ever rode the line, was he afraid of flying? "No", he replied with his thick Dutch accent, "but I am always thinking of those breaker points", and he held up his hand snapping his index finger and thumb back and forth together. There were two sets of breaker points on each DC-3A Twin Wasp engine, which had to open and shut 14,000 times a minute at 2,000 rpm. If they stopped, the engine stopped.

Back at my office I spent much time on the problem of communications between all of us in the pilot group. I had never attended or even heard of a pilot meeting in the ocean divisions. I once asked Harold Gray why. He said, "No point. In a large group everyone sits in silence, disagreeing with you on everything you say; but you have no way of knowing that". He was quite right, at least for pilot meetings. But I was determined to have regular meetings whether wanted or not. At first there was some attendance—just out of curiosity to see me, I suppose. Then I began to invite spokesmen from other departments to each meeting from sales, reservations, accounting, public relations and so on. Most of their talks appeared to produce only boredom, but I felt a little exposure to other departments might make for less arrogance in the pilot group. At least I hoped so.

One day I received a complaint from the chief controller at the Miami Airport control tower on the slowness of our pilots in responding to instructions from the tower. I spent most of one day sitting in the tower listening to our pilots and those of Eastern, National, the non-scheds, and general aviation. I was appalled at the slowness and inattention of our pilots by comparison.

Of course, Pan Am had no airways to fly so it was to be expected that they would be less competent in dense traffic on a tightly controlled Federal airway than the domestic pilots. Rather than put out bulletins or plan some training section routine, I scheduled all the captains and all the first officers, with the help of the chief traffic controller, to spend part of the day when traffic was heaviest in the control tower. Results came fast. Soon the Pan Am plane responses to the tower became the snappiest and fastest executed of any to be heard. The tower would call—TOWER: "Pan Am 37" / PLANE: "Pan Am 37" (at 8,000 feet on flight plan) / TOWER: "Descend to 6,000 feet" / PLANE: "Roger". / One and a half minutes later—PLANE: "Pan Am 37 at 6,000 feet, over" / TOWER: "Roger".

The time elapsed from beginning to end of the exchange was now less than two minutes; before it had often been as much as five minutes or more. Of greater importance was the mutual under-standing of each other's problems which came about between the pilots and the tower operators. Previously, the pilots disliked the brusque, matter-of-fact tone with which the tower gave them or-ders. Now they knew what a tower operator had to contend with —a very exhausting, high tension job at which a man could only remain efficient for three hours at the most. Mutual respect grew. Previously the tower had not understood a not so pleasant response from a pilot coming in from San Juan, low on gas, seeing a huge thunderstorm to his left over Homestead, being told by the tower to "Hold at 4,000 feet over Homestead until you get an approach time".

One morning in the spring of 1946 while we lived in our house on San Marino Island on the Venetian Causeway, a visitor pulled up at the vacant lot next to our place. Out of the Rolls Royce, an unusual sight anytime in Miami and especially now with gas ra-tioning, stepped a footman with an easel, canvas paintbox and campstool, followed by Winston Churchill. I was not there, being at my office at the airport; but our Canadian nurse was out with Woody, about six months old, and Johnny, about two years. She knew exactly who it was. Winston Churchill painted happily away at a scene of the rather dramatic Miami skyline across Biscayne Bay —dramatic chiefly because of the enormous towering clouds over the Everglades and behind the city.

While Robbie (the nurse) remained in the background, Johnny toddled over to inspect what Mr. Churchill was doing which didn't bother him in the least. After a couple of hours, the Prime Minister left, but returned each day until he finished the landscape. Hope and I, swimming on Sunday at the Bath Club beach, saw him dozing peacefully in a beach chair under a big umbrella with a bottle of brandy. No one spoke to him, asked him for an autograph or anything like that. The great man's privacy was totally respected.

No reference to his vacation in Miami ever appeared in the papers or in conversation.

It was only much later that I discovered how he came to take a vacation in Miami Beach. He was returning to England from his famous "Cold War" speech in Fulton, Missouri and was staying in the house of a Canadian, Colonel Robertson, who had put him up in Quebec for the meeting with Mr. Roosevelt in August, 1943. Colonel Robertson had offered him his Miami place whenever he might like a spell of warmth and sunshine.

VE Day and then VJ Day came and went. We were getting new equipment—Pan Am was always first with each new kind of air transport. After the Douglas DC-4s came Lockheed Constellations referred to as Connies on all airlines. The Connies were for the Atlantic. We were to have some Convair 240s and some Martin 402s or 404s. We were entering an era of war surplus aircraft. DC-3s and DC-4s (C-47 and C-54) were obtainable at a fraction of their new cost and we converted them from cargo into passenger planes in the Miami shops. Pan Am began to take delivery of Lockheed Constellations in New York, and we got one for training at Miami. Pan Am always got the first new planes, in this case the L-049s, which were real dogs. The later 749s and 1049s were good airplanes.

As we introduced Douglas DC-4s, Vice-President Morrison set up a promotional flight down to Buenos Aires to display and promote our new four-engine equipment. I was captain and took Captain Dick Vinal with me. On the way down, before we even got to Trinidad, No. 4 engine gave us trouble and would produce little or no power. It turned out to be a defective carburetor and there was no spare in Miami. Clearing it with Mr. Morrison, I just continued on three engines; but for the sake of photographers, I started all four engines before leaving the ramp to taxi to takeoff point and just left No. 4 idling until we were out of sight when we feathered it. Upon landing we would start the engine on final approach and let it windmill till we shut down on the ramp.

Then Morrison had a commitment to fly a demonstration flight for local celebrities. "Could I do it?", he asked. "Sure", I answered.

The next day was overcast with a lowering ceiling and looked very gloomy. We took off, climbed up through the overcast and showed our passengers the sunny sky; but I was not about to do any sight-seeing at 300 or 400 feet with only three good engines. It would be an instrument approach back into the field and I turned it over to Vinal. As I expected, it was a smooth, absolutely perfect let-down, approach and landing. Vinal was very good. It must be re-membered that this was a radio range approach with no outer or inner marker beacons, no Instrument Landing System, no high in-tensity flashing approach ladder and none of the ground aids upon which all instrument approaches are based today.

Next day we were starting home and glad of it. I was at the airport early, carefully checking the entire plane. In the cabin I found two local cleaners sitting in the aisle and devouring the spe-cial box lunches loaded for Morrison and his party. I didn't bother with my not-so-good Spanish. I just seized the first man by his collar, marched him to the cabin door and pushed him down the loading steps, followed by the second. At the bottom of the steps stood Morrison talking to George Rihl, an old Pan Am official and the founder of Compania Mexicana. Rihl was the expert on all Latin America and well aware of the sensitivity of the Latins to the Yankees whom they generally hated. After startled looks of sur-prise I could hear Rihl telling Morrison "this guy Brock has to be fired. He can't get away with assaulting an Argentine employee", and so on. Morrison just mounted the steps, followed by Rihl ex-postulating "He'll never be allowed to leave". I retreated to the cockpit to start the engines on the opposite side as they boarded and taxied away for the quickest possible takeoff. We had no trou-ble leaving and Morrison stuck by me. Once again I survived being fired when no doubt I should have been.

We were indeed glad to change to DC-4s and I argued daily for eliminating all flying boats. The landplanes were much safer. No one in the operations department, that is, ground personnel above the pilot group, had any idea of the hazards of flying boat opera-tions. The main problem now was lack of the very high level of experience and competence required of seaplane pilots. The Company was still expanding. Our boat pilots went to the oceans which now were being flown by landplanes, the Boeing B-377s. We had to check out new pilots for the S-42s and they were probably the most hazardous seaplanes ever built. It took super pilots to insure successful landings in them in all sea conditions. The remarkable record of the S-42 which made the ocean surveys across the Pacific and Atlantic was due to its always being flown by very good seaplane pilots.

Now in Miami, we had to turn out super pilots from all kinds of material. I had Johnny Nolan in charge of all flying boat training, assisted at times by Cy Goyette. They had little to work with. We had accidents.

I remember an S-42 crashed on landing in Antilla on the north coast of Cuba, a seaplane refuelling point on the route to Port-au-Prince and San Juan. I think most of the passengers and crew were drowned. As soon as I got the message in my office, I ran down and out to the line, grabbed an S-43, collected an inspector from the hangar, a representative from the operations manager's office, a public relations man and Dr. McDonald; and took off for Antilla. By the time we arrived the bodies had all been recovered and were laid out on the floor of a warehouse in town for possible identification. I went out to the wreck with our inspector, and Dr. McDonald went to town to work on identifications.

It was mid-summer and Cuban law, like the law in most tropical places, required burial before sunset. To see how many were identified, I later went to town with our local agent who had to coordinate the list with Miami where notification of next-of-kin and the newspapers was being handled. Sitting on a bench outside the warehouse, I found Dr. McDonald. "Don't go in there", he said, "I cannot take it anymore. I'm going to be sick". I was astounded and had not realized that anything could make a doctor sick. But there was trouble with making any identification other than male or female, and the local coroner was disembowelling all the bodies to make the possible identifiable parts of the bodies last a little longer. Buckets of entrails were being removed. I returned to our seaplane base, a shack with a runway to a float on the bay, more convinced than ever that the S-42s should be ended.

In the Antilla accident, as in virtually every one, the purser was the hero. The entrance hatch in the S-43 and S-42 was in the top of the cabin to keep the sides closed and watertight. Access to the entrance hatch was by a gangway run over to the top of the hull from the shore or dock, and the passengers then went down a short companionway inside in the cabin to their seats. In a crash it was the purser and steward, if there were two cabin attendants, who would carry or push the passengers up the companionway and out into the water. In these landing crashes there might be no time for inflating rubber boats or formal evacuation procedures. No purser ever left the cabin till he had gotten all of his passengers out of it, and some died in the attempt. The stewards and pursers were all, at this time in LAD, Cuban-speaking men, and we held them in esteem as crew members.

Usually with airline accidents, the other pilots who know the plane and crew involved have a pretty good idea of just what happened. Determining the cause, with all the related legal consequences, is a different matter. The Federal government accident-investigation boards were under the CAB at this time. They became expert in determining the "probable cause" of an accident. In Pan Am cases, the crash was usually in a foreign country which would appoint a national official to conduct an investigation. In most cases that official merely watched and helped the U.S. team which arrived at the site from Washington as soon as possible. The wreckage would be located on a map indicating where it was found. It was then tagged, collected and laid out in a tent at the site. Later, it was taken back to the United States for study.

The search for cause, especially where a mechanical problem was suspected, was very thorough, and the mechanical detective work was often brilliant. The board would hold a hearing in Miami to take testimony and much later a report and the findings would be issued in Washington. The conclusion was often "Probable cause: Pilot error". The term was like a red flag to all pilots and the Airline Pilots' Association. If the pilot was blamed, the ALPA head-quarters in Chicago would issue tirades against the incompetence, stupidity, self-interest, etc., of the CAA and the regulations it issued; and, while I sometimes disagreed, I came to find the accident boards fair.

Nevertheless, as an example of how to be unpopular, at almost every pilot meeting I would say: "If I am ever involved in an accident, I want you to know now that the cause was pilot error—mine". Then I would say, "The same goes for all of you. You are in command of your plane. You have total authority. Under government regulations you have emergency authority to disregard any and all Company or government regulations and do as you think best, and you alone determine what is an emergency. I have fought to get us all that authority and I shall continue to do so, but, with it goes responsibility. The prima facie cause of any accident is pilot error and the burden is on the pilot to show that what happened was beyond his control and would have happened to anyone else".

I only remember one puzzling and unsolved accident. A good and trusted pilot, taking off from Piarco in Trinidad in a DC-3, rolled over on takeoff; that is, the left wing dropped, scraping the runway, and the plane turned over and was wrecked on the field with some of the occupants killed. When the news hit my office, I rushed down the hall to Jimmy Walker's office—he was the operation manager—who said he wanted to go at once. I got a DC-3, the chief maintenance inspector, and a couple of traffic men and we left within a few minutes. I did not need to speak to the chief inspector, a good friend, knowing he and I thought the same; but I asked him anyway, "What do you think it was?" We both could only guess that loss of lateral control on takeoff with a competent pilot had only one possible cause—crossed aileron control wires so that the controls were reversed. Such a mistake was not unknown after major overhauls, but, just to be sure, our pre-flight checklist called for testing full left and full right aileron on the ground while observing the aileron to move up and down correctly. The plane had just had a major overhaul and inspection and he was sure it couldn't have occurred. Besides, how had it gotten from Miami to Piarco? "Please", I said, "as soon as we land you get over to the wreck and check the cables. I want to hear from you and no one else that they are hooked up correctly". (In a wreck it would be difficult to check the correct connection unless you were very knowledgeable.) Shortly after landing and while waiting for the inspector's report before rushing to the hospital in Port of Spain to join Jimmy Walker, I began to think back to the BT-13s at Mitchel Field which had a way of doing a roll on takeoff, later corrected by the addition of spoilers to the wing to prevent a "wing root stall" which would progress out to the tip causing loss of lift in one wing but not the other. Such an occurrence had never been heard of on a DC-3. The chief inspector came up: "OK", he said, meaning that the ailerons functioned properly.

In the hospital the injured were well looked after by good doctors, including some U.S. Army surgeons. The captain had survived. He had no idea of what happened. The wing just dropped and he lost control. We never came up with any rational explanation for that crash.

As a chief pilot with a policy of giving a check ride to every captain in the division, I found a wide discrepancy in skills among the old-timers who chose to stay in Miami and not go to the oceans. Some couldn't qualify for the oceans, but many had put their savings in small two- or four-apartment houses which they rented to provide income and a home for themselves and their families upon retirement. There was no retirement or pension plan yet in Pan Am. One saved for one's old age. They stayed to look after their real estate or local business rather than move to Long Island or San Francisco for slightly more money. I had held these men in very great esteem as having been the world's greatest pilots, but now the planes and new techniques were changing too fast for them.

One day I scheduled a check ride at night for Captain McGlohn. He was primarily a boat pilot and had come to Pan Am from the New York, Rio and Buenos Aires Airline at the very beginning of the Company. Boats were almost out now and McGlohn was on

DC-3s. It was a mean night with occasional drizzle and a wind blowing 30 to 35 knots. For training flights and check flights we often used a nearby county airport far enough out so the traffic patterns did not mix. The county airport was closed, had no tower, no lights and no facilities; but we got permission to use it for training. There were two intersecting runways, one of which was directly into the wind and the other was 90 degrees to it that night.

I said to McGlohn, "Let's just go over to the county airport and make three landings". There Mac made a very smooth landing with only the plane's landing lights, in the rain and gusty wind. By the operations manual, the DC-3 was limited to something like 20 knots at 45° for crosswind landings. McGlohn knew this of course. We taxied back, McGlohn took off again and I shouted: "Land crosswind on the other runway". I expected Mac to say "No", but without showing any emotion at all, he just nodded and changed the pattern to come in 90° to the wind. Our drift angle was very large as he came across the fence, but McGlohn, kicking the plane straight at the last fraction of a second, set it down to a smooth perfect landing. It took full rudder and almost full power on the upwind engine to keep straight. I merely said, "Let's go home". Mac was supposed to make three landings, but I had had enough with two. My report and the log showed three landings and the comment read "excellent", a word rarely used by me.

McGlohn had survived two in-flight fires. It was generally held that no pilot ever walked away from one. We had total contempt for the current fire extinguishing systems in the engine nacelles. Mac's first fire was in a Commodore when flying for NYRBA in South America. He landed, ran up on a beach, unloaded all his passengers and then, with the co-pilot, got the fire extinguisher and put out the fire. After a careful check, the passengers boarded again and Mac completed his schedule.

The second time was in a DC-4 during the start of the war when he was ferrying a DC-4 to Africa across the South Atlantic via Ascension Island. After refuelling at Ascension, shortly after takeoff No. 4 engine caught fire and Mac turned back. It was night and he came in as the whole island watched. It looked like a meteor with a fiery tail. Other pilots watching looked and prayed. They gave him no chance. But Mac landed on the short runway, parked and came out with his co-pilot carrying his logbook, and walked unconcernedly over to the operations office as the plane finally blew up behind him.

McGlohn was one of the smoothest and best pilots I ever flew with. At retirement he went to live in Belém and became an Amazon rancher and trader.

By the end of 1945, practically all of LAD's routes had been converted from seaplanes to landplanes, using the ADP airports which now covered Latin America and the Caribbean. All S-38s and S-42s had been sold or junked but, as I breathed a sigh of relief to be rid of all the boats, we received the last of the M-130s from the Pacific. Two of those boats had crashed, one with Terletzky and a second with Bob Elzey who hit a mountain north of San Francisco on an instrument approach. Only three were ever built. Both oceans had gone entirely into landplanes, the new, big, luxury clippers, Boeing B-377s with a lower deck lounge. Lockheed Constellations and DC-4s were also in service. With the last of the big boats we were to start service between Miami and Léopoldville, Belgian Congo. (Today it's Kinshasa, Zaire.)

When the maintenance department was through rebuilding the M-130 which was an old wreck, the hull gas tanks leaked and the air in the cabin smelled like an explosive mixture of gasoline and air. But the CAA inspectors OK'd it which I could hardly believe. There would be *no* smoking on this ship.

We set up a survey flight with the CAA and mail officials to "prove" the route. As there were no new segments on the route for Pan Am, it would only take one survey flight.

I put Johnny Nolan in charge as captain, Cy Goyette as first officer, myself as a check pilot and assigned a navigator and some extra relief pilots with ocean experience as crew. We would fly day and night, Miami, Trinidad, Belém, Natal, Fisherman's Lake, Léopoldville. On the way across the South Atlantic, I pointed out to Johnny Nolan and Cy Goyette that beyond the point-of-no-return, we had no alternate. I would like to make a blind landing at

Fisherman's Lake. Our approved landing minimums were 1,000 feet and one mile visibility below which the pilot was to go somewhere else, but where? I thought it would be a good idea to know we could do what we might have to call on one of the pilots to do someday. I talked Nolan into the landing "under the hood" with Goyette as safety pilot and myself as observer. Both were somewhat reluctant but finally agreed to try it. The M-130 was a good, stable hull and easy to land; I would never have tried or asked anyone to try it in an S-42.

"Blind landings" which are commonplace today were unheard of then, although a few had been made to test experimental automatic landing systems.

Nolan came in, totally on instruments, using a low powered non-directional beacon and the plane's RDF as the only radio aid. He made a perfect, smooth landing with no assist whatsoever from Goyette. What the CAA inspector on board thought, I do not know and never asked.

We had an interesting time in Léopoldville, crossing the incredible Congo over to Brazzaville, two miles across to the other side. The ferry had to detour around the huge islands of water hyacinths which drifted down the Congo, and we speculated on the consequences of a breakdown of the ferry's engine. The river ran so swiftly that we crossed at almost a 45 degree angle and the river plunged down falls and rapids for 200 feet to the sea a few miles downstream. We talked to local Belgians who loved the Congo and would never go home, having seen what the Germans had done to their country in two world wars; but this was before Moise Tshombe and Patrice Lumumba.

The return to Miami was uneventful and on January 7, 1945 the first passenger flight went out, with a younger pilot in command and Captain Goyette as check pilot. All went well until the approach into Port of Spain, Trinidad. Then the third and last of the China Clippers crashed into the water off Cocorite. Once again with Jimmy Walker, I grabbed a DC-3 and we pushed it all we could to Piarco.[1]

The station manager met us and rushed us to the dock from

which the rescue operations were being conducted. They were still getting bodies out of the sunken hull. Almost as soon as he got out of the car, Jimmy had his shoes, shirt and trousers off and was in the water, diving for bodies still trapped inside. Jimmy was a very good swimmer and a natural athlete as well as one of the best pilots. He would get two bodies for every one the natives brought up, and we laid them on the dock. Most seemed to be children and so many little corpses was a singularly sad sight. Goyette and some others had survived but were in bad shape at the hospital. The water at the site was covered with a layer of gasoline. The survivors had a lot in their lungs. The whole hospital smelled explosive. No smoking anywhere. No turning on or off fans or even light switches. But no one died in the hospital.

Now, what had happened? As usual, we were besieged with people who "had seen it all", "knew just what happened", or "had figured it all out". It had occurred at night, the darkest tropical kind. No one had really seen the crash. The most plausible reason was that given by many natives who claimed to have seen the Clipper hit the mast of a boat. But, where was the boat? I searched the Port of Spain area by boat and plane; local police and government officials talked to hundreds. Finally we had to conclude that there was no boat. Just the usual case of everyone, perhaps to gain fame if they happened to be right, perhaps to try and be helpful, proposing loudly anything they could think of.

We never knew what happened. Goyette, who recovered, never knew; the pilot at the controls was killed. The CAB accident board found, and it was hard to disagree, that the two pilots just didn't see the water and so flew into it. The type of accident was not unusual and not understood then. It was always over water, either with boats or landplanes. The first I remember had occurred on an approach to Shushan Airport in New Orleans where the approach was over the glassy water of Lake Pontchartrain. There were many such crashes until it came to be understood they were due to an optical illusion. In most cases, the experienced pilot who survived swore on a stack of Bibles that he was at least 200 feet in the air when the plane was seen to hit the water in normal descending flight. This was before the days of low altitude wind shear which has caused recent accidents on approach and which applies only to large, heavy planes with their great inertia and slow response to control forces. So ended the day of the great seaplane Clippers.

Before long, a full-dress hearing was held in Miami by the Accident Investigating Board. I seemed to be the principal witness. Trippe had sent his right-hand man, Howard Dean, administrative vice-president, to see what was going on. It was a tough hearing on us, unfriendly and sometimes abusive. I must have behaved all right on the stand for several days because when it recessed, Dean asked me to come to New York as his assistant. I said, "God, no". Another move for Hope and now the first for little Woody. I was pressured. They needed someone in the Chrysler Building who knew what went on in operations. I would keep my flight salary. It was a real move up in the Company and so on. Most reluctantly and only because I liked Dean very much, I agreed. So, we moved again, this time to a house in Glen Cove, Long Island, that Hope found.

So I sadly left the Latin American Division for New York. Pan Am needed more pilots; the War was over and the military services were being cut back and men discharged to civilian life as quickly as possible. The Washington office arranged with the Air Force to interview flight officers being discharged who were interested in airline pilot jobs. A committee was set up to interview them, and to try to persuade them to come to work for Pan Am. Captain Lodeesen went from the Latin American Division as a member of this committee.

The point system for discharge, based on more than just length of service, favored outstanding men, mostly ranked as majors or colonels with many decorations visible only on their discharge papers. Captain Lodeesen reported that they were the most attractive and the finest bunch of men he had ever met. We hired all we could get. Within six months the New York office decided to cut back on the number of pilots and almost all of the newly hired Air Force officers were laid off. They were very bitter, and some said they would never fly for an airline again. This was the beginning of my disillusionment with the Company.

CHAPTER VIII

—————————◇—————————

Pan American Airways, Executive Office, New York

SEPTEMBER 1946 – OCTOBER 1947

THE shift from chief pilot to office work was not something that I looked forward to; I intended to keep on flying when I could. Shortly, I received a telegram from vice-president Dean in New York instructing me to report to him on September 3, 1946. Also, to my surprise, he advised me that I had been elected a director of Panagra (Pan American Grace Airlines). The headquarters of the latter were in Lima, Peru where Grace had most of its principal offices for South America. Grace virtually ran the west coast of South America, owning or controlling almost everything from wine and sugar to banks and shipping. The regional Grace manager was more powerful than the American minister or ambassador in each country.

Harold Roig, a Grace V.P., was president of Panagra, and Messrs. Garni and Patchin were other Grace directors. Pan Am's Erwin Balluder, another Pan Am V.P. and myself were the Pan Am directors of Panagra. The reason for my election or appointment soon became apparent. It gave me something to do. Otherwise I had absolutely nothing to do in my little office on the 58th floor of the Chrysler Building next to Dean's office and one down from Mr. Trippe's. Another reason was that Trippe had signed an agreement with Panagra for through-flights of Panagra's trips from Santiago, La Paz, Lima and Quito into Miami over Pan Am's route from Panama to Miami, and a similar agreement between Panagra and National Airlines so the Panagra plane could go through to New York.

234

In October I was sent down over Panagra's routes as a new director to look over the operation. It was a Company inspection trip and my wife, Hope, could go too. Panagra's top V.P. and general manager in New York City, Douglas Campbell, one of the great pilots in the first World War and, I believe, the first American Ace, saw us off. He was a man of singular charm, a Henry James character. Gustavo Vidal, the treasurer, an intimidating man with the appearance of a gangster, feared in Panagra but all the same a nice guy, accompanied us on the trip. The Panagra group in Lima was of very high caliber. I ran into our old friend Jimmy Walker, now their operating head in Lima; John Shannon, later to become V.P.–Operations for Pan Am; Ned Wright, an ex-Pan Am operations man and friend; Tommy Kirkland, the operations manager; Captain McCleskey, an old China hand like Chilie Vaughn, and a really top-flight group of men, all totally bilingual.

In her diary Hope recorded her impressions of the trip. "We left Miami at midnight November 2, 1946 and slept in our seats in a jam-packed DC-4 to Balboa where we let down shortly after dawn with a very calm and gray Pacific on one side and the hills of Panama on the other. The usual irritating ordeal of government inspectors and then on to a Panagra DC-4 and off for Lima, stopping only once at Guayaquil, a dreadful looking city on the coast of Ecuador. Famous for straw hats—all of a five and one-half million dollar business annually, I was told!

"The Andes started showing up after we left Guayaquil but were pretty well obscured by clouds, unfortunately. Really magnificent scenery for about two hours of the Andes and hard baked orange-brown coast with its dried up river beds and ragged coastline edged with the lace of what must be terrific surf. Then all was blotted out by a thick coating of clouds which lasted until we let down through them and came out in the green world of Lima. Lovely flowers everywhere—geraniums, gigantic roses, everything—wide boulevards and avenidas and enormous squares with statues to some admiral or general (none of whom ever won a battle) dominating the scene. Lima is surprisingly clean and really quite lovely with the sun out and the mountains rising like a backdrop for some musical comedy.

"We were put up at the country club by Jimmy Walker and his wife, Liz, who met us at the airport. The club is most attractive— stucco and tile with a wonderful panelled oak bar. Reminded me of the smoking rooms on the old *Berengaria*. It was very well laid out with a polo field in back and golf links in front.

"We arrived around six P.M. and adjourned to the bar where we met Tommy Kirkland (vice-president of operations for Panagra) and Gustavo Vidal. Dinner with Jimmy, Liz and Tommy at Chez Victor's—very good with excellent red vino. Much PAA talk which is always interesting.

"Sunday morning was bright and clear with the sun out which is unusual for Lima, and after a leisurely breakfast we set forth with Jimmy and Liz to see the sights. Drove through an olive grove that was planted by Pizzaro. It is used as a public park and a completely tone deaf Peruvian band was playing at full force to the obvious pleasure of old and young. We proceeded down to the road by the sea where we had lunch at the Herradura beach (horseshoe) out in the sun with a hard surf pounding at our feet and enormous barren hills rising behind. The beach, the fields and the hills are all exactly the same dry, baked, wholewheat color, and the absence of any green whatsoever is startling. Even the sea seemed drained of any color.

"And then the bull fight! It was the last day of the season and the ring was packed. We had good seats halfway up on the shady side and at 3:30 promptly the parade came in with the matadors in their gold coats and shocking pink socks. The picadores looking like Don Quixotes, the banderilleros in violet and silver and pink, and the cleanup crew in saffron yellow. The band played fast Spanish music and the crowd cheered. Quite a sight to put it mildly.

"The three matadors were Ormellita, Ortega and Procuna. Ormellita, tall, ugly to the point of charm, and a master showman, gave the best performance I've ever seen. His first bull, after placing the three pairs of banderillos *himself*, he killed with his first try; and the second bull he played with such skill and contempt that the crowd went wild and gave him the most tremendous ovation although he had to make three thrusts to kill el toro. To show his opinion of his performance he threw the ears of the bull in the middle of the ring and stalked off leaving the crowd howling with delight. Men threw their hats down and women flowers; he finally circled the ring at a slow run waving the bull's tail. Everyone was extraordinarily pleased and the band got so excited they lapsed into college songs. Very strange to hear 'Crash thru that line of blue', with a dead bull being dragged across the ring.

"It was much better than the fights I saw in Mexico City and my only regret was that I didn't see the great Manolete in action. I saw him in the bar of the country club the day we arrived, and a more fascinating character I've never seen. He is rapier slim, about six feet tall, gleaming black hair shot with silver, narrow El Greco face with a jutting beak of a nose. He was obviously very aware of the heads turned in his direction and played it to the fullest. I regret very much that I didn't see him with the bulls as I know it would be like seeing Nijinsky dance.

"That night we dined at the country club with the Walkers and Tommy Kirkland, and went to bed at eleven on account of a 4:00 A.M. rising. The DC-3 took off on schedule from the Limatambo Airport at 5:30, and we next let down at Arequipa, a small mining town up in the Andes, 8,000 feet up with large, snow capped mountains rising in the distance to 19,000 feet or so. The air was cool and marvelous, and the little airport was very pretty . . . rather like a Swiss hut, and I bought Johnny a pair of Indian dolls. Then on to Arica, the border town of Chile, a frightful, arid, God-forsaken spot if I've ever seen one. As Horace said, it looked like a lunar landscape. No green, nothing but the grey-brown clay earth stretching into eternity, with stark grey-brown hills ribbed by erosion rising into a cloudless sky".

The next stop was at La Paz, 11,909 feet high: the highest large city in the world. One moved slowly getting out of the plane at that altitude. The route south from La Paz was across the Altiplano stopping at Uyuni and Oruro, and on to Santiago, Chile. The area is a flat moonscape devoid of any vegetation, but still inhabited by a few Indians. It is something over 14,000 feet with the towering Andes to the east.

We spent a night at Santiago and then rode a DC-3 across the Andes, sniffing an oxygen bottle, going through the Uspallata Pass (12,464 feet) in the middle of which is a statue of Christ (Cristo Redentor) which we grazed over by a few feet. The pass was said to be normally overcast. With Mt. Aconcagua sticking up to 22,834 feet a few miles to the north, Tupungato, 22,310 feet to the south, terrain generally above the ceiling of a DC-3 and the absence of any radio aids that worked reliably, the route was both risky and scary. It could be flown only by visual contact with the ground. We could see the thread of road winding up and through the pass, past the Cristo, the same road on which San Martín marched his ragged Army of Independence in January 1817, a feat that ranked him with Hannibal and Napoleon.

The survey flight ended in Buenos Aires, and we returned to New York on Panagra via Salta, Argentina—a direct flight to Lima cutting off Santiago and called the "diagonal".

Back in my office in New York I began to hear a bit about what had been going on in Pan Am, especially in the Pacific and China. The War was now over and the tight security—censorship—which had wrapped our Pacific War was being relaxed. It had been so effective that one wondered if our Allies in Europe even knew that there had been a major war going on between us and the Japs. The Burma Road from Lashio in Burma to Kunming in China, across the Himalayas, was unable to carry much in the way of war supplies by truck. The Japs had taken all of Burma by April 1942. A resumé of the China National Aviation Corporation's (CNAC) operation over the Hump, since CNAC was a part of the Pan Am organization, is appropriate here.

OVER THE HUMP

By 1940 Chiang Kai-shek's government had been pushed back to Chungking and was being supplied from India by the Burma

Road. Supplies went by rail from Rangoon to Lashio and then by truck on the Burma Road from Lashio to Chungking. Sometimes supplies went by rail from Calcutta to Sadiya, then by air to Myit-kyina, then back by barge to Bhamo on the Burma Road and then by truck over the road to Chungking. In 1940 CNAC was flying a scheduled passenger service between Chungking and Rangoon via Lashio in Burma, started in October 1939. Now the Japanese had cut the rail link between Chungking and Hanoi and demanded of the British that they cut off supplies to China going through Hong Kong and Burma. The British resisted. In September 1940 the Japanese forced the Vichy government to accept occupation of northern Indo-China by their Imperial army, making Lashio exposed to Japanese air attack.

William Langhorne Bond, the General Manager of CNAC, knew he would have to develop a more northern route from Chungking to Calcutta. In December 1940 he boarded a CNAC DC-3, flown by Hugh Woods, for a survey flight from Lashio up the Irrawaddy valley to Myitkyina (pronounced Mitchina), selected a site for a proposed airport and then flew on to Chikiang, Suifu and Chungking. This was the first flight over what was to become known as the "Hump". It should be remembered that not only did China's government need supplies to exist but that CNAC flew out needed exports of tungsten ore and tin bars.

Bond, who ran CNAC for Pan Am and the Chinese government from 1931 to 1949, was an extraordinary man. He said he never had but one problem—survival. "Striking parallels can be drawn between Bond and Didier Daurat, the great managing director of Latecoère and model for Revière in St. Exupéry's *Vol de Nuit*. (See *The Dragon's Wings* by Wm. L. Leary, Jr.)

On the morning of December 8 (local time), 1941, the Japs hit Hong Kong and Kowloon's Kai Tak Airport, destroying half of the CNAC fleet of DC-2s, DC-3s and Condors, as well as the Pan Am Clipper, an S-42, which was there under Captain Ralph. Bond immediately evacuated all the surviving CNAC aircraft, personnel and high Chinese officials to Manyung. From there they went to Chungking. The Japs took Kowloon on December 12th. General

Stilwell, commander in chief of Chiang Kai-shek's troops in 1942, then commander of all U.S. forces in the CBI (China-Burma-India) theater was pushed out of Burma by the Japs and into Assam to the north. He was largely supplied by CNAC as the Army Air Force at that time was not up to the job.

The British evacuated Rangoon on March 7, 1942. Stilwell urgently needed 200 tons of supplies from India each month. In March the Army delivered 12 tons and CNAC 27 tons. M. X. Quinn Shaughnessy, adviser to the China Defense Supplies Office, wrote Louis Johnson, President Roosevelt's personal representative to India: "I prefer to see Pan American and CNAC handle the whole business" of supplies to Stilwell. Lashio fell to the Japs in April 1942 followed by Mandalay and Myitkyina.

Only counsels of despair were heard in Washington. Louis Johnson returned to the U.S.A. in May and reported "that Burma is completely gone and that with the loss of Burma, particularly Lashio, all possible routes to China are closed". Only Bond disagreed; he could provide a cargo airlift, given enough planes, over the Hump from Assam. In May President Roosevelt declared, "It is essential that our route (to China) be kept open, no matter how difficult". In July the Army delivered 73 tons to Stilwell with 35 aircraft, while CNAC delivered 129 tons with ten aircraft. Johnson finally telegraphed the Secretary of State, "I am convinced that expeditious and vital aid to China can most quickly be accomplished by Lend-Lease contract through the Army to Pan American and CNAC". General Stilwell opposed the idea as he believed that military personnel should not be placed under civilian control in a combat area and because CNAC was controlled (55%) by the Chinese government.

CNAC flew 873 round trips over the Hump between August and December 1942 carrying 1,804 tons to China and 1,833 back out. Calcutta's Dum Dum Airport became the main maintenance base with Dinjan and Kunming main operating bases. CNAC had demonstrated that China could be supplied by air. On December 1, 1942, the Army Air Transport Command (ATC) took over the

Hump operation. Their C-46s, supposed to carry twice the load of the DC-3s, were full of bugs. The carburetors iced up. Pilots called them more hazardous than the Hump. The Hump operation became the place to which obstreperous or undisciplined pilots were transferred from other ATC runs. Many never came back. The pilots were poorly trained. The administration was worse. General Stilwell wrote in his diary about this time that "the ATC record to date is pretty sad. The CNAC has made them look like a bunch of amateurs". C. R. Smith from American was brought into the ATC as a brigadier general. The CNAC's superior performance was attributed to the greater experience of the airline's pilots. In December, Smith observed, "We are paying for it in men and planes" when Colonel Hardin had pushed the tonnage up to 10,000 tons a month. "The kids are flying over their heads", said Smith, "at night and in daytime, and they bust them up for reasons that sometimes look silly. They are not silly, however, for we are asking boys to do what would be most difficult for men to accomplish". ATC was then carrying 15 tons per plane in much larger planes, to 37 tons per plane for CNAC.

In late January 1947 Bond flew a CNAC DC-3 from Chungking to Calcutta via Kunming and Dinjan. Here he writes about such a flight over the Hump, quoted from *The Dragon's Wings*:

"About sixty miles out of Kunming we ran into bad weather and started going up trying to get above it as ice began to form. I went into the control room partly to watch the flight carefully and partly because I knew it was going to be a tough flight at high altitude and I wanted to get up with the crew so I could get oxygen occasionally. I found recently that I could not take the high altitudes without oxygen like I used to. I acted as co-pilot for the flight.

"We got into solid soup at about 14,000 feet and ice began to form. The temperature began to go down and although the alcohol spray on the front window was working, ice began to form slowly. It also began to form on the props and about every four or five minutes would let go and bang up against the cabin. It got a little rough but not too bad in that respect.

"We continued to go higher and the thermometer went lower. The ice on the windows closed over completely until we had the most perfect hood you ever saw.

"Then our heating system gave out. It was then 25 degrees below zero. I believe it got to 30 below at the lowest point. The engines were running perfectly. The Bendix radio had died. The Telefunken was perfect, except that the loops for our Telefunken are not housed and (radio operator) Joe Loh had to keep cranking the loop around to prevent it freezing up and sticking. We got as high as we could at about 20,800 and were just running in and out of the tops of clouds. The temperature inside the cabin got so low that the windows were frosted up on the inside. We could get bearings that told us where we were. We knew we were bucking a very stiff headwind.

"The icing condition outside got better and we had very little coming off the props and we could see the sun every now and then. Or rather you could tell every now and then the sun was there and that gave you a warm feeling—inside. Actually it was still cold as the deuce. We tried pumping up the window de-icer spray pump until the pressure got so high that the alcohol, which we use in it, worked out around the pump system. We could then catch this on our fingers and rub it on the inside of the window but it didn't help much and the rapid evaporation on our fingers plus the already cold conditions nearly took our fingers off. I found out, however, that I could press the palm of my bare hand against the side window and hold it there for awhile and I could thaw out a small part that would enable me to get a quick peep at the top of the engine and a part of the wing. This showed a little ice on top of the engine cowling and a little ice on the wings but not enough to cause any trouble, and most important, was not getting any worse. This lasted about 400 miles and four hours. Then we finally got safely down and the thermometer got up to zero and we felt like giving three cheers for the luxuries of life. The passengers stood it remarkably well. Really, it is amazing, almost pathetic, the licking CNAC passengers will take without any complaint".

CNAC flew more than 80,000 trips over the Hump between April 1942 and September 1945. There were several routes. The northern went from the Dinjan Army DF Station, Ft. Hertz DF, Lake Cheng Hai and south to the Army DF at Kunming. A middle route went direct from Dinjan to Kunming and could be flown at 16,000 feet. A southern route went from the Army DF near Dinjan to a fork of the Tanai River and thence to Kungming with a CNAC DF at Yunlung for a check. The latter was very vulnerable to Jap attacks but could be flown at 14,000 feet. Under instrument conditions, westbound went via Ft. Hertz and eastbound via Yun-lung. The ATC dominated the aerial supply route in 1944 and 1945 and expanded considerably when General Tunner took over from Colonel Hardin in September 1944, but CNAC continued over the Hump until the end of the War in August 1945.

CNAC at its peak in early 1943 had 58 senior captains of whom nine were Chinese, 175 Chinese co-pilots and radio operators, and some 60 planes. From April 1942 to September 1945 22 crews were all killed, 16 of them over the Hump.

After the War there was considerable resentment over the fact that none of the personnel of CNAC was offered a berth in Pan Am nor was any gratitude ever expressed. According to Woods, the chief pilot (from *Wings Over Asia*, privately printed by China National Aviation Association Foundation): "Earlier the Pan Am people had indicated that, when the War was over, the boys who had joined the CNAC operation in Assam and China would become 'members of the family'. If so, they were treated as illegitimate members".[1]

The American pilots who usually had Chinese co-pilots checked out quite a few Chinese captains and must have been among the bravest men ever to have flown. Chief Pilot Woods, hired by Pan Am with 1,800 hours in 1932, had over 10,000 in 1945. One day he asked a new recruit from Flying Tigers how much time he had.

"Wait a minute and I'll add it up . . . including my cadet time at Pensacola", he said. "It comes to 277 hours". One pilot, Donald McBride who joined late in 1943, kept a diary. It is thrilling reading and parts are recorded in *The Dragon's Wings*. A long list of entries such as in January 1944: "Last flight over the Hump was one of the worst in memory—snow, ice, rain and high winds. Today four ships went to Suifu. Ours was the only one to make it back to Dinjan. . . . Japs shot down three A.F. transports over the Irrawaddy River today. . . . Two more transports shot down over Ft. Hertz today. . . . One of my best friends, Mickelson, is 24 hrs. overdue. Probably hit a mountain or was shot down in a pass".

And yet, another entry by McBride reads: "February 27, 1944: The scenery here is probably the finest anywhere, and undoubtedly the wildest and most isolated of any in the world. There are places in the Himalayas where we fly over dense tropical jungles and a few seconds later are over regions of eternal ice and snow. There are gorgeous waterfalls from the melting snow and beautiful sea-green rivers winding through canyons with vertical sides two and three miles high. I have seen mountains split in two by earthquakes, and freaks of nature like the "Devils Slide" in Nevada have been duplicated on a scale that make the original look like something in miniature. There are valleys in which the Creator could easily have lost the Grand Canyon. I found a valley west of Likiang that is an excellent replica of the "Garden of the Gods" in Colorado, only much larger. Between Likiang and Sichang there is a range of mountains that have tipped over on their side, completely revealing the layers deposited during the various geological ages. In a small valley on the west side of the Salween Range west of Paochan are three newly formed volcano craters, so recent that no vegetation has regrown. High up on the west bank of the Mekong River west of Weishi, stands a tremendous natural stone arch. There are hundreds of crystal blue lakes hidden in watersheds slightly below the snow line. Sometimes there are native huts and villages on the shores of those lakes and I often think how peaceful their existence must be, surrounded as they are by an excellent climate, good hunting and fishing, plus plenty of pure cold water. I almost envy them".

In time I became on familiar terms with my neighbors in the New York office. Sam Pryor was on the other side of Mr. Trippe, followed by Erwin Balluder, Frank Gledhill and coming around to me again, Dave Ingalls. Mr. Ingalls represented the political arm of Mr. Trippe, and up and down the hall by Trippe's office often circulated top figures in the Republican party such as Bob Taft, a cousin of Dave Ingalls and Ed Stettinius, Trippe's brother-in-law, ex-president of U.S. Steel and ex-Secretary of State. During my sojourn there, there also appeared on the floor Admiral John H. Towers whom Trippe had hired as a vice-president. He never knew why as he was never given anything at all to do and complained to me that when he passed Trippe in the hall, his boss not only didn't speak to him but didn't seem to know who he was. Towers was perhaps the most distinguished admiral in the Navy before the War. He was the first Naval aviator, and he was the pilot of the NC-3 which was on the first transatlantic flight in 1919.

The three NCs which started all came down at sea. Only the NC-4 reached the Azores and by taxiing. Admiral Towers was the youngest Chief of the Bureau of Naval Operations, the top job in the Navy. He retired and was called back to active duty in Hawaii after Pearl Harbor. I became very attached to him and was able to occupy some of his time by chatting. He had much charm. Dave Ingalls was also a very attractive man, a good private pilot, and held a high position in the Navy in Hawaii during the war.

During the hearings before the CAB in Washington on the Panagra, Pan Am and National through-flight agreement from Lima to New York, I was a witness for Pan Am and consequently spent some time in Washington. I would fly down with Mr. Trippe and Henry Friendly in the Company plane, a converted Douglas B-23, flown by Trippe's personal pilot, Al Ueltschi. I got to know Ueltschi well and thought him a very good pilot, especially on the airways, for he flew into Washington in any weather, even when all the airlines were grounded. Henry Friendly was general counsel for Pan Am. He was said to be the brightest student ever to graduate from Harvard Law School. He drafted the Civil Aeronautics Act of 1938 almost overnight at the direct request of President

Roosevelt. In time he became a Federal judge on the Circuit Court of Appeals and was often mentioned for the Supreme Court. Harold Gray once told me that working on a project under Henry Friendly was the most stimulating experience of his life.

In Washington I stayed at the "House on F Street". This was rented and staffed for the Company as Mr. Trippe spent much of his time in Washington, not merely to push his desired routes, but also at the beck and call of the White House and the State Department. Trippe's House on F Street was run very circumspectly and about the only Congressman ever entertained, as far as I knew, was Senator Brewster (Me.) and only at breakfast, which sometimes lasted until noon.

The Pan Am offices in Washington, D.C. were in the Bowen Building, in charge of Mrs. Anne Archibald, widow of a Marine officer buried at Arlington. She was an assistant vice-president and there were two political vice-presidents in the offices, J. Carroll Cone, a figure in the Democratic party, and William McEvoy, a Republican.

With little to do in Dean's office, I tried to keep my hand in at flying. On June 21 I took a charter to Madrid, to be the first Pan Am plane into Madrid. I went via Bermuda and Lisbon—15 hours nonstop in a DC-4 from Bermuda to Lisbon. On the return, I flew from Madrid to Santa Maria in the Azores, to refuel on the way home to Bermuda and New York.

Landing at Santa Maria, the first time I had seen the place, the weather was bad and, shortly after I refuelled and left, the field shut down to zero-zero. About an hour out, No. 4 engine quit and had to be feathered. Knowing that if I reported it to New York I would be ordered back to Santa Maria, and not wanting to make a three-engine landing on instruments into that unfamiliar field surrounded with hills, I kept quiet and went on. When about halfway to Bermuda I reported the emergency. Before long a PBY, air-sea rescue plane from Bermuda, appeared ahead, turned around and followed us back to the islands. We were very glad to see it and learned later, that it even had droppable life boats by which plane crash survivors at sea could be directed, under sail and under cover, to the nearest land.

On September 20, 1947 we had an accident to a DC-4 coming back from Bermuda. Captain Carl Gregg had No. 3 engine catch on fire about halfway to New York. The fire extinguishers had no effect, and the engine burned merrily with a long trail of flames streaming out behind under the wing tanks and in plain view of the awed passengers. Soon the right landing gear tire, concealed in the wing under the No. 3 engine blew out. As the hydraulic lines and the electrical junction box were contained in the No. 3 wheel well, all hydraulic and electrical systems were lost. Then the No. 4 engine quit and could not be feathered as most of the controls and other lines to it were no longer operating. Now Gregg had only two engines, the two port ones, and one half the gear hanging down. He had asymmetrical thrust and drag, all pulling to starboard. With full power on both good engines, Gregg and his first officer could barely keep the plane straight with all four of their legs pushing as hard as they could on the left rudders. But they were still losing altitude. Simple calculations made it doubtful that they would reach Long Island, but if they could just reduce their rate of descent by a small amount, they might have a chance. Ditching was discounted due to 35 foot swells. Gregg applied full takeoff power to engines one and two, and they just pushed harder on the rudder.

The engines were limited to five minutes at takeoff power after which they were supposed to fail, probably by one or more cylinders blowing up. Gregg had about one hour to go to reach Long Island. On they went, getting lower and lower, the Pratt and Whitneys running smoothly. Now they saw they would not make LaGuardia because of distance and they were too low to clear the buildings. Idlewild (today, Kennedy Airport) was not finished.

A very slight change in course would take them over Floyd Bennett Field, a Navy airport right on the edge of the water. Gregg crossed the fence at about three feet and, still with full power, no gear or flaps, made a belly landing on runway 01 in line with their approach, pursued by all the emergency equipment on the field. The fire was still burning. As the props were sliding on the runway, the No. 2 nose section broke off and slid under the left wing, rupturing the fuel tanks. The entire left side of the aircraft then was enveloped in flames. As soon as the passengers were taken off through the forward crew entrance door, the fire was put out. Later a hole was chopped through the floor and all baggage recovered. Not a scratch on the 41 passengers or crew. The aircraft was a total loss. Busses for the passengers had been rushed over from Idlewild. Gregg was as cool and nonchalant as always, and there was almost no publicity as reporters were not allowed on the Navy base.

In my office, I wrote a letter of appreciation and commendation to Captain Gregg, knowing that no one else would. No one in Pan Am ever had or ever would get recognition for anything. Trippe didn't believe in it and perhaps he was right. I did not believe in medals. In short, people who collect medals were not the sort I would check out as Pan Am captains, but I did believe strongly that recognition of achievements was the most important motivating force for loyalty, team work, and performance above and beyond the call of duty. So I wrote an official letter to Gregg. I showed the letter to my boss; and Dean, reading it, merely said: "Why all the flowery language?" I realized that a cockpit and an executive's office were not the same kinds of places. The people in each were subjected to various kinds of strains but different. There was a mutual lack of recognition.

Technically, what impressed me most about Gregg was that he was in control. The plane wasn't going to control him. If he needed more power, he took it—to Hell with engineering limitations, warnings or predictions. When a well-trained pilot is so indoctrinated in procedures that he never violates a rule or instruction, it may be hard to throw away the book in an emergency but he may have to do so. As an example, shortly after, a captain in LAD was going into San Juan with one engine out and another giving trouble. He went down in the water off Morro Castle with less than full power on the operating engines. Gregg would have made it.

Pan Am paid the lowest salaries of any airline, due, perhaps, to Trippe's desire to present a picture of parsimony in his applications to the CAB for more mail pay. Trippe had to approve, personally, every salary of $10,000.00 a year or more. I believe his salary, as president and chief executive, was only $30,000.00 at this time whereas that of C. R. Smith of American was $75,000.00. Pilot salaries rose automatically with each new kind of plane under the ALPA contract. Ground personnel seldom got a raise, and a pilot was soon paid more than a top executive. Nevertheless, there was extraordinary enthusiasm, loyalty, and pride in the Company on the part of all employees in every category. They were all, to put it mildly, top grade people. For example, the head of our flight kitchen in Long Island, where the meals for the Pan Am flights to Europe were prepared, was Albert Tuinman, a Dutchman who had been chief chef at "21".[2] There was almost a caste system among the cabin attendants on the Atlantic (before stewardesses were adopted) and the "special" ones who lorded it over the lesser ones often came from the Piping Rock Club where Tony, the head-waiter, was a stern disciplinarian who terrified the staff but pro-duced the best trained waiters and the best club dining room service in the country.

Nevertheless, I took strong exception to the policy of ignoring any outstanding achievement. About this time, Mr. Priester retired at the compulsory age of 65. He just stayed home one day, advised the comptroller that he was retiring and going off the payroll. Priester was legendary. He was one of the first men hired by Trippe, as chief engineer. He was responsible for virtually every-thing in Pan Am operations and for the success of the Latin Amer-ican and Ocean Divisions. Pan Am procedures and practices which became the standards for the world, followed by the British, French, German and all others to say nothing of TWA, had all been established by Priester. When it was learned that Priester had retired, grumblings came to my ears from our operations personnel all over the world. No memo even announced his leaving. No let-ter of thanks. No present; no dinner; no recognition of any kind.

I told Mr. Dean in no uncertain terms what I thought. He listened and said nothing, knowing Mr. Trippe. In time, a pleasant but hardly appreciative memo was issued by the president's office. To Trippe's credit he had invariably picked exceptional men—up to that time. On the 58th floor where I was, I saw the top vice-presidents almost daily. I became very fond of and thought highly of Mr. Gledhill and Mr. Balluder whose offices were on the other side of the 58th floor. Franklin Gledhill of Pan Africa fame was vice-president of purchasing, meaning that he was the principal negotiator for the purchase of new planes. He was a tough bargainer. The enormous prestige of Pan Am enabled him to get the first Convairs, series 240, at $250,000.00 each. They subsequently cost other airlines $750,000.00 each as 340s.

Erwin Balluder was in charge of all Latin American affairs. He was born in the Virgin Islands of Dutch parents and lived most of his early life in Mexico. He had come to Pan Am via Mexicana. He was fluent in Dutch, German and Spanish as well as English. One day I was in his office when some important looking Latin was shown in. He was the Pan Am representative in El Salvador. He spoke his best English, not very good, and was complaining about his remuneration. He had been president or vice-president of his country and thought himself very much a Central American big shot. Balluder chatted courteously and then suddenly changing to Spanish which I understood better than I could speak, he said: "You're nobody. Your country isn't much. Your only position in Central America is as an agent of Pan American. Now get out". This was not exactly diplomatic protocol, but Balluder knew much more about who was who in Latin America than anyone in State. The Salvadorean left unescorted.

Not long after, a serious defalcation occurred when the general manager of Pan Am's affiliate, Panair do Brasil, skipped with over $1,000,000.00. It was easy. Money was transferred by slow boat from Rio to New York. During the month or more it was in transit, the money was not in the Rio bank nor in the New York bank —a real "float" not accounted for anywhere. In this case it never showed up in New York. John Woodbridge, Pan Am's comptroller, was a brilliant man and probably the best in any airline. Pan

Am was the first to have all IBM machine-tabulated reports and the first to have all accounts on a modern IBM computer. After the Brasilian loss comptroller Woodbridge set up an internal audit system whereby a group of special auditors travelled the world, dropping in unannounced at all places where Pan Am funds were held. I do not think Pan Am ever had another loss.

Howard Dean, who had brought me to New York, was an old friend and Yale man of Trippe's time. He had the title of administrative vice-president and was second to Trippe over all other vice-presidents. A big, bluff man, ex-Wall Street broker, able to drink any man under the table—some of the vice-presidents were pretty hard drinkers when on a party—always amusing, Howard Dean was the perfect adjutant for Trippe, to handle all his hard and sometimes temperamental associates. Dean could take care of any situation and was, I think, a very good judge of men. I liked him a lot and he liked me; otherwise I never would have stayed in the New York office as his assistant after the first year, and he knew it.

There was a problem of who was to run the Atlantic Division. James Hopkins Smith was in charge and Robert Cummings had been his division manager. Cummings had originally been in charge of the ADP which grew into such a large venture that it was a bit beyond him, and he assisted in finding San Pryor who was hired for overall supervision of the program. Pryor later became the senior vice-president after Trippe although his duties were mostly political. Cummings was a very strong and aggressive personality and so was Jimmy Smith. It was not very long before Cummings left, and he became assistant director of the Marshall Plan in Paris.

Now there was again a vacancy for division manager. Dean proposed me and offered me the job. I think it was felt that Smith needed a little more operating experience under him, so I was chosen. I was to have full authority to run the operations. I accepted hoping I might survive a little longer than Cummings.

CHAPTER IX

<> ─────

Pan American Airways, Atlantic Division, Division Manager

OCTOBER 1947 – SEPTEMBER 1954

THE Atlantic Division which I now headed involved an airline covering half the world. Things had changed since my previous tour on the Atlantic in 1944. Now they had stewardesses as well as pursers and had gone from the big seaplane Clippers (B-314s) to landplanes—Connies (Lockheed Constellations or L-049s), DC-4s and the giant B-377s.

I was in charge of flight and ground operations; stations and sales offices in Newfoundland, Iceland, Ireland, Scotland and England; Paris, Rome, Lisbon, Copenhagen, Brussels and Frankfurt; Oslo, Stockholm and Helsinki; Dakar, Monrovia, Accra, Lagos, Léopoldville and Johannesburg; and, besides, Beirut, Teheran, Karachi, New Delhi and Calcutta. Also we had just set up a intra-European operation based at Brussels with DC-3As which flew to Frankfurt am Main, Munich, Belgrade and Vienna.

The Brussels base was staffed with crews from New York on temporary assignment, without their wives; except that we hired local Belgian girls as stewardesses who were required to be fluent in most European languages—a requirement we could not meet with Americans.

The Pacific Division besides now going southeast to Sydney and Aukland, went east to meet us at Bangkok for round-the-world schedules set up by Jimmy Smith in February 1946.

The Latin American Division under Wilbur Morrison in Miami,

operated from New Orleans to Panama; from Brownsville, Texas down through Mexico City and the capital of every Central American country to Panama; across the north coast of South America from Trinidad to Venezuela, Colombia and Panama; and from Miami to the Bahamas and to every country on the east coast of South America and Paraguay. Panama was a connecting point with the Panagra routes which covered every country on the west coast of South America.

The Trippe theory of decentralization, that is, three separate and autonomous divisions in Pan Am, didn't quite work as it should have in my case. Gray in San Francisco and Morrison in Miami could be quite unreachable by headquarters in New York. It was more difficult for me, first at LaGuardia Field and then in Long Island City, to avoid the 25 or more vice-presidents in the Chrysler Building, few of whom had anything to do. Naturally, they took a lot of interest in me.

Each division was set up like a separate airline except for two things. All revenue accounting was done by a system accounting office in New York, and there was a system sales office under the vice-president–traffic and sales which produced most of the revenue for the Company, from both cargo and passengers. Under the same system vice-president there was also a mail superintendent who handled all matters relating to mail, foreign and domestic; and a fare superintendent who issued to the divisions the schedule of fares between all cities in the world. The vice-president–traffic and sales, ran the sales offices in the United States, in most major U.S. cities, but not the sales offices in foreign countries which were operated by the divisions. However, foreign sales were limited by quotas designed to fill the seats not sold in the U.S.

As a consequence of the separate airline concept, I had, under me in the Atlantic Division, three main departments: Operations, including all flight personnel and all the airport stations; Maintenance, with about 800 airline mechanics in New York; and Traffic and Sales, which ran the sales offices and the sales counters at the airports in some 30 foreign countries. Lesser departments such as passenger service, which included a flight kitchen, the corps of stewardesses when Pan Am came to have female cabin attendants; communications, which supervised the flight and ground station radio operators; an accounting department (about 100 men); and a medical department all of which reported directly to me. In addition there were many separate offices such as press relations, public relations (publicity), a statistician, a photographer, an insurance manager, a manager of buildings and facilities, and others now forgotten. Of course, there were many sub-departments: under the operations manager was the chief pilot, superintendent of stations, ground facilities and baggage handlers, flight radio operators, navigators and others; under the traffic and sales manager were superintendents of passenger sales, cargo sales, mail, rates and fares, advertising and others. When I took over, there were about 4,500 men in all.

I tried to meet and speak to every single man and girl in my division at least twice a year while, at the same time, never being away from New York more than four or five days at a time. It was an impossible job, but I nearly succeeded; and I did know everyone in my division, which could not be said, I believe, by the head of any division before. I doubt if most of the personnel in the New York office had ever been to most of the Pan Am stations. For example, I found I was the only Pan Am official they had ever seen in Oslo.

The work of the sales personnel at foreign stations, ticket agents, reservation clerks, etc., was so governed by regulations emanating from the system office in New York that I interfered little with these offices. Most of the top traffic and sales officials in New York, however, seldom saw the foreign sales offices or met the personnel in the field, and seldom knew anything about the areas in which we were trying to sell Pan Am.

Perhaps my only disagreement with Willis Lipscomb, the vice-president–traffic and sales, involved passenger service, i.e., flight service. As long as the cabin attendants were almost all girls, I thought the head of that department should be a woman, and I had one picked out. But Lipscomb prevailed and we kept a man in that job. I concerned myself only with passenger service in two cases. In one I helped get our aircraft meals which were obtained abroad, prepared by Maxime's in Paris (Mr. Vaudable); and I obtained a liquor license for my division which enabled us to avoid the high taxes on liquor by not unlocking the liquor locker on the plane until outside the three mile limit. I did this on my own, obtaining the correct form from Albany which required me to swear that no member, director or stockholder of Pan Am had ever been convicted of a felony. I sent the form to Henry Friendly, Pan Am's general counsel in the New York office, with a note: "OK to sign this?", and he sent it right back: "You must be out of your mind". So I changed the form to read, "To my personal knowledge", signed it and in due time got the license. The embarrassing question of felons on the board or among the stockholders was avoided, but I believe it was the only time this question ever was overlooked. Liquor licenses were very hard to obtain in New York. No doubt the magic of the Pan Am name had something to do with it.

The Atlantic Division offices at this time were in a wing of the Marine terminal building at LaGuardia with vice-president Jimmy Smith at one end of the hall and myself at the other. Harold Gray had left the division to head a system planning board in the Chrysler Building. Frank Hankins, an ex-pilot with degrees from Dartmouth and M.I.T., was operations manager. He was brilliant and personable, but I wanted a different personality for operations manager and finally selected "Mutt" Fleming from Brownsville, a product of Kraigher—affable, knowledgeable and with the personality of a good Texas politician. Everyone liked him. I took it for granted that Priester's office would make a place for Hankins or that San Kauffman, Priester's assistant, would. He was needed there and would have been one of the best men in that office. To my horror, he was offered nothing when I replaced him with Fleming, and he left Pan Am to become a vice-president of Curtiss-Wright.

My boss, Jimmy Smith, was one of the most colorful characters in Pan Am. A paper he wrote at Harvard Law School on International Air Rights got him a job with the State Department which put him in the middle of the disputes between the British government and Trippe. Trippe hired him and soon sent him to Pan Africa. He was on his way there on Pearl Harbor day, and he was then called to active duty in the Navy and served as a torpedo bomber in the Pacific, ending up on Admiral Radford's staff. After the War, Trippe rehired him and made him vice-president of the Atlantic Division.

Jimmy told me of one mission for Trippe during his early employment just before our entry into World War II, and now I'll put it in his words: "I was in Cairo when the Germans were chasing Montgomery to Egypt and the fall of Cairo was imminent. Roosevelt had made Alexander Kirk minister to Egypt and Saudi Arabia. King Ibn Saud's capital at Riadh was a hard three days' trip from Cairo. Kirk asked me to fly him from Cairo to Riadh to present his credentials. I asked Ibn Saud for a cleared, level, place to land and that it be marked by four smoke pots.

"Kirk and I took a C-46 from Cairo, located with difficulty a small group in the desert near a solitary smoke pot—one tent, some Arabs and six ragged looking soldiers. Our C-46 landed alongside. Ibn Saud was there. Kirk presented a $50,000.00 gold bar from the President. The King asked the sex of the plane. Kirk replied, "Female, of course". The King was pleased. It developed that to prepare a landing field the King had asked what was the largest in America. Told that the longest runways were 10,000 feet, he had laid out a flat area 10,000 feet by 10,000 feet with a smoke pot in each corner, and had turned out much of the population of Saudi Arabia to pick up every rock and to smooth any bumps in the area. We landed on a billiard table of sand.

"A state dinner that night in the tent required eating sheep's eyes and all the rest amid a solid cloud of flies. The temperature was about 120 degrees F. in the tent. Departure the next morning was set for 6 A.M. because the engines might not start after that. The departure was delayed while the King showed me his falcon killing a bustard. After closing the door at 11:00 A.M., the temperature inside the C-46 was at least 130 degrees, four men rushed out with a present from the King. It was a pig-skin (made into a bladder) filled with ewe's milk. I said, "No". Kirk said, "You have to accept it or it will be an insult, an international incident". We left with the pig-skin and its cloud of flies, but opened the door of the C-46 in flight and threw it out as soon as we were out of sight".

I was in London on an inspection trip when one of our Connies crashed on approach to Shannon on April 15, 1948. It hit the ground just short of the runway and burst into flames killing all the crew and passengers except one man, a Lockheed employee, who crawled quickly through a hole in the fuselage which miraculously appeared next to him as the plane came to rest. He ran away as fast as he could, proving the theory that one had about five seconds in a violent crash to escape before the fuel from the ruptured wings ran out, caught fire and exploded.

When I arrived at Shannon from London that afternoon, pausing only to send a message to Hope that I was not on board (Jimmy Smith had already called her), I found the immediate problem was how to deal with the bodies. They were badly burned—clearly unidentifiable. They had to be buried with a religious service of some kind. The passenger list disclosed passengers from China, Japan, India, Iran and other places.

On the round-the-world flights special meals were carried to suit the dietary laws of most religions, Hindus, for example, and we were familiar with such laws, but burial customs for all the religions of the world were beyond me and inquiries were of little help in the short time allotted.

Next, the station manager took me to call on the bishop in Limerick. He proved to be a jolly, red faced Irishman, dressed in a cassock with both feet clad in purple socks. He sat in front of a fire with his feet propped on a pillow. He extended his hand for me to kiss his ring, which I did, respectfully, and he said: "What can I do for you?"

"Your Worship", I said, not knowing the correct address (perhaps "Your Holiness?"), "I would like to arrange a funeral for the persons killed in the crash of our airplane at Shannon yesterday".

"Well, well", said the bishop, his face lighting up. "A funeral did you say?" and he sent an acolyte out of the room who returned soon with an enormous flask of wine, sacramental, no doubt. After we all had full tumblers of the wine, it dawned on me that I had made a terrible mistake in saying "funeral". I was to learn that a funeral in Ireland involved a parade through town followed by several hundred mourners and a wake when all the mourners and everyone else would be plied with spirits by the bereaved, in this case Pan American World Airways.

"No, No", I interrupted the enthusiastic comments the bishop was making to plan the greatest parade Limerick was ever to have. "No funeral. We just have to bury all the deceased and want you to read the service over them". "How many?", said the bishop. "Well, we need six individual graves for identified persons, and one larger grave for the unidentifiable bodies, 56 of them".

"What?", said the bishop, thinking perhaps of 62 burial services tomorrow morning. "How many good Catholics?" "Thirty-five", I said promptly. Quickly I added, "We are arranging to have the graves dug, but you will have to show us where they should be". "I will indeed", said the bishop, quite obviously figuring the charge. I intended to leave that matter to the station manager who lived in Limerick and went to church.

"By the way, your Worship", I said as our tumblers were refilled, "some of the bodies are of Asiatics and Iranians so is it all right if priests of other religions also participate in the services so that their faithful may be properly consigned to God according to their faiths?" "Certainly", said the bishop with a pleasant look, apparently having settled in his mind on the charge.

I promptly got in touch with Jack Kelly, our Pan Am regional director in London, and gave him the job of getting to Shannon the next day a rabbi, an English clergyman (whose funeral services I hoped would satisfy the heirs of any Presbyterian, Lutheran, Baptist, etc.), representatives of Confucius, the Shinto religion, Vishna and even Zoroaster.

The burial took place on a gray and drizzly day; and I gazed at the cavernous grave at the side of which the bishop said mass, followed by six holy men in their varying robes, intoning in their different tongues. That afternoon I flew back to New York.

At this time we were trying to convert all the routes of Pan Am from carrying radio operators to direct radiotelephone between the pilots and the ground. So far we had only short-distance radio-phone with control towers at airports. Communications systems had to be approved by the CAA after demonstrated reliability before the primary system could be changed from telegraph to telephone and the radio operators taken off the planes. Pan Am, that is Lynch and McLeod, successfully achieved this revolution in long distance communications when it was still quite beyond the capabilities of the Army, the Navy, RCA or the American Telephone and Telegraph Company. How it was done is quite technical and is explained in the notes.[1]

Approvals of the countries overflown had to be obtained and were obtained promptly except for Switzerland and Brazil. We detoured Switzerland between London and Rome, but we had to carry radio operators flying over Brazil for some years.

Each Monday at lunch time there was an operations committee meeting held in a private room in the Cloud Club on the top floor of the Chrysler Building, and Mr. Trippe was always there. The regular members would be the three vice-presidents of the three divisions, but Morrison from Miami and Gray from San Francisco were only present when they were in New York for some other reason. The other members who varied over the years I was present were Dean, Pryor, Balluder, Gledhill, Woodbridge (comptroller), Ferguson (treasurer), Lipscomb and also Ingalls, Towers, Al Adams, and Sam Meek (account executive of J. Walter Thompson, advertising).

First I would report on the load factors in each segment of the Atlantic Division routes during the past week, there were no reports from anyone else. Anyone might raise some matter that interested him, but one didn't ask questions of Mr. Trippe. Other than operations matters, all of which seemed to always be referred to me, the only other matter of general interest would be the progress of any applications to the CAB for route changes or new routes. Mr. Friendly answered those.

Trippe always listened intently but seldom spoke. I never heard him give an order, make a request, or even make a suggestion. He ran a Quaker meeting. People only spoke when so moved. Frequently Trippe seemed deep in thought. No one moved. No one spoke. Hours could pass. At the start of the meeting waiters took the orders for lunch. Cocktails were always offered, but none was ever ordered. Lunch was always a numbered "special" served with coffee. Our meal was served and the dishes were removed. About 5:30 or 6:00 I would quietly ask permission to leave for a moment and do so, calling Hope to say I didn't know if I'd ever be home.

Long after sunset, Trippe would look up, smile and say good night. He was a man of great personal charm. You were always flattered to be spoken to by him. I never heard him raise his voice or say anything forcefully, and yet. . . .

Sometimes at such a meeting a controversial subject would come up, and there would be a heated debate among those present, with the exception of Mr. Trippe who never said a word. But when the discussion would die out, there would be left an unspoken agreement, totally unanimous now, which was understood to be what he wanted, and it would be done.

Sometimes, when leaving the meeting, sensing how I disagreed with what he wanted done, although unspoken, he would walk out with me and, putting his arm around my shoulders in a most fatherly way, would say: "Harold" (my name is Horace, but never in seven years, did he ever use my correct name), "we must experiment. We must not be afraid to try things. Some things may be mistakes, but we must try". Trippe greatly admired Alfred P. Sloan, the management genius of General Motors, and was said to try and pattern Pan Am after General Motors. It was also said that he never could remember anyone's name. Maybe so, but a suspicion always lurked that his forgetfulness might be a put down. Once, when he took the directors to Paris, the Pan Am special representative there, Clem Brown, gave a cocktail party for Mr. Trippe and his party. Clem then lived in a beautiful town house, a small palace off the Étoile. When they arrived, Clem met Mr. Trippe at the door and greeted him effusively: "Juan, so glad to see you. Hope you had a good trip over". Mr. Trippe shook hands and wandered over to the bar saying, quite audibly, "Who was that?"

Shediac,
New Brunswick, Canada

Foynes,
Ireland

Lady Ashley and
Douglas Fairbanks
at Foynes

Southampton store, 1939

Southampton shelter, 1939

PAA—ACD-3A—25M—6-1-39

WEATHER REPORT

TELEPHONED

TO ....
BY ....
TIME ....
CHECK ....

2255 GMT

    BROADCAST FROM BRITISH COASTAL RADIO GCK:

    BRITISH SHIPPING BOUND MEDITERRANEAN FROM ATLANTIC CALL AT

    GIBRALTER AND AWAIT ORDERS --- SHIPS IN THE RED SEA PROCEED

    TO SUEZ OR ADEN --- SHIPS BOUND FOR RED SEA FROM INDIAN OCEAN

    PROCEED TO ADEN AND AWAIT ORDERS --- NO SHIPS ARE TO VISIT

    ITALIAN PORTS--- SHIPS IN BLACK SEA REMAIN IN SEA OF MARMORA

          39:09 NORTH   21:30WEST

          "S.S ASHBURY" SIGHTED SUBMARINE 1455

45:37N   14:35W   SS AGAIN CHASED BY SUBMARINE 0051GMT

COASTAL RADIO GCK

ALL BRITISH MERCHANT VESSELS ARE TO CONTINUE ON THEIR VOYAGES EXCEPT THOSE

BOUND FOR THE BALTIC SPECIAL INSTURCTIONS FOR SUCH VESSELS WILL BE ISSUED--

VESSELS IN PORT SHOULD CONSULT BRITISH NAVAL REPRESENTATIVE OR CONSULAR

OFFICER BEFORE SAILING --SHIPS AT SEA SHOULD AVOID FOCAL AREAS AND PROMINENT

LANDFALLS AND SHOULD MAKE A LARGE DIVIRGENCE FROM THE TRACK NORMALLY

FOLLOWED---SHIPS AT SEA IN OR SUBSEQUENTLY ENTERING AREAS NOS 1,2,3,4A,5A,

6,7 OR 9 IN ADMIRALTY NOTICE TO MARINERS NO 3 SHOULD DIM NAVIGATION LIGHTS

AT NIGHT AND EXTINGUISH ANY OTHER LIGHTS WHICH SHOW OUTBOARD THEY SHOULD

TRY TO ARRIVE OFF PORTS AT DAYBREAK.........

              0840 GMT

Radio traffic picked up on my last North Atlantic trip, August 27, 1939

ADMIRALTY MESSAGE

ANNOUNCE FOLLOWING ARRANGEMENTS FOR PROTECTION OF HOMEWARD BOUND

BRITISH MERCHANT VESSELS HOMEWARD BOUND VESSELS OF LESS THAN

15 KNOTS IF BOUND FOR BRISTOL CHANNEL OR IRISH SEA SHOULD PASS

THROUGH RENDEZVOUS LAT 51 DEGREES AND 10 MINUTES NORTH LONG

7 DEGREES 56 MINUTES WEST BETWEEN 0500 AND 0700 7TH SEPTEMBER

THEN STEER 060 DEGREES AT 10 KNOTS IF POSSIBLE AFTER DARK OR

ON APPROACHING THE SMALLS VESSELS SHOULD PROCEED AT FULL SPEED

TO THEIR DESTINATION ALL VESSELS APPROACHING RENDEZVOUS SHOULD

BURN DIM NAVIGATION LIGHTS IN ORDER TO MAKE A RENDEZVOUS VESSELS SHOULD

ZIGZAG OR REDUCE SPEED BUT SPEED MUST NO REPEAT NOT BE REDUCED BELOW

8 KNOTS VESSELS WHICH HAVE ALREADY PASSED THIS RENDEZVOUS BY 0500

7TH SEPT ALSO VESSELS BOUND ROUND NORTH IRELAND AND ALL VESSELS

OVER 15 KNOTS SHOULD ZIG ZAG AND PROCEED TO THEIR DESTINATION

AT FULL SPEED KEEPING WELL CLEAR OF THE RENDEZVOUS AND ROUTE MENTIONED

IN THIS MESSAGE FURTHER RENDEZVOUS WILL BE PROMULGATED DAILY VESSELS

BOUND FOR ENGLISH CHANNEL FROM OVERSEAS ARE TO PROCEED ON THEIR

VOYAGES UNLESS THEY RECEIVE SPECIAL INSTRUCTIONS 1626 / 5

More radio traffic

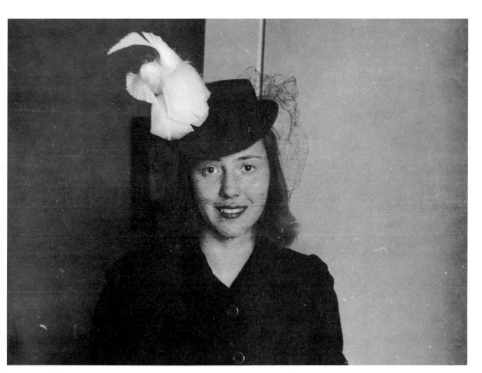

Hope Brock

The author

Guanabara
Bay, Rio

Copacabana

Gavèa

André Tarnowski

Captain Everard C. Bierer

Copacabana Beach,
Ambassador Caffery,
Hope, Mr. Lage,
Xanthacky

John F. Kennedy on Copacabana Beach, Rio, January 1941

Portrait of Fuji Walker by Hope, done in Rio

Douglas DC-3

Boeing S-307

The author

Boeing B-314 at Dinner Key

Douglas DC-4

Lockheed L-749

Lima, Peru.
Olive trees planted
by Pizarro. Jimmy
Walker and Liz.

Altiplano.
Uyuni, Bolivia

Highest pass
crossing the Andes,
Santiago to
Buenos Aires

Boeing B-377 over London

Welcomed by a local chief at Accra, Ghana, on inaugural flight
from New York to Johannesburg

Juan T. Trippe

Samuel F. Pryor

John C. Leslie

Andre Priester

Erwin Balluder

Franklin Gledhill

Wilbur L. Morrison

Captain Edwin C. Musick

Harold E. Gray

In 1949 and 1950 Pan Am was being subjected to increasing criticism as a high-cost operation whose unit costs per ton mile flown did not go down as costs were doing on the other U.S. airlines. Some of the domestic trunk lines, such as American and United, no longer needed subsidies. Many local service airlines such as Mohawk and Allegheny would soon be off subsidy, too; but it seemed as though Pan Am would never be. Routes like those to Teheran or Johannesburg had few paying passengers but were flown in the national interest, greatly desired by both the White House and the State Department. Pan Am would fly anywhere, anytime, with no apparent interest in normal business considerations.

Major competition came from foreign carriers which were heavily subsidized by their governments, and many of which operated with American airplanes given them by our government through outright grants or purchased with dollars loaned them on long-term, low-interest rates. Before the War our only competition had been Imperial Airways, operating British aircraft. Right after the War, TWA operated across the Atlantic with a huge backup from domestic routes which were denied us. Every type of unfair competition was used against Pan Am. We paid higher landing fees than foreign airlines in their respective countries, but they paid the same as we did in the U.S. Currency restrictions made foreign travellers to the U.S. travel on foreign airlines. Americans could travel on any airline.

One evening in 1949 Howard Dean took me to dinner at the Union Club and after plenty of drinks told me gently that "Juan" wanted a 10% reduction in the number of personnel in my division. I knew the AOA acquisition would bring more personnel and some new European routes to fly. I blew up, for I knew almost every employee in the division by name, and they all knew me, both in New York and in more than 25 foreign countries. I had already, as an approved economy measure, terminated all company meteorologists, professional navigators, flight radio operators and one class of ramp personnel.

I pointed out to Mr. Dean that you could not fire ten percent when you only had one employee on duty at any time, as at some places. The station managers at more than 50 cities we served had to load and unload passengers' baggage, handle the mail and sell or collect tickets, etc. Firing 10% of these people merely meant that I would have to contract outside for the same services at a greater expense. Nevertheless, Trippe wanted a 10% cut in the number of heads in the division. "Yes sir!" I said. Another drink, and I left, wrecking my car on the way home.

When I took over the Atlantic Division, it had 4,500 employees. At the merger I turned over 2,600 employees to Harris, a reduction in heads of 42%. Not one single one had been surplus. Costs did not go down, they went up; but we continued to give first class service.

I wrote a personal letter to each employee laid off or fired. There would be no hope of reemployment. Many were old crewmates and friends, and their crafts were being abolished. Almost all came up to my office to shake hands before they left.

Labor relations took up most of my time during these years. There was a system industrial relations department, under Gledhill. I fought hard to keep the flight personnel. Our radio operators were really expert radio mechanics and technicians. I wanted to transfer them to the ground radio shop and fire the much inferior and often incompetent mechanics there, but the union refused. The shop men had their own seniority list, the flight men theirs. The lists could not be integrated. Gledhill agreed to keep two and only two navigators, and he picked them. Fortunately one became the world's authority on celestial navigation.

Once, I was sent to the Douglas Company in Los Angeles on improvements to the DC-4. We were flying a lot of these at that time, but all were surplus C-54s. Now a postwar passenger transport was coming out and the old C-54s would be converted into cargo planes. Trippe spoke convincingly about cargo service, predicting a phenomenal growth, possibly exceeding passengers in revenue. I started an all-cargo service across the Atlantic as directed, but the payload was so small in a DC-4 that it lost money. But, as usual, Pan Am was the first.

On a visit to the Douglas factory, I attended a meeting with top engineers from Priester's office plus all the top engineers of Douglas and with Donald Douglas, Sr., himself. After one engineer had given Douglas certain specifications for the size of cargo doors, seat arrangements and so on, I outlined the pilots' ideas on what could be improved. Because no one else there was a pilot, I was given close attention. After damning almost everything in the DC-4 such as the cockpit instrument arrangement, emergency exits and other things, Mr. Douglas, very impressive, finally spoke, quietly and with a smile to me: "Captain Brock, less than a year ago I decided to try and find out why we made our airplanes the way we do. I wrote the head of each engineering section and asked them. The replies astonished me. I found out that we don't know how to build an airplane. Seventy-three percent of the pieces are made the way they are only because someone did so first and it worked". "Yes, Sir", I said, and I have always remembered the charm and wisdom of this man, probably the greatest of all airplane designers.

At an operations committee meeting early in 1950, Morrison announced that he had acquired a large facility at the Miami Airport —hangar, shop and office space—at a very low rent. It was to become a system overhaul base. Previously each division had had its own independent maintenance base although most major overhaul work and modification work had been done at Miami. Now it developed that all the maintenance work of the Atlantic Division was to be done at Miami, and the planes would be ferried down there.

I can only suppose that the plan was Trippe's and not Morrison's. Wilbur Morrison was a very good friend of mine and I thought so highly of him that I hoped to see him take over the Company after Trippe. He was bright, tough and very loyal to his men. I liked him the best of all the vice-presidents.

The reasons given for the Miami base were the usual ones of economy of scale, lower wages, cheap space and other specious reasons. No doubt the maintenance ferry service between New York and Miami would provide an argument in Washington for a domestic route. When the change became operative costs soared and quality of work plummeted.

On February 1, 1951 I wrote Mr. Trippe in great detail about the effect of transferring most of the Atlantic Division aircraft maintenance from New York to Miami. Here are some excerpts, MOB standing for Miami Overhaul Base:

On September 30th R-4360 engine ⚹2041 failed 32 hours after overhaul at MOB from a "crankshaft failure at front-end of B Row crank pin".

On October 16th R-4360 engine ⚹1147 failed five hours after overhaul at MOB because "engine seized due oil line not properly tightened".

On December 16th R-4360 engine ⚹753 failed five hours after MOB overhaul "due to broken link rod strap at A-3 piston". Failures such as these just don't happen on other airlines.

On December 12th, Flight 150 left Léopoldville for Joburg. It turned back shortly after takeoff for a cylinder change. It took off and turned back a second time for an engine change. It left again and turned back a third time for a cylinder change on the new engine, overhauled at MOB.

Two weeks later ex-Governor Stassen was to ride with us from Joburg to Lisbon where a dinner at the Embassy had been arranged. The plane broke down at Joburg so he rode BOAC to Brazzaville to wait for us to catch up. We did, but our plane again broke down at Léopoldville and Stassen had to take Air France to Paris and missed Lisbon completely.

My letter never even drew a comment from Mr. Trippe—but nothing ever did. My anger at the Company, however, increased at what I thought to be Trippe's promotional theory of management. It seemed to me that no consideration of efficiency or cost would ever influence a decision of his which would increase the size, importance or fame of Pan Am. I believed that Mr. Trippe thought Pan Am was so important to the U.S.A. that it would always be supported. It couldn't go broke. It would always be subsidized if necessary, although he would try his best to keep down the subsidy requirement. I did not think, at this point, that Pan Am was a viable business or ever would be under Mr. Trippe. But, he had created the greatest airline in the world out of almost nothing. Congress was getting restless, and it was hard to believe that it would support Pan Am forever. Trippe was sure it had to—or so it seemed. If so, he was wrong.

One day in 1951, the operations manager, Mutt Fleming, dropped in my office. Captain Kim Scribner was the chief pilot. "Is it all right for Kim Scribner to go down to Miami to fly in the Air Races?", he asked.

"Certainly not", I said. "I've never allowed any pilot to appear in any air show with the attendant publicity, as a Pan Am pilot. Let's leave that to the domestic fly boys".

"But I'd like to let him do it", said Mutt.

"So would I", I said, "so OK, but nothing about Pan Am".

Captain Kim Scribner was a good friend and a very good and somewhat special pilot. Not an Army or Navy graduate, he still was a consultant to the Army on parachutes. Kim even had several patents on them. In the pre-World War II days, long before parachuting became a sport, Kim had been an authority. Three problems interested the Army, and Kim knew more about them than anyone else. These were: quick opening to permit drop from low altitude; quick release from the harness so as not to be dragged if jumping in a wind; and steerability to avoid hi-tension lines, lakes and other hazards while descending. Kim built and jumped the first steerable parachute.

Kim was also a world champion acrobatic glider pilot, holding the world's record for speed over a measured 100 kilometer triangle and distance flights. He had a glider act which the Miami Air Races sought. So Kim went down. On the first day, January 6th, 1951, a friend was to tow him up to where he would release himself over the field and do acrobatics on the way down. He intended to be towed by the stands inverted, then roll out of the inverted position and be towed up to 3,000 feet, then release the tow, do an outside loop, etc. and land, stopping the sailplane on a newspaper in front of the grandstand.

The day dawned, but his Stearman tow plane was up north, as

was his tow pilot. He rented a sign-tow Stearman and pilot. The pilot had never towed a glider before. Kim had the new tow pilot tow him the day before the air show—he did very well; but Kim did not roll over inverted until they were at 500 feet.

On the day of the air show, however, Kim filled his wing tanks with water (to provide weight for his inverted dive to reach 200 miles an hour to do the outside loop). After completion of the outside loop, he would jettison the water and climb back to almost 3,000 feet again. The tow pilot changed airplanes (unknown to Kim), and he now had an under-powered Stearman. At 50 feet and being inverted, a high negative angle of attack was required for the sailplane to remain at 50 feet. The tow pilot, seeing this high angle of attack through his mirror, thought he should *climb*. The result of his attempt to climb without sufficient power—he would have had it with the original airplane—and with Kim's water in his wings, resulted in the tow plane stalling as seen by Kim from his inverted position in the sailplane. Kim released the tow, but he could not roll out. Upside down he went into the grass beyond the runway. Kim was thrown against his instrument panel. He had multiple fractures and was unconscious for several days with head injuries, dual vision, right leg broken in three places, right foot pushed up through his ankle, left leg through his hip, and internal injuries. However, many months later, in a wheelchair, he was in New York and back to work and soon thereafter he was back flying.

In April 1952 I heard an LAD B-377 had gone down in the impenetrable Amazon rain forest southwest of Belém. An expedition was being set up hurriedly in Miami to go in and look for it. There was no word of crew or passengers. I had also heard of a special Air Force paratroop school at France Field in Panama which trained "jungle jump" teams. Graduation entailed being dropped on the Darien peninsula and making one's way back to France Field with no supplies. This peninsula was considered about the most impenetrable terrain in the world. The Inter-American Highway construction stopped when it got to the Darien peninsula. Steep hills and most of the most venemous insects and reptiles we know, lived in it. The training was the ultimate in survival.

I called the commanding officer at France Field and promptly got him on the phone—such was the magic of Pan Am's name. "Sir, we have a plane down in the Brazilian jungle. Could you possibly drop a rescue team in there?" "I know about it", he said. "There is nothing we can do. The trees are solid there and over 100 feet, maybe 200 feet high. Our men would hang up in the trees. Their ropes to get down with are only 60 feet long". The Air Force did, however, send a rescue team which was based at Belém. The wreckage was found and all the passengers and crew had been killed.

In 1948 after he had been the vice-president over me for about a year, Jimmy Smith left Pan Am and, not long thereafter, was made Assistant Secretary of the Navy. I then reported to Admiral Towers and, in 1950 to vice-president Balluder. I saw little of them except when I needed them, and they gave me a complete free hand. In July 1950, however, Mr. Trippe announced the acquisition of American Overseas Airlines. Pan Am had to take over not only all the assets of Overseas but also the 300 non-union employees and, by name, Harold R. Harris. It would be over a year before the acquisition was finally completed.

C. R. Smith had acquired a transatlantic flying boat operation with two Sikorsky S-44s from a steamship line, American Export Lines, which started American Export Airlines from New York to Lisbon. Lacking any rights to land in Portugal or any other foreign country, it nevertheless got CAB and U.S. government backing. The CAB forced Pan Am to give up its exclusive rights to the Azores and Portugal. The CAB had plenty of muscle as it fixed the mail pay (part subsidy) on which Pan Am depended to stay in business.

Pan Am had previously attempted to block another steamship company airline in the Caribbean. Waterman Lines once set up an airline which was totally dependent on Pan Am for weather service, communications, navaids and even runway lights, all of which had been installed and were privately owned and operated by Pan Am. Pan Am just turned everything off when a Waterman schedule came along. Very bad publicity resulted because it was said that the Federal government supplied free airways inside the U.S.A. and, in effect, equipped airways beyond the borders of the U.S.A. by granting Pan Am higher mail pay (and subsidy) than to the domestic airlines, with which to build airways in foreign (mostly Latin American) countries where the U.S. had no control but Pan Am had exclusive rights.

Pan Am lost the argument; but the Civil Aeronautics Act of 1938 prohibited control of an airline by a steamship line, railroad, or any other form of surface transport. So Waterman gave up its air operations and American Export Airlines was acquired by American Airlines and became American Overseas Airlines.

As in the above cases, the U.S. government broke the exclusive franchises which Trippe had gotten without government help. These were the first indications of the bitter opposition to the size and power of Pan Am in the White House (after Roosevelt) and in Congress.

Another indication of Pan Am's disfavor with the government was the certification of TWA to serve Paris and Rome, right after the War, leaving Pan Am with only Lisbon and Marseilles, the original seaplane terminals. The transatlantic routes would all be operated with landplanes from now on, huge airports having been built by the military or the Marshall Plan at all major European cities. American Overseas was promptly certificated to London, as was Pan Am, and on to Frankfurt which became a major traffic point in Europe. By dint of supreme effort in Washington, Trippe was able to get Pan Am certificated to Paris and Rome after TWA was well set up in both cities. It seemed particularly unfair that, having pioneered the Atlantic, Pan Am was denied access to the major traffic points merely because it started with flying boats. TWA and AOA, which operated with weather services, communications, and cruising and navigation procedures all developed by Pan Am, were given the choice routes. We would meet many old friends from Pan Am who left to be instantly hired as important executives by TWA.

Now I had to assimilate American Overseas. The only personnel problem was the integration of the American Overseas pilots into the Pan Am seniority list. An integrated list was worked out by the ALPA with some difficulty and the Company stayed out of it. The Pan Am pilots did not exactly welcome the American Overseas ones. Nevertheless, among the group, we picked up three of the best pilots Pan Am ever had, Charlie Blair, Champe Taliaferro and C. T. Robertson. There were many other very good pilots, but I did not know them.

General Harold R. Harris, a college football star as a young man, had been an Army aviator in the First World War and a test pilot afterwards, charged with testing and evaluating World War I planes which were brought back to the U.S.A. In the course of one such test flight the plane fell apart and he bailed out to become the first member of the Caterpillar Club.[2] Harris had started and operated an airline in Peru which was absorbed into Panagra, and from there he went to American Airlines to head up American Overseas. He was rough and tough and a somewhat picturesque character with a record of great courage and skill as a pilot. In World War II he was drafted into the Air Transport Command, as was C. R. Smith, each with the rank of brigadier general. He came to Pan Am with the purchase of American Overseas.

Harris, my new boss, promptly removed Fleming, my operations manager, one of the best and the one who had been responsible for the transition from flying boats to landplanes and for the installation of two-way radiotelephone communications across the Atlantic. He replaced him with his old friend from Panagra, John Shannon. Shannon was a Navy Academy graduate, a pilot for NYRBA, one of the first to fly across the Andes, and the operations manager for Panagra in Lima. Fortunately Harris left my chief pilot, then Sam Miller, intact.

Harris hired a male secretary who turned out to be not only an excellent secretary, but also an expert on bugging. I do not remem-

ber that we used the word "bugging" then, we just called it recording. Harris quite openly told me that he recorded all phone
conversations that he knew or thought might be important, and
Frank Lord, his secretary, was soon at work equipping the General's desk with a most elaborate recording system—omitting, of
course, the beep which the law required to be sounded during the
recording of any telephone conversation. Mr. Trippe's secretary,
whom I knew quite well, was Bob Lord, and Frank was his
brother.

Harris equipped himself with an intelligence infrastructure that
would have pleased even Himmler. I was not so happy with this
initial introduction to the way some people work in big business.

There were, of course, outstanding exceptions. Two come to
mind right away: Nelson David who was a senior representative
for AOA in Frankfurt, a very good man who left shortly after the
takeover to become an official of ICAO in Montreal; and Norman
Blake[3] whom Harris sent to Beirut to be in charge of the Middle
East. He did an outstanding job there, becoming close friends with
Saeb Salaam, six times Prime Minister of Lebanon and head of
Middle East Airlines, then family owned; with Sheik Alamuddin
who ran the airline; with Fawzi el Hoss who ran another air service; as well as with almost everyone else of importance in the area.
In time Blake was returned to New York and became vice-presi-
dent of traffic and sales.

Harris next removed my division engineer, Joe Dysart, and replaced him with a Bob Moore from AOA who turned out to be
a very good man. Joe was promptly taken on by Boeing. Next
Harris replaced the Company photographer who produced the in-
ternationally famous Pan Am calendar color pictures. They were
so beautiful that they became collector's items, and people wrote
me from all over the world asking for a calendar each Christmas.
Harris installed Blackie Kronfeld, the ex-AOA photographer.

Planning was totally non-existent in Pan Am except, perhaps, in
Trippe's head. When we were expecting the first landplanes, the
B-377s from Boeing, to replace the long-range flying boats, a spe-

cial committee was set up to plan the introduction of these super luxurious and enormous (then) planes with their 28 cylinder engines. Planning involved the location of spares, especially spare engines, and the training of mechanics along the routes to be flown. Trippe had decided to introduce the new super-planes on the route to Buenos Aires, and the route to South America was set up with spares and ground equipment. When the first B-377 arrived at New York, Trippe put it into service immediately to London, calling it the "President Special" service. This was another example of the promotional type of management. Trippe was always first with the best, and major decisions would be made on the spur of the moment as publicity dictated, and it was left to us below to implement them instantly.

I had been attending the weekly operations committee meeting in the Chrysler Building almost every Monday. Jimmy Smith had attended, representing the Atlantic Division when he was in New York but Jimmy was away on higher Pan Am business much of the time so I had usually taken his place. Now Harris attended but, shortly he had a heart attack and was confined to his house. I was summoned to New York in his place. The day following each meeting I would report to him at his house in Connecticut on what had transpired.

Before long, Harris recovered and was offered a job as president of Northwest Airlines, headquartered in Minneapolis. He accepted. I gave a farewell company party for him, made a speech of praise and regret, presented him with a present from the division, and wished him well. Before he had been president of NWA for three months, he had a falling out with the board of directors over moving the main offices from Minneapolis to New York, and he resigned.

Just before Harris came to Pan Am, I had word from Beirut that Middle East Airlines would like to acquire some new planes. This privately owned airline was owned by the Salaam family and operated a passenger and cargo service principally between Beirut and Dahran. Aramco (Arabian-American Oil Co.) was building a large base at Dahran on the Arabian Gulf and TAP (Trans Arabian Pipeline) had constructed a pipeline from the Gulf to the Mediterranean in Lebanon. Cargo and passenger traffic were heavy across the Arabian peninsula. Aramco was flying DC-4s from Beirut, but Middle East could well use more planes. Its only rival in the whole mushrooming Mideast was MISR, an Egyptian airline out of Cairo.

Salaam wanted DC-4s, but Pan Am couldn't spare them, so Trippe gave him several DC-3s which were better than the planes they had. In return he acquired a minority position in the company, making me a director. MEA grew, serving the Arab world and flying from Cairo to London, but Trippe finally got out of MEA and British European Airways took it over. But at this time V.P. Erwin Balluder went out to Beirut with me to sign the deal for the DC-3s.

We called on Saeb Bey who was president of MEA and he gave us tea. Saeb Bey spoke perfect English from having gone to the American University in Beirut, as had all the leading men in the Mideast Arab world. His very pretty wife, Tamima, spoke French, but his brothers spoke only Arabic. They all came into the room, or at least four or five of them, shook hands and sat in chairs around the room just looking at Balluder and me to size us up while they silently polished their beads—an Arab custom, rubbing beads between their fingers as others smoke tobacco or chew gum.

That night we went to dinner with Sheik Najeeb Alamuddin, then general manager of MEA, later to be president of MEA and to end up as a member of the executive board of IATA (International Air Transport Assoc.). Najeeb Alamuddin was a Druse and a cousin of Kemal Jumblatt, the Communist political leader of the Druses, who much later featured in the terrible 1975–76 war in Beirut. Najeeb was married to a Swiss girl who was an M.D., and they had a child who was presented before dinner. As conversation dragged, Erwin asked for some sheets of paper out of which he folded a whole zoo of animals, boats and planes. It was the finest exhibition of the Japanese art of origami I have ever seen. Not only the child, but his parents and I were spellbound.

The next day, Saeb Bey and his family were dragging their feet on the deal, so Balluder said goodbye and announced we were going home. In the beautiful old St. George Hotel, he explained to me that Arab protocol for any deal required two things, rank and patience. He said, as I remember, that TWA, seeking a connection with the Ethiopian Airline, was made to keep a vice-president waiting two years in Addis Abbaba before the deal was made. They had mistakenly sent someone at first who was below the rank of vice-president. Balluder said he was going to Cairo as he had never been to Egypt and would return to Beirut in a week. On our way over I had left Hope in London to stay with my cousin, Isabel Ames. Johnny Ames was an aide to Ambassador Aldrich. I told Balluder I'd be back in Beirut in a week to meet him. We met, saw Saeb Bey again and signed the deal. Saeb Bey came to the airport to see us off. We were in a waiting room full of Lebanese, all standing there as there were no chairs or benches. By custom, I suppose, everyone stood around against the walls with no one in the middle of the room. Saeb Bey entered and proceeded in a circle around the room, shaking hands with everyone, speaking only to those he knew, stopping to give Balluder and me each a present, an inlaid box of Arab candy. Then, having circumnavigated the room once, he went around again, shaking hands silently with everyone a second time, to say goodbye. Such was the custom for a public figure.

Another time I accompanied Balluder to Johannesburg for the opening of the route to Léopoldville and Johannesburg. I had asked him to come to lend a little more top level publicity to the flight. It was a good thing that I asked him. The South African government gave a dinner for us. *Time* magazine had just come out with a scathing article on apartheid and the magazine had been banned. Copies on our plane were confiscated. The Prime Minister himself, Verwoerd, was present at the dinner, surrounded by high officials, all unsmiling and very glum. They often spoke Afrikaans across us, deliberately and rudely. I think Balluder could understand as he spoke Dutch but he did not show it. After the dessert there was champagne but no toasts. Verwoerd rose to speak. His only ex-

pression was a scowl, and, in thickly accented English, he was stud-
iedly insulting about America, black slavery and I forget what else,
and sat down. Not a word of welcome or pleasure at the new direct air service to New York. Then Balluder rose to reply. He
spoke gracefully, with a touch of humor, praising the country and
everything in it with the notable exception of the Afrikaners. He
ended with a toast to South Africa. The contrast between the two
speeches was not lost even on the humorless, bigotted officials
whose utterly impassive faces showed, I thought, just a touch of
embarrassment.

The navaids on the 1,720 mile route from Léopoldville to Johannesburg left something to be desired. There were none. The route,
flown at night, was totally black, the earth below lit only occasionally by blinding flashes from huge thunderstorms which formed,
exploded and vanished with frightening rapidity. Occasionally one
would see a faint spotlight on the earth below, a campfire of some
village to remind one there were some human beings in the blackness below. Later, with the coming of jets, we flew the route in
daylight with a slight diversion, to fly over Victoria Falls. But now
we needed at least one radio beacon on course. I gave the problem
to Waldo Lynch, system superintendent of communications, back
in New York. In a short while he said they could put a 100 watt
non-directional beacon at Vila Luso in a Portuguese colony, on
course about 600 miles from Léopoldville, for $75,000.00. It was the
only practical location considering availability of power and access
for repairs. Now all that was needed was the money and permission
from the Portuguese government. Trippe promptly approved the
RCA (Request for Capital Appropriation) for $75,000.00, and I
wired Pedro Pinto Basto, our senior representative in Lisbon, to
try and get the required permission. He replied that it was practically impossible as I.T.&T. had a monopoly on public radio de-
vices. Pan Am didn't rent radio aids from others and installed and
operated its own airway aids where possible, often designing and
manufacturing the equipment besides. So I went to Lisbon and
Pedro arranged a meeting with the minister of communications.
It was probably the only interview he ever gave to the representa-

tive of a private company, but such was the name of Pan Am that any door would always open. The minister of communications in many governments at that time was the top cabinet official, often having the Army and Navy under his jurisdiction, and I think it was so then in Portugal.

At the appointed time Pedro took me in to see the minister whose office was in a government palace on Black Horse Square in Lisbon. The room was enormous. The ceiling was about 20 feet high, and the room was panelled in dark, tropical woods. Thick embroidered red and gold draperies hung the full length of the room on each side of the windows. It was definitely medieval. At one end was a desk, very large and ornately carved, which was almost lost in the vast room. Two chairs were placed in front of it. As Pedro and I approached the desk, the minister rose from behind it. He was a small man, with black hair that was well brushed down, and was immaculately dressed in a black suit, black tie and black shoes and socks. He came around the desk, shook our hands warmly, motioned to us to sit down and returned to his seat behind the desk. I didn't know what to say; so, with Pedro interpreting into Portuguese, I stated my request and explained the need, elaborating on the long, black night and the difficulties of navigation. An overcast sky blocking any star sight was much more frequent over land than over the seas. Flares on which to take drift sights could not be dropped on land, and so on. The minister listened patiently. I finished and he asked me one question, "How much would it cost you?" I replied promptly, through Pedro, "Seventy-five thousand dollars". The minister rose. We rose. He came around the desk, shook hands and we left. Pedro said, "Absolutely no chance. His deputy told me a foreign company, or even a Portuguese company, could not possibly own and operate a radio aid in Portuguese territory. You are wasting your time". Next morning Pedro called me to say we had received the permit. He couldn't understand it. Much later Pedro told me he heard that I.T.&T. had bid $250,000.00 to install the same beacon for the Portuguese government.

Due to the almost total dislocation of all currencies by the War, in the immediate postwar era, many currencies were non-convertible into dollars or "blocked" so they could not legally be exchanged for the currencies of any other nation. In the Atlantic Division we were building up a large account of Turkish lira which was blocked and for which we had no need in Turkey. I asked the comptroller what he proposed to do with them. "Nothing", he said. "Wait until they become convertible into dollars. They will some day". George Doole, our regional director in Istanbul, and I discussed the problem, and shortly thereafter, Doole picked up an American tobacco buyer in the hotel in Istanbul where he lived, and sold him all our Turkish lira for dollars. He needed the lira to pay for tobacco. Some time thereafter, I found a regular customer on one of our flights who turned out to be a special agent for Paramount Pictures. His job was to get rid of the large bank balances that had built up from worldwide movie house receipts in currencies not convertible into dollars. He travelled the world continuously on Pan Am buying, exporting and trading all sorts of goods and commodities so as to end up with dollars. It seemed to me that Pan Am could well have used such an agent. Before long, however, came Bretton Woods and the exchange problem vanished. The New York banks such as National City and Chase with worldwide branches, had been of no help whatever in disposing of blocked foreign currencies.

When Harold Harris had come to the Atlantic Division, George Doole had left and gone to Washington. There he ended up in charge of the world's largest conglomerate airline—bigger than Pan Am—run by the U.S. Central Intelligence Agency (CIA).[4] Doole had Jimmy Walker, my ex-boss who had been operations manager in Miami, as the operations head of the entire organization in Taiwan. There Jimmy married a Chinese girl and died in March 1976, in Hong Kong.

I survived three more years, first under Harris, then Harris was superceded by Gray. In the spring of 1954 I sent a letter of resignation to Trippe. It was never acknowledged and, after a suitable interval, I walked into Gray's office and said I would not be back. He got up, shook hands, said he was sorry and returned to work. I went home, my last trip from Long Island City to Jericho.

CHAPTER X

---◇---

What Happened to the Company?

"There is a tide in the affairs of men
Which, taken at the flood, leads on to fortune"[1]

TRIPPE, blessed with great vision, saw the tide and took it
at the flood, building an investment of only $400,000 into the
greatest transportation complex in the world with over a billion
dollars in assets. Pan Am, at its peak when I left, rivalled or ex-
ceeded the greatest of the railroad empires built by Vanderbilt or
Harriman, and the greatest of the steamship lines such as Cunard
or P & O.[2] The founders of those empires created them in the days
before income taxes and heavy government regulation with both
of which Trippe had to contend. Shakespeare omitted comment
on what happens when the tide turns, as all tides must, sometimes
leaving the affairs of a man stranded high and dry.

The tide which Trippe saw was a mushrooming public demand
for air transport. It did not happen instantly with the invention of
the aeroplane. In fact, the first twenty years of aviation are marked
with the bankruptcies of almost all who went into this glamorous
new venture. The tide turned with Lindbergh's flight, even though
that flight had nothing to do with air transport. Still, in the 1940s
we found that only about 3% of the U.S. population had ever
been up in a plane.

Trippe promptly hired Lindbergh as a consultant and went all
out to promote air travel. He believed in cheap mass travel, and he
pioneered the concept of tourist or economy fares in high density
seating. The European airlines, all arms of their governments, with
a 19 year start on Trippe and firmly indoctrinated in cartelization,

fought Trippe on everything. They stood for high fares and limited service. Local nationals had to travel on their own country's airline and show the ticket to be able to take money out of the country. Pan Am, extending to everywhere in the world, usually found no hotels, or poor ones at best, which led Trippe to build 65 International Hotels (IHC) using no Pan Am money—all were financed locally. Pan Am hotels appeared from Kabul to Dubai.

The Atlantic Division, which I ran, flew to 22 countries in Europe, Africa and the Middle East. The other two divisions flew to more than 40 other countries. At one point Pan Am served 84 countries. But today the Atlantic Division no longer flies to Paris nor to Sweden nor Finland, although Pan Am still goes to some 56 foreign countries besides five outside states and U.S. possessions. What happened?

There is no biography of Trippe and probably there never will be. He has had no Colonel House nor Harry Hopkins. He is a man of extraordinary persistence and real charm. The question I pose here, "What happened?", is routinely answered: "Trippe's fault". That is not so. Three spurious reasons for the decline of Pan Am are often given.

ONE. Trippe ran a one man show and made no provisions for succession. It is not so. Almost from the start, Trippe had someone to take over if ever necessary. Howard Dean may well have been in that position, but he, unfortunately, died young. Believing he could do better outside the Company, perhaps because all the second echelon were about the same age and would retire about the same time, Trippe brought in Roger Lewis, ex-Secretary of the Air Force. Clearly slated to take over when Trippe retired, Lewis was executive vice-president from 1955 to 1962. In the latter year the White House called him to take over failing General Dynamics which had just turned in the largest corporate loss in one year on record. General Dynamics was among the Defense Department's largest and most important arms suppliers, especially for submarines and aircraft. I had left Pan Am by then and was in business as an aviation consultant in the Graybar building across from Pan Am's offices. One day Roger Lewis came across to my office and asked me whether I thought, if he took over Trippe's job, Trippe would let him run the Company. I replied that, while I doubted it, I fervently hoped to see him take over Pan Am. But President Kennedy called him again and heat was put on until he had to leave Pan Am and become chief executive of General Dynamics as his patriotic duty. Trippe's plan for succession was aborted again.

Next, Trippe turned to the Company and made Captain Harold Gray president. Gray had a son who was a carrier pilot on the *Enterprise* off Vietnam. One day, shortly after he took over as president, Gray had a doctor's appointment to see about a lump on his neck. That morning he received notice that his son had been killed over Vietnam. He did not make the doctor's appointment until long after. By then the lump was diagnosed as inoperative and terminal. Once more fate had intervened.

Trippe cast about again for a successor and hit on Najeeb Halaby whom he had hired as second to Gray before Gray's illness was known. I knew Halaby and was not enthusiastic about the appointment. Halaby had an impressive and forceful personality and little else. He had been administrator of the Federal Aviation Agency. It was said—so I was told—that he announced that Pan Am had no management and he would supply it. Shortly thereafter the Company was infested with young men supposed to take over most of the departments. They wandered about asking what the various departments were supposed to do. None had any noticeable airline or other experience. The old Pan Am staff would not speak to Halaby. I heard that one night he appeared on the hangar line and, finding some mechanics asleep, promptly fired them. The next day the maintenance manager called on him and explained that a small emergency crew was kept on duty with nothing to do until the last departure was well on its way so that any turnback, such as a faulty fire warning light giving a false cockpit signal, could be quickly repaired and the plane resent on its way with minimum delay. Politely, the manager explained that he himself and only he would fire any mechanic and that he had been hard put that morning to keep the entire force from quitting work, and he with them.[3] Many of the board of directors saw the need to replace

Halaby. Soon a majority of the board did so and shortly thereafter procured William T. Seawell who proved to be excellent.

Two. It was claimed that Trippe was an incompetent business-man. Not so. I believe that, under Trippe, Pan Am had the best management of any airline in the world. The financing of new, improved and more economical aircraft was always completed long before the aircraft were and long before any other airline. Pan Am's engineering was responsible for many of the improve-ments in safety, economy, navigation, instrumentation and passen-ger comfort over the years.

It must be said, however, that Trippe did not run the Company to make money or maximize profits. He ran it to grow, to cover the world, regardless of any other considerations, and it did. There were no management frills. Executive salaries were much less than those of comparable positions in American or United Airlines. Trippe must have been convinced that the Civil Aeronautics Board would always, as provided in the Civil Aeronautics Act of 1938, see that Pan Am would, through subsidy if necessary, earn a "rea-sonable rate of return on its capital used and usefully employed" in the business. But the CAB did not do so. Why?

Three. It was said and believed, especially among long time Pan Am officials, that Trippe's arrogance made so many enemies in Washington that the permanent bureaucracy was solidly anti-Pan Am. Trippe dealt only with the top, usually the President himself, and never even spoke to officials lower down who often represent the real power. They were left to "Mrs. Archie".[4] There may be some truth in this idea of antagonism in the bureaucracy, but Ambassador Henry Cabot Lodge, three times senator from Massachusetts, told me that he never heard of any senators, or even congressmen who "had it in for Trippe". On the contrary, he re-members both houses as having only respect and admiration for Trippe and Pan Am.

Not so long ago at a Wings Club meeting, Jim Farley was heard to say: "When I was Postmaster General, Trippe was in Washing-ton all the time. He seemed to be always around asking for something. But I cannot remember his ever asking for anything that wasn't in the public interest".

Nevertheless, there were a few ex-Pan Am personnel in the government who felt ill-treated by Trippe. He did seem a little arrogant. Once Saeb Bey Salaam of Middle East Airlines came to New York and I tried to arrange for Trippe merely to speak to him. I was a director of the airline and a friend of Saeb Bey. Trippe was too busy to see him. Saeb Bey went to Washington, called at the White House, and President Eisenhower promptly saw him.

One day, right after the war, George Kraigher came to see Trippe to get his job back. Kraigher, ex-chief pilot at Brownsville, the man who had set up and run Pan Africa under Gledhill, had supported the ATC when they wanted to take over Pan Africa. With the North African landings in the offing, it was only reasonable that the Army would want control of all supply operations in the area. Trippe was determined to keep the route civilian and operated by Pan Am for the post-War period. Trippe lost. Kraigher sat in Gledhill's office all day. About 6 P.M. Gledhill took him out for a drink, telling him to come back the next morning. He did, and, after another day in Gledhill's office, he left and took a job with Aramco to run their big air operation from MacArthur Field on Long Island to Dahran on the Persian Gulf. Trippe never saw him.

Trippe had some enemies at the top in Washington, but only because they wrongly believed it was his ambition to be a monopoly. Actually, he had offered to merge Pan Am with other airlines and even railroads to give the United States of America control of the world's air routes. Public opinion was far more anti-big government than anti-Pan Am.

In the diary of Harold Ickes[5] we find:

"Apparently Trippe, who is President of Pan American, is an unscrupulous person who cajoles and buys his way. He has made quite an unsavory record in South American countries. He has what amounts to a worldwide monopoly and the President is against this. . . . The President said he had talked personally with

Trippe. He described him as a man of all-yielding suavity, who could be depended upon to pursue his own way".

It is well known that Ickes was a man of deep prejudices and, to the best of my knowledge, the comment about "unsavory record" is completely untrue. Elsewhere we find:

"One of the most influential people to speak out clearly against PAA was Harry Hopkins, who said as early as December, 1941: 'I have never liked the idea of Pan American having a world monopoly of our airlines'."

The tide which had carried Trippe to the pinnacle of power was receding. Foreign governments and even our military had always gone to Trippe to get things done they couldn't do themselves such as Air Ferries, ADP, Pan Africa and the operation over the Hump in China. Initially, Trippe's great vision had almost total public support. By the 1960s it no longer had. The glamour and adventure of flight was turning to boredom. There was no public interest in having American planes, pilots and airlines supreme in the world. A new tide was setting in and Trippe knew it.

We all felt that Pan Am, after the War, was wrongly and very unfairly treated by the government—White House, Congress and the CAB. It seemed to us that Pan Am had become so persona non grata in places where it had once been favored, that only the personality of Trippe could be responsible. That is just not so. The tide against bigness argued herein was indicated by the passage of the Federal Aviation Act of 1958 which was clearly designed to promote competition among the airlines and which repealed most of the Civil Aeronautics Act of 1938, which had been designed to promote the growth and the health of the infant airline industry. In addition to the competition from other American carriers and the exclusion of Pan Am from domestic routes, of far more importance to the decline of Pan Am was the U.S. support of foreign airlines. The U.S. government, at taxpayers' expense, financed their equipment and even trained their crews and mechanics through the Agency for International Development (AID) and technical assistance programs in many of which programs Pan Am participated. Soon Pan Am faced ruinous competition from more than 20 foreign airlines across the Atlantic.

In 1947 England was bankrupt. It was becoming evident that the future of our civilization depended on the U.S.A. to rebuild Western Europe, which was not recovering from World War II and never could by itself. How to explain the crisis to the American people fell to Truman, Marshall and Acheson. They succeeded, not without great difficulty, and the Marshall Plan, NATO and the Military Assistance Program worked. In saving the world, Pan Am's interests came to be sacrificed.

"Instead of pursuing trade and investment policies designed to give United States business the maximum advantage, the Truman administration felt America would prosper in a prosperous world: American private enterprise would be encouraged to export capital, technology, skills and management to foster economic growth. It was Acheson's economic policy to see that Europe and other countries were endowed with the capacity to compete with the United States economically which they eventually did, as a means of making them stronger, more prosperous allies and trading partners".[6]

It is a very subtle argument but it is certainly possible that Pan Am's subsequent difficulties were in no small part due to our government, for the first time in the history of any government, putting the welfare of the world, our western world, ahead of the commercial interests of its own people.

The rising tide that was almost to wreck Pan Am by making government support impossible, we may call a tide of anti-big business. Anti-monopoly is too narrow a term, for a monopoly may be beneficial, as our monopoly of helium was thought to be when Ickes denied it to the Germans for their zeppelins[7] long after World War I.

Of course there was no antagonism to big business at first after the Industrial Revolution and the steel and railroad giants tied our country together as nothing else could have. But with size and power went abuses, and the tide started. It may never recede. Perhaps the start was marked by the Sherman Act in 1890, and it went in spurts with Teddy Roosevelt's trust busting and Wilson's progressive legislation till it even touched the infant airlines (backed by big bankers) in the Air Mail Contracts cancellation in 1934. After World War II Pan Am was a principal target for anti-bigness, wrongly called anti-monopoly. Immediately, competition was created for Pan Am. TWA was certificated to fly into London, Paris and Rome, the major traffic generating points in the Pan Am system, while Pan Am was left to fly unprofitable but national interest routes to Oslo, Teheran, Johannesburg, Bangkok and so on. In the Pacific, Pan Am had developed air service to New Zealand, Australia, Southeast Asia, China and Japan, very much in the national interest but hardly profitable; and United Airlines was promptly given the only money-making route segment, from our west coast to Hawaii, which it flooded with service from all over the United States.[8]

At the time I left the Company, it seemed quite clear that Pan Am was not a viable business any longer, and possibly might never be again. Trippe, however, continued to fight like a tiger for government support for which there now was not a chance.

I attended a meeting of the "Clipper Pioneers" on May 13, 1975 at which Trippe spoke. It was to have been a short, extemporaneous speech, but he talked for more than half an hour. He was just reminiscing about his aims and the Company's accomplishments in which we had all taken part. He began with the justification for subsidy. The Civil Aeronautics Act of 1938 authorized the granting of air route franchises with subsidy support, if necessary, based on a finding that the route would serve the needs of the commerce, post office and national defense of the United States. All Pan Am's routes did. Pan Am had become the major air cargo carrier in the world. Its foreign earnings provided a major contribution to the balance of payments. Pan Am even subsidized the post office since it was paid less per ton mile of mail carried than the post office received from the stamps on such mail. The entire operations of Pan Am were turned over to government service in World War II for a fee of 4% versus the 10% determined by the CAB to be a "reasonable rate of return". During the Korean and Vietnam wars,

Pan Am provided most of the air lift to Taiwan and Guam for the Marines and the Navy. Following a proposal by Pan Am, a Civil Reserve Air fleet was created whereby commercial airline planes would be equipped with certain instruments and gadgets to be compatible with military air operations and be ready to go at a moment's notice under military command. All Pan Am planes are so equipped, few others are.

When the desperate race was on to build an A-bomb before the Germans did and the two major problems were solved, i.e., how to separate U-235 from the natural U-238 and how to detonate an A-bomb, there was left a third problem: where to get the uranium and enough of it to make a bomb. It is found in pitchblende and about the only source then known was in the Belgian Congo. Once again the government turned to Trippe and almost immediately a special Pan Am cargo plane landed at Léopoldville and took on a full load of unmarked boxes. These boxes contained the uranium for the bombs that were to end the Pacific war, but no one in the crew knew their contents nor its intended use.[9]

Trippe realized he was talking too long. He stopped, smiled and sat down. I turned to Harry Canaday next to me and said: "It's a funny thing, but it seems to me that no one cares any more". "I think so too", said Harry. "Nobody gives a damn".

As Trippe sat down, appearing as charming and indomitable as ever, someone was heard to mumble: "Sic transit gloria mundi". A more appropriate comment from the room full of old-timers who had flown all through the rise and fall might have been: "So what".

So what happened to the Company, or rather, Mr. Trippe? The answer is plainly, bad luck. This quite extraordinary man had the misfortune to be born into the waning days of the age of Kipling and to finish in the present era of anti-heroes. Trippe believed in "One World" far more than Wendell Willkie ever did, and Trippe did something about it. He used to say that we would never have had a Civil War if the railroads had run north and south instead of east and west. Trippe, more than all other entrepreneurs of the air, brought the peoples of the world closer together.

At a reception in Tokyo in the early 1950s, a young Army lieutenant was introduced to Mrs. Anna Chennault, the Chinese widow of the famous General Claire L. Chennault who set up the Flying Tigers in 1941. In somewhat embarrassed flattery, he said to her: "Mrs. Chennault, your husband must have been the greatest man in aviation". "No", she replied, "he was not. Juan Trippe is the greatest man in aviation and always will be".

ENVOI

I have always loved the sea. I first saw it as a small child from the beach at Cape May, N.J. At school I studied Greek and, when I settled into the *Iliad* and the *Odyssey*, the Aegean became my whole world. I followed Agamemnon collecting his armada at Aulis and leading 1,140 ships to the shores of Asia Minor where they were all beached north of Troy. Compared to our 800 ships used for the invasion of North Africa—some convoy! When Theseus came home from Crete with the wrong colored sail, he hit Cape Sounion on the nose—some navigation! The onomatopoetic phrases of Homer still sing in my ears, such as:

βῆ δ'ακέων παρὰ θῖνα πολυφλοίσβοιο θαλάσσης
([Chryses] went silently along the beach of the loud-roaring sea.)
Iliad, Book I

In Pan Am I first went to sea over the Caribbean. Few explorers wrote about it, perhaps because it is so rough and unpleasant. The constant trades, never less than about 20 knots, kick up a sea that isn't too friendly and didn't look so to us as we dead reckoned along across the middle, five hours at about 100 feet of altitude all the way.

Then came the Pacific, so named by Magellan after getting through his straits and finding it smooth and peaceful. As we droned across those limitless wastes of water, always tense to hear the slightest break in the 112 spark plugs firing 56 cylinders 15 times a second, we were a little north of Magellan's tracks but we thought of him and of Captain Cook who sailed the waters right under us and found the Hawaiian Islands. We could see a far-fetched resemblance to Alan Villiers' description: "On sailed the little vessels, feeble, man-made, windblown chips upon a hostile immensity, held to their course only by the ability and iron will of the great seaman commanding them". All of us had a pretty good idea of how Cook's sailors felt and, had one of our engines

287

ever failed and had we gone down, in our little rubber boats we would have seen the ghost of the *Victoria* or the *Endeavour*.

There are still countless oceans to be explored but I no longer have any interest. They all have Latin names and besides, they have no water in them—they are on the moon.

THE END

PAN AM PERSONNEL
1936 – 1955

I have noted before the extraordinary achievements of Pan Am, conceived, planned and directed by Trippe; and I have noted the lack of recognition of the men who executed the projects and made the Company. Probably Trippe never heard of most of them. Certainly few of them ever laid eyes on Trippe. The more conspicuous pilots of course did. Having finished my story, I feel impelled, however, to mention many of these remarkable men.

Operations managers. William L. Bond must have been one of the greatest. He ran CNAC and the early operation over the Hump. Harold Gray who went on to be president must be included as an operations manager, both in the Pacific and the Atlantic after Dutch Schildhauer, a Naval Academy man, set up both of those operations. Ed Critchley, an Englishman who ran the Eastern Division at Miami, and George Kraigher, the chief pilot at Brownsville, were outstanding. So was Fritz Blotner, based in Rio, who ran the far end of the Latin American operation. He had surveyed, on foot, guided by Indians, the "cutoff" route from Rio through Barreiras to Belém, walking days through the forest without seeing even a patch of sky overhead. Jimmy Walker at Miami and after him O. J. Studeman were great men. So was "Mutt" Fleming, operations manager of the Atlantic when it grew to cover half the world, and so were D. G. Richardson and Randy Kirk.

In the *engineering* groups, after André Priester, world famous, came Captain L. L. Odell. Odell was chief airport engineer who planned the construction of the Pacific island bases from his office in New York down to the last nail. The manager during the construction of these bases at Midway, Wake and Guam was William Grooch, a former NYRBA pilot. I did not know either of these two, but their names often came up in Company conversation. In Priester's office there was John Borger who worked on the Pacific bases construction crew, and ended up as Priester's right-hand man as a top aeronautical engineer, well known to every aircraft manufacturer. Under him Lou Allen, Norm Smith and Bob Blake were top engineers.

Quite a few *flight engineers* were superior persons in every technical or non-technical group. First of all was Chan Wright who was on all the original Pacific flights with Captain Musick. Then Vic Wright, also famous on the Pacific, who ended up as a captain. Then Etchison, Doc Lee, Jake Nagle, Bill Miller, Ray Comish and others whom I remember as clubmates, as we were on many first flights together when total confidence in each other among the crew was essential. They were all tough, unflappable and expert with aircraft engines and the increasingly complex aircraft systems. Among *navigators* there were Judd Ingram, our original instructor in the Pacific when you had to be good, Charley Lunn and finally Pat Reynolds. Among *flight radio operators* there were Poindexter, Jarboe and Bob Dutton, all hand picked for the pioneering ocean flights.

Other outstanding men in any league were: Ben McLeod,[1] perhaps the top communications engineer in the world; Captain Waldo Lynch, vice-president and chief communications engineer; Ray de-Haan who rose from a chief airline mechanic to superintendent of all the ground stations in the Atlantic Division; and Bill Mullahey, ex-Jones Beach lifeguard and famous surfer. Another great was John Boyle, station manager at Wake, then Hong Kong and later at San Francisco.

When I was Atlantic Division manager, I replaced our long time Dr. Shillito with a new medical director and flight surgeon, Colonel Otis Schreuder. Shortly before I resigned, the chief pilot called me one day to say: "We have a captain with cancer. What should I do?" I replied, "Do nothing and I'll call you back". I then called Dr. Schreuder and our conversation went like this:

"Dr. Schreuder, I understand that Captain So and So has cancer".

"Yes", said the doctor who was not garrulous.

"Terminal?"

"Yes".

"How long?"

"Don't know. You can never tell. Maybe months".

"Does he know?"

"Yes".

"Will it affect his flying?"

"No. He is an unusually well-adjusted and stable man".

"Will he know when the time comes to ground himself?"

"Yes".

"Keep him flying".

"Good", said Dr. Schreuder, "I will".

He did, and it was shortly after I left the Company that I heard that Captain So and So had died.

In the *traffic and sales department* where I did not know many well, Vic Chenea was the first vice-president of these activities; then Phil Delaney, Paul Rennell, Jim Montgomery and Norm Blake became well-known in our industry. Paul Rennell was the best and became a vice-president. Jerry Roscoe, a famous Yale '35 quarterback, left to go into advertising when General Harris took over the Atlantic. Harry Snowdon, ex-Yale wrestling captain, dropped out early due to illness. Fife Symington, a good friend of mine, was stationed in Baltimore, his home town, when the Atlantic Division was started there. Later he was based in Lisbon, then Assistant to Bixby at the New York office. He left one day, much missed, to end up as our ambassador to Trinidad.

Among ground personnel in foreign stations, one found the kind of Americans rarely, if ever, found abroad. For example, our station manager at Bangkok, Dick Fisher, was an ex-Army colonel. Within a few days after arriving to take up his duties running the station, which only involved meeting two round-the-world transits each week, he was fluent in the Thai language. By the end of his first year, he was teaching math at the Royal College in Bangkok, in Thai.

At Damascus our senior representative was my cousin, Johnson Garrett. During a revolution the airport was closed; all other non-Arabs had gotten out of the country, and there was shooting in the streets. Each morning Margie Garrett would set forth from their house to go down to market. At the appearance of this slender and very pretty blond, all shooting would stop, snipers and troops from both sides would appear and wave to her, exchanging pleasantries as she spoke fluent Arabic. She was the daughter of Dr. Dodge, the president of the American University in Beirut.

In *public relations* Van Dusen in New York was surely the best man in that field in the country at that time. Fred Tupper in London was among the best public and press relations men I ever knew. Fred covered the tennis at Wimbledon for the *New York Times*, as well as handling press matters for Pan Am all over Europe. Dave Parsons, my press relations man in Atlantic Division headquarters, was the brother of Jeffrey Parsons, the noted editor of the Paris *Herald Tribune*, and was certainly among the best in his field.

The *station managers*, almost legion in number, included many never to be forgotten like Johnny Donahue at Havana or Johnny Nash at Dinner Key—both of them characters.

We had *regional directors* in various parts of the world who reported directly to Trippe, although administratively, they were in the divisions. In London Jack Kelly was in his flat and went to his office on Picadilly every day throughout the War, experiencing the buzz bombs and later V bombs, which gave him a camaraderie with all the shopkeepers and bartenders in the west end. He usually knew every prime minister of every country in western Europe, which he covered. Under him Clem Brown in Paris was a top salesman for Pan Am and was well known throughout France. In Lisbon and later in London, Bill Lyons, married to a Portuguese girl, Catusha, was one of Pan Am's best sales executives. George Doole (an ex-captain) in Istanbul made it his business to know all the top Arabs and oil executives in the Middle East where the great fields in Saudi Arabia were being brought in.

In the Bahamas, Sidney Farrington represented Pan Am. He was a charming gentleman, friend of the Duke of Windsor when the latter was governor general at Nassau during the Second World War, and was knighted by Queen Elizabeth.

Now I come to *pilots*. I knew virtually every pilot, of the 1,500, in the Company by 1954 and had flown with all but one or two.

The "old-timers" in Pan Am were mostly ex-barnstormers, and Ed Musick was one of the very few to make the grade as an expert airline pilot. Pan Am's seaplane captains commanded a great deal of respect among the flying fraternity who recognized the extra demands of seamanship which flying ocean routes imposed on them. I considered Johnny Nolan the best seaplane pilot in the Company. Two outstandingly good ones were Chilie Vaughn and Marius Lodeesen. Fame is rare among airline pilots. The good ones shun it, and their feats of courage are known only within the group.

Charlie Blair, an ex-Navy pilot, graduate of Pensacola in 1942, was hired as chief pilot and acting operations manager on American Export Airlines when that company was set up in 1940. Later he was chief pilot of American Overseas when American took over Export in 1945, and he came to Pan Am when we took over Overseas in 1950. Charlie's particular love and interest was navigation. He bought a war-surplus P-51 and flew it solo from Bardufoss, Norway, across the North Pole to Fairbanks, Alaska on May 29, 1951, while on vacation from Pan Am where he was flying Stratocruisers across the Atlantic. His personally developed and simplified navigation system so interested the Air Force that they made him a consultant with the rank of colonel and later put him in a "think tank" as a brigadier general. He also won the Harmon Trophy and got a D.F.C for heading the first flight of jet-fighters across the North Pole. It is all told in his wonderful book, *Red Ball in the Sky*.

I believe the most famous Pan Am pilot is Doug Moody, nephew of Helen Wills Moody of tennis fame. Doug is one of the best pilots in the game. When the President (U.S.) began flying around the country and had an Air Force jet assigned to him, he soon needed a second plane for the large number of officials, press and security people who went with him. The White House promptly chartered a Pan Am 707 as a second plane and Pan Am assigned Doug Moody as its pilot. He so served four Presidents, Eisenhower, Kennedy, Truman and Johnson. Doug was a good looking and very likeable person and became a favorite at the White House.

Soon he was demanded for every presidential flight, by E. J. (Jiggs) Fauver, the White House transportation executive.

Any flying machine carrying the President was always designated "One" which meant he was on board. Hence "Air Force One" would be any Air Force jet carrying him. "Marine Corps One" would be a Marine Corps helicopter carrying him, and so "Navy One" would be any Navy plane carrying him. Three Marine Corps helicopters were usually assigned to carry the President between Andrews Field in Washington, and the White House lawn, but it was never known which of the three he would board. When he got on one it became "Marine Corps One".

Once President Johnson, probably under political pressure, asked for an American Airlines' plane and pilot. The fortunate American pilot complained so about the details of his schedule that no other airline nor its pilots ever flew again with the President except on a few short flights. Pan Am and Captain Moody were thereafter always specified. The Pan Am 707 and its crew had to be and were totally compatible with the Air Force 707. The Pan Am plane could be cannibalized if necessary for any immediate repair to the President's plane, and it always carried a full load of spares of practically every part of the Air Force 707. The Presidential plane could *never* be delayed and must *always* be ready to go. A portable GCA system would be flown in ahead and set up at any airport lacking ILS or other zero-zero landing and takeoff aids. The Air Force 707 always made a dry run of the route before the Presidential SAM (Special Air Mission), but Moody did not. Each President picked his own Air Force pilot, from his home state; so Eisenhower had Colonel Draper from Kansas, Kennedy had Colonel Swindel from Massachusetts, Johnson picked Colonel Cross from Texas. They all knew Doug. The airport to which the President was going would be "sanitized" and closed to all but the party until the President had come and gone.

The most fantastic trips were with Jack Kennedy. He liked a good time away from home on weekends and he especially liked Palm Springs, California. But there had to be a public reason for each flight, supposedly non-political. The stated purpose was usually the dedication of a new Air Force base or other such installation. There was one in almost every state, and a dedication brought out all the important political figures to meet the President. It was especially helpful in weak Democratic states or ones which might go Republican in the next election. The ceremony was always Friday or Saturday morning and everything stopped for R & R (rest and relaxation) promptly at noon on Saturday.

As Doug tells it: "Such flights required detailed preparation. The correct jet fuel, loading steps, tugs and other ground equipment would be flown in a day ahead of time. After briefing at Andrews I would take off immediately before or just after Air Force One and fly ahead, with AF 1 above and behind, and I would land first. As soon as I came to a stop, a Bell Telephone Company vice-president would jump out, get into a waiting car and, with a police escort, race into town to the main telephone center to take over all lines into and out of town. By the time the President arrived, all circuits for the hot line to Moscow and to activate SAC (Strategic Air Command) headquarters deep underground at a western base, and the missile silos, were checked and secure and sure never to be interrupted.

"One flight was to Jackass Flats, Nevada. There had been some problem finding anything to dedicate as they were running out of new bases, but this unheard of base, which didn't even have an airport, was discovered near the New Mexico border. It was developing nuclear propulsion motors for future space flights. We would land on a nearby airport from which helicopters could take the President to the base. Then we would go to overnight at Albuquerque and on to Palm Springs the next day.

"We landed on a DC-3 size airport and, on takeoff, the wheels of Air Force One which left first, made great holes in the runway where the surface was pulled off. I took off immediately behind and was able to miss the holes. Those presidential excursions were on a scale that dwarfed anything ever put on by Alexander the Great, Hannibal or Julius Caesar, and they grew in scale with each successive President after Kennedy".

Doug was in Dallas with the Pan Am plane when Kennedy was assassinated.

Later Doug was put in charge of all checkouts on the superplane, the Boeing 747. It was by far the largest, weighing 710,000 pounds and accommodating 450 passengers, and the most complicated flying machine ever built. It had seven computers among the flight and navigation systems. New techniques for approach and landing had to be developed. New terms came into use such as "bug speed", "sink rate" and so on. Ruthlessly, any pilot who could not satisfy Doug was weeded out and sent back to the 707s. Checkout took up to four months and much was done at Roswell, New Mexico. By agreement with the Air Line Pilots Association, any pilot whose seniority entitled him to bid on the much higher paid 747s but who could not check out was paid 747 pay anyway. As a result, the introduction of this monster was the first time new equipment was ever put into service, flown only by thoroughly competent crews.

A very few Pan Am pilots voluntarily quit flying, and I have always felt it was due to the terrific strain, physical and emotional, that the dawn to dusk, low altitude, tropical flights imposed on us. We were always over water with no "one engine out" performance on the early flying boats, so an engine failure always meant ditching in rough, shark infested seas with little or no hope of rescue. My belief was challenged, even ridiculed, by some of my bosses who were the ground operations managers but were never pilots. Nevertheless, the following pilots quit, showing no signs of strain at the time; but we Pan Am pilots, and we alone, knew how they felt:

Walt Allen had a forced landing in an S-38 and landed safely in the Caribbean, but he gave up flying.

Carl Dewey had an aileron fall off an S-43. He landed safely in the Caribbean, but he gave up flying. However, this tough, ex-Marine went on to supervise all the Latin American ground stations and to be operations manager in Pan-Africa.

Robin McGlohn, long after coolly surviving an in-flight fire twice, finally quit to be a trader on the Amazon.

R. J. Nixon, big, tough, unflappable, never showing strain of any kind, was overheard in Manila one day after the Terletzky and

Musick accidents saying, "I think I'll quit. I've had just about enough". His first officer couldn't believe his ears. Pilots never quit, but R.J. did a year later to buy and run a bar high in the Rockies.

Champe Taliaferro, after a very tough instrument approach to Kennedy, coming from London through the traffic mess of those days with all the foreign planes, many of whose pilots could not speak English and were not well trained, all in near panic on their radios and none knowing where they were, decided he had had enough. He was made chief flight instructor on the Atlantic and, upon retirement later, took to crossing the Atlantic in a small sailboat, once with Captain Lodeesen. Champe, although not old enough to be really an "old-timer", was one of the few modern transport pilots who had never been a co-pilot. He got his license at 16 and was hired as an airline captain, the youngest ever, by Pitcairn Airlines, going on to be an Eastern captain, then American Overseas and finally, one of Pan Am's best.

Harry Canaday, chief navigator for the initial Pacific crossings after the demise of Fred Noonan, was grounded for physical reasons after checking out as a captain at Miami and flying in the Caribbean and became head of all ground schools. He was ex-Annapolis and Pensacola.

A few pilots also gave up flying for Pan Am Airlines for reasons that are probably not included in fatigue and strain, such as Walter Fitch, Sid Adger and Bill Atterbury.

Of course some Pan Am pilots upon reaching the compulsory retirement age of 60 for jet pilots, retired but kept right on in the flying business. Charlie Blair ran Antilles Air Boats, a charter flying-boat airline based at Christiansted in St. Croix. Cass Szmagaj flew as an instructor in the Yugoslav Airline.

Bob Ford became assistant chief pilot–technical for Trans Ocean. Kim Scribner is an official with Embry-Riddle Flight School. Quite a few more have made new careers in aviation and are still flying.

The type of extraordinary men who built Pan Am were by no means all engaged in flying operations. Take Mario de la Torre as an example. He was born in Ecuador, got a B.S. as a civil engineer at the University of Maryland, and was hired as an airport engineer by Pan Am's ADP in 1942. On July 13, 1942, a U.S. Army B-24 went down in the Amazon jungle somewhere southwest of Belém. The pilot landed safely on a hard, ancient lake bed, relatively flat. The crew of nine, unhurt, made it out, mostly by their rubber life rafts, going down rivers for nine days until picked up. The Army decided to fly the plane out. That would require finding it, fixing it and building a runway. The Army called on Pan Am and de la Torre was assigned to the job. The plane was located after a three day search by a Beechcraft, 71 miles from Belém. Engineer de la Torre started into the trackless jungle. On August 12, leading the expedition, he was bitten in the left index finger by a bushmaster. He was carrying a double-barrelled shotgun. Without breaking stride, he put his finger over the end of both barrels, fired both and kept right on going. In 22 days a 5,000 foot takeoff strip with a 2,500 foot runway had been built and, on September 12, the same crew flew the B-24 out and on its way to fight the Axis.

NOTES

NOTES TO CHAPTER I

1. The Harvard Flying Club, according to Crocker Snow, was formed about 1910, as the Harvard Aeronautical Society, to promote aviation. It then held the first International Air Meet (or so it claimed) in 1911. At the meet, Claude Graham White flew from a field around the Boston Light and back. Bleriot and other notables attended. The Club went out of business in the First World War but was reorganized in 1926 by Crocker Snow, August Pabst and Freddy Ames, as the Harvard Flying Club. They first operated with an OXX-6 Travelair and are still going strong.

2. The First Troop, Philadelphia City Cavalry is the oldest regular outfit in the U.S. Army and was General Washington's bodyguard throughout the Revolution which it antedates.

3. From *Under My Wings* by Basil Rowe: "Gradually pilots were beginning to have a bit of confidence in instrument flying, but it was still too doubtful to proceed rapidly in that direction. . . . A bird can't fly without a horizon for visual reference. We were uncertain if a human could do it safely for any length of time, guided solely by flight instruments. . . . There was no night flying, no blind flying, no lighted runways." But the Western Division was flying on instruments on schedule at that time and had been doing it for several years, mostly due to Kraigher.

4. Under Soviet direction an International Brigade was organized and attracted volunteers from all over the world to fight in Spain in a crusade against Fascism. In the U.S.A. the Abraham Lincoln Brigade was formed as a division of the International Brigade. The Spanish Civil War, 1936–1939, was fought between the Republicans backed by the Communists, and the Falange led by Franco and backed by Hitler. Franco won. It is interesting that no such volunteer groups ever appeared in other civil wars (disregarding the French, German and Polish generals who fought with Washington). The American young were very sentimental about the Spanish Civil War and Hemingway wrote one of his best and most popular books about it—*For Whom the Bell Tolls.*

5. I have always felt that too little attention is given to the fact most of the tremendous advances in science in the U.S.A. were achieved by foreigners who found, only in the U.S.A., a climate conducive to their best work.

So, in Roosevelt's Manhattan Project, the principal brains were mostly foreign: Bethe (German), Fermi (Italian), Kistiakowski (Russian), Oppenheimer (German), Von Neuman (German) and Teller (Hungarian).

So, we achieved supremacy in space at the Redstone Arsenal in Huntsville, Ala. where were housed Dr. Dornier, Werner von Braun and the German V-2 experts who surrendered to the American Army under the noses of the Russians. These men, the world's foremost rocket experts, were brought into the U.S., along with their families. In time they came to be known to the good citizens of Huntsville who just took them in with their children, forgetting their enemy origins, and made them feel at home. None has ever left as far as I know.

NOTES TO CHAPTER II

1. Kraigher started in this country working for Brock and Weymouth, my cousin Norman Brock. It was an aerial survey and precision machine company which developed the first stereoscopic aerial camera photographs from which exact contour lines could be drawn on a map.

2. Loops were sometimes large ground stations, two crossed loops maybe 10 ft. high, fed into a small goniometer for taking null bearings. The arrangement could be in a house to eliminate rain static on the loop. It appeared to be a wash between the advantage of a large receiving loop on the ground with a low power transmitter on the plane, and a large, high power transmitter on the ground received by a small loop on the plane, mounted outside the fuselage and affected by precipitation static.

Bearings taken with a loop antenna were greatly overrated. The main reason was, perhaps, the very broad null obtained with a loop. The operator had to average two readings where the signal became too weak to read. Furthermore, only bearings taken on low frequencies had any accuracy and low frequencies did not carry very far. A loop exposed to the elements was usually put out of operation in the rain from precipitation static. A ground loop in the radio shack would avoid this problem, but only an airborne loop permitted taking bearings on any ground station, such as a broadcasting station.

Tudor Leland, a friend and old-time TWA pilot, told me he remembered their early loops—ground stations. When the weather was bad and an incoming pilot needed help, pilots off duty volunteered to stand by at the radio station. One would stand outside and, when he heard the plane, would point in the direction of the sound. The radio operator, watching him from inside through a window could then send the incoming pilot a bearing to get him in to the field.

"Homing in on your destination by radio bearings" always sounded very reassuring in publicity releases. We pilots knew better and wondered if our superiors did.

3. The transmitter was a simple Hartley oscillator and power amplifier, as I remember, with a trailing antenna which the operator had to reel out in flight and remember to reel in before landing, because it had a lead weight on the end. Communication was only by CW in Morse Code. The transmitter tuning coils were plug-in ones which had to be changed manually to change frequency. Leuteritz was a nut on reliability. All components were thickly covered with a special varnish he developed and guaranteed to be impervious to moisture. The sets were also very rugged and Mr. Critchley, the operations manager at Miami, said that Leuteritz had thrown a transmitter and receiver out of his second floor window in Coconut Grove to the sidewalk below, after which they still worked perfectly.

The receiver was a simple regenerative receiver with one stage of tuned RF and two of audio. This simple, primitive circuit as opposed to the then standard superheterodyne was not selective and it picked up a maximum amount of static. Atmospheric noise in the tropics is very heavy so that the long radio watches were deafening and gave one a terrific headache.

The trailing antenna was not infrequently hit by lightning when all the tubes would burn out and the coils would jump out of their sockets. When the radio operator got over the shock, he could reinsert the coils, replace the tubes with spares and again be in business.

4. Johnny Donahue told me about the rum running. He may have invented it for it made a good story and having been a rum runner was "the thing to have been" at that time. In Grooch's "From Crate to Clipper with Captain Musick Pioneer Pilot", a biography from personal records of Mrs. Musick in 1939, there is no mention of rum running. However, Captain Briggs told me that he showed Musick a picture of an old Curtiss flying boat alongside a large boat loading liquor at Bimini. He asked Musick if he were the pilot because he looked like him. Musick's only reply was: "My how that skipper loved that boat!" So Musick never admitted and never denied the rum running.

5. The Mayan ruins at Chichén-Itzá had only recently been discovered and had aroused world-wide interest in the Mayan civilization. The Maya settled in northern Guatemala about 2,500 years ago, on barely-seen hills in lowland jungles, descended from ancestors out of Asia about 1,000 years before that. Their civilization flourished from about 600 B.C. to 900 A.D. The center of archaeological research today is at Tikal in northern Guatemala. Chichén-Itzá postdates Tikal. The Spaniards subdued the Maya in 1697 but their descendants are the present Indians of Guatemala and still speak Mayan.

6. Admiral Rickover was the father of atomic submarines. He was a very

brilliant man and would only bother with very brilliant men under him. The kind of men he could tolerate were so hard to come by that he wrote a book on *Swiss Schools and Ours: Why Theirs are Better* (Little Brown, 1962). He would put the following problem to applicants for a job under him and often said that a ten-year-old Swiss school girl could solve it but no American college graduate could. It took me over an hour the first time, but I tried it on Billy McFadden, a friend of my son who had just graduated from Harvard and he gave me the right answer in less than five seconds. The problem is: "A stock of pamphlets is in three piles. The first pile contains one-sixth of them; the second contains several fifths of them; the third pile has four pamphlets. What is the total number of pamphlets?" (120).

7. An Agouti is a rabbit-sized rodent, a nocturnal forest dweller with rough, coarse, brown hair. A Manicou is a similar but bigger animal; the name is not found in most encyclopedias and is probably a local one.

8. One day a delapidated old Ireland Amphibian landed in front of the terminal at Dinner Key and taxied up to the ramp. The mechanics seemed to know the scarecrow, Jimmy, who got out and asked to have his crate overhauled. James Angel was a well known explorer and prospector who lived no one knew where in the Guianas. He had discovered the highest waterfall in the world, or so he said, but few had ever heard of it much less seen Angel Falls at the time. Some reputable geographers have located it since but the latest Columbia Encyclopedia says: "One of the highest uninterrupted waterfalls in the world, it is said to be between 3,300 and 5,000 feet". The National Geographic Society is more specific and here is a comparison with other famous falls:

	Height	Width
Victoria Falls	420 ft.	1 mile
Niagara Falls	165 ft.	3,500 ft.
Iguassu (Paraguay)	200 ft.	wider than Niagara
Angel Falls	3,200 ft.	—

Later we used to fly over Foz de Iguassu on the corner of Argentina, Brasil and Paraguay to show it to passengers, and much later over Victoria Falls in Africa. We never, however, flew over or saw Angel Falls which is somewhere in southeast Venezuela, about 100 miles from the border of British Guiana, on the Caroni River.

9. See *Under My Wings*: "The biggest hazard at that time was due to errors made by map makers. The best we had were hydrographic charts printed by the government. . . . They didn't help much. We had to rely on maps we tore out of children's school geographies. Most of these . . . were copied from old Spanish maps which indicated elevations in meters and were copied with the same figures shown as feet".

NOTES TO CHAPTER III

1. *Cruise Control* was principally the technique for obtaining the most ground miles per pound of fuel. It was also called Long Range Cruising. It is not the same as Endurance which is just staying in the air as long as possible. Pounds were used and not gallons and the gallons loaded were converted to pounds because energy was a function of fuel weight and not volume. The pounds were corrected for temperature between 6 lbs. and 5 lbs. per gallon.

The plane was flown at the angle of attack for maximum L/D (Lift over Drag for the wing section). To maintain this constant angle of attack it was necessary to reduce speed periodically during flight as the gross weight decreased with the consumption of fuel.

The father of Long Range Cruising was John C. Leslie who developed it in 1934 and tested it with Musick in the latest S-42 at Miami. This plane was equipped with extra fuel tanks for the Pacific survey flights. Igor Sikorsky, the designer; Gluharef, the top engineer at the Sikorsky Company; and Tillinghast from Pratt and Whitney, the engine manufacturer, all provided advice.

Experience taught us a lot. At the best speeds, the M-130 wallowed so that the automatic pilot could barely maintain control. We were flying at just above stall speed, about 90 kts. when fully loaded decreasing to about 78 kts. at the end of the long Honolulu flight. We soon increased those speeds 10% to 15% and found we used no more fuel due to the smoother flight. On the shorter flights the cruising speed at the normal 70% rated continuous engine power was about 130 kts.

A "How-Goes-It-Curve" was designed by Captain Gray to give a quick picture of progress at all times. It immediately showed troubles such as excessive fuel consumption or unexpected head winds in plenty of time to allow choice of options before the troubles became critical.

The flight engineer always plotted fuel consumption vs. time, and the navigator plotted distance vs. time. Gray combined both into a curve of fuel consumption vs. distance. Its use was limited only by the ingenuity of the navigator who kept it. The example below, entirely theoretical and not an actual curve from an actual Honolulu flight, assumes the following figures:

	4 engine	3 engine
Fuel consumption	600#/hr	500#/hr
True airspeed*	100 kts	90 kts

The projected progress line is based on Ground Speeds projected from the met forecast which would give average winds for each of the zones into which the route would be divided.

Whenever the actual progress line crosses any of the emergency curves

coming down from the two top corners, you have reached a point of no return on that curve. If you get in the triangular area above all those curves,
you can no longer make it ahead or back should one engine fail.

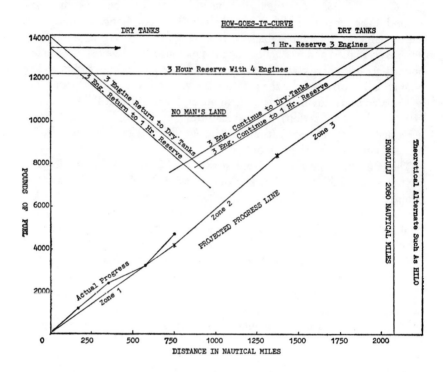

2. Leuteritz developed Adcock ranges for long-range bearings which were
supposed to give accurate bearings. They did not. The famous Pan Am long-
range radio bearings system was perhaps better than nothing, but not much
better.

As an example of our instrument approaches—and this was on the CAA
radio range at San Francisco—Musick, coming in from Hawaii to San Francisco, was making an instrument approach when his flight engineer, Vic
Wright, saw the ground and let out a yell. Instantly the navigator, Fred
Noonan, called to Musick, "Climb and turn right". Just then First Officer
de Lima saw everything green outside his window. Musick did a near
Chandelle with the Clipper. They had been getting an "on course" or solid
dash signal from the range, which would have put them out over the
Pacific. When Musick found a hole and got down in the South Bay, it
developed that the CAA range had failed so that all planes were getting the
same dash in all sectors. The Clipper was believed to have gone right over
the range at Alameda, without getting the normal "null", and to have been

letting down in the clouds into the hills behind Oakland.

The Adcock (A-N) ranges on the Pacific islands each had four vertical towers in a square, each with leads into a central metal box from which a cable went to the radio station. These central boxes were supposedly sealed, but leaked moisture and, when wet, gave a false "on course" indication. It might be fatal to rely on them. We didn't. They only served as a check on the celestial navigation.

3. Duke Kahanamoku, then the Sheriff of Honolulu, was one of the great surfers as well as an Olympic swimmer. Surfing with some friends at Balboa, California in 1925, they swam out through a fierce surf with their boards to a burning fishing-party boat off shore and brought back safely 12 out of 17 passengers. Duke brought back eight of them. It was a feat quite beyond the Coast Guard or anyone else. He was recommended for the Congressional Medal of Honor and it was about to be bestowed when a Southern Senator saw him and noticed his dark color. The medal was withdrawn and never bestowed.

4. "Point of No Return" is the point along your route where you no longer have enough fuel to go back and must keep on. Its calculation is the classic radius of action problem. There are three variations:

    1. Returning to your point of origin.

    2. Returning to an alternate.

    3. Returning to a moving base such as a carrier.

We altered the problem slightly by using a three-engine speed and fuel consumption rate.

The formula for calculating the distance from the point of departure to the point of no return is:

$$\frac{\text{Ground Speed Out} \times \text{Ground Speed Return} \times \text{Fuel Hours}}{\text{Ground Speed Out} + \text{Ground Speed Return}}$$

5. A flare pot which lighted up when it hit the water was dropped at night.

6. *Top Side Ricksha* by Harold M. Bixby, 1938 (privately published). The title of these delightful and extremely interesting memoirs was "pidgin English" for an airplane. In full it was: *Top Side Ricksha, Coolie No Got.*

7. From a letter to my mother dated October 18, 1937: "Today I feel completely worn out and extremely depressed. I missed my vacation last spring which I had counted on and if anything happens to this one (due in December and to be my first one with the Company) I shall resign and come home anyway. These long flights are not only terribly exhausting physically, but equally so mentally and emotionally from the prolonged excitement and worry which go with them".

8. There was always a search for methods to simplify the calculations required to solve the celestial triangle. The first American shortcut was devised by Dreisonstok (H.O.208) in 1925 and was largely patterned after an earlier

work of Ogura, a Japanese. Ageton followed in about 1932 (H.O.211). When I was navigating in 1938 we used Dreinsonstok but the Hydrographic Office was just preparing a much better shortcut by calculating the solutions for almost all triangles, substituting a huge amount of tables for the slim little volume of Dreisonstok. They were published as H.O.214 and we were sent copies, a volume for each 10 degrees of latitude, to try. I promptly found some 161 errors and sent the copy back to the Hydrographic Office. They had been computed as a WPA project but now were redone by computer. They came out finally after I had finished navigating. H.O.214 called *Tables of Computed Altitude and Azimuth* was replaced in about 1949 by H.O.249, *Sight Reduction Tables.*

Today as I write, most of these tables and methods are obsolete as the triangle can be solved in seconds by pocket computers. With such programmable calculators as the Hewlett-Packard Model 65, and with the right program which can be purchased, complete reduction of a celestial sight for any body, yielding the Altitude Intercept and True Azimuth of the Line of Position can be had in seconds. The Nautical Almanac can be used without interpolation and one need not remember the rules for relative names of declination and latitude or the sign of the local hour angle. Navigation becomes simple.

Calculating the great circle distance and initial course, formerly a long and tedious computation, can now be done almost instantly on a calculator with the appropriate program. The great circle initial course was of interest to us using only Mercator navigation charts because long-range radio bearings came on great circle courses. This problem, DF correction for meridional convergence, disappeared when Mercator charts were discarded for Lambert Conformal projections.

9. The story from Harold Bixby's book, supra, is: "The only floating objects ever seen are corpses, and those are by no means rare. The Chinese will not touch a corpse—it is bad joss (luck). Then too, if they pull a dead man out of the Yangtze the retriever must buy the coffin and find a place of burial. Human life is not regarded as dearly as in less populated countries. Also, if a Chinese saves the life of a drowning man or woman, he is responsible thereafter for that person: for had not the rescuer saved that life, the community would not have had that person to contend with. In short, there is no percentage in saving a life. If the life turns out to be a useful one, all honor to the parents and relatives of the survivor. If, on the other hand, the person saved turns out to be a bad person, then the life-saver is the one to blame.

"Pilot Chilie Vaughn tells an amusing story. He had landed his flying boat at this small town of Wanshien. After the plane was refueled, the barge crew of three coolies lifted up the wing pontoon as was the custom. As the motor was started, they pushed the wing clear of the float. In pushing it clear, the wing hit a girl who was gawking at this strange boat, knocking her into the lazy current. Vaughn, taxiing away, noticed that no one went to her rescue. He turned the controls over to his Chinese co-pilot and dove into the water.

Before he dove Chilie kicked off his shoes. As it was summertime he was wearing shorts which uniform included white socks. In the dive both his socks were stripped off. When the coolies saw the socks floating downstream, all three of them dove in and fought to recover the socks. Chilie dragged the girl back to the pontoon and told our agent to get a doctor for her. When he returned the next day, the agent presented him with a bill for two dollars to cover the doctor's call—and that was all that was ever heard of the incident. It was fortunate for Chilie that the girl turned out to be a dutiful daughter or wife and did not take any samples from a money shop. Otherwise he no doubt would have been called upon to make good."

10. Senior pilots, with no or little experience in boats, actually were transferred to Miami before being sent to the Pacific. Captain Barrows, for example, in addition to seaplane experience in Alaska, was sent to Miami for a year for transition experience on boats before being transferred to the Pacific.

11. John Leslie told me as I was writing this chapter in 1975: "There's not a shred of evidence that the fuel was sucked up over the trailing edges of the wing into the engine exhaust. There is another explanation which is much more likely to be correct. (Although I did not know it at the time.) On previous dumping tests, gasoline fumes had penetrated the wing and into the center cabane strut and had actually dropped onto the navigator's chart table directly below. More importantly, the flap motor was located precisely in this cabane strut. It is much more plausible that this caused the explosion. Unfortunately, there could be no proof."

The above and new explanation does not seem plausible to me. At the time, all operating people were told that the cause was operating the dump valves with the flaps down. We were told that the dump valves had never been tested with the flaps down. In fact, all S-42s were modified shortly thereafter with dump shutes extending back of the trailing edges to permit safe dumping even with flaps down. We also heard at the time that a native or natives of Tutuila had seen the explosion and the plane fall into the sea.

P. St. John Turner writing in 1973 and acknowledging Pan Am as the source of his information, wrote about the accident at Pago Pago: "It was afterwards found that the petrol dumping valves were positioned too close to the hot engine exhausts making an explosion almost inevitable when actuated."

When South Pacific service was resumed, I had left the Pacific. Preparations began in 1938 but this time through Canton and New Caledonia. A problem was not knowing who owned Canton. Mr. Trippe asked our government to stake out a claim which it did by sending a sub-chaser which took along a Pan Am construction crew and claimed the island for the U.S.A. Two days later an Australian cruiser arrived claiming the island for Great Britain and ordering the Americans off. No doubt the respective sizes of the two warships and the fact that the sub-chaser was unarmed had something to do with it, but the Americans withdrew and the Australians left one lone postal official in a hut to hold down the claim for the British. By the end of the year the U.S.A. and Britain had agreed on joint sovereignty over Canton with rights for Pan Am to use the island. Next the French gave Pan Am operating rights to Noumea in New Caledonia, but the English adamantly refused such rights to Suva in the Fijis which would have given a more direct route. Service to Sydney in Australia did not start until after the War, but it was resumed to Aukland in 1939.

To supply Pan Am's empire of lonely Pacific islands, it acquired, in 1939, a four-masted diesel schooner *Trade Wind*; so then we had a real, genuine Clipper ship.

NOTES TO CHAPTER IV

1. "Piggyback" refers to a small plane attached to the back of a large one for the purposes of takeoff and then released from the larger in flight. The *Mercury* was part of a composite aircraft with the *Maia*, eight engines in all, all running for takeoff. *Mercury* separated after the composite got well into the air. The *Mercury* was lifted off near London and released over Foynes.

From the *Air Line Pilot*: "On July 28, 1938, *Maia*, commanded by Capt. Wilcockson, and *Mercury*, commanded by Capt. D. C. T. Bennett, rose together from Foynes, Ireland: 20 minutes later *Mercury* unhitched from the flying boat (*Maia*) and was on its way to Montreal with 1,000 lbs. of mail, newsreels and freight. After 20 hours it landed in Montreal, the first aircraft ever to carry a commercial payload across the Atlantic."

2. A "step" in a hull is a break in the keel line, changing the draft. Its purpose is to shorten the length of the keel in the water and hence reduce the water drag when the speed makes the boat ride up on the step of a shortened hull.

3. A "water loop" is a very sudden change in direction occurring on the surface while landing and still going at great speed. The whole seaplane just flips around so the bow is pointing aft while the tail now points ahead. In this sudden, high speed flip, a seawing or even half the wing may be torn off by contact with the water.

4. Weather ships were put on permanent stations all over the world on ocean air routes and named A, B, C, etc. . . . after the phonetic alphabet used in radiophone, which was then Able, Baker, Charlie, Dog, Easy, Fox, etc. . . . hence Hotel. These were arranged for and maintained by various countries through the postwar Provisional International Civil Aviation Organization (PICAO) which later became ICAO in Montreal.

5. The most authoritative book on instrument flying at the time was *Instrument and Radio Flying* by Karl S. Day, chief instrument flight instructor

for American Airlines. It was published in 1938 and says: "One of the greatest hazards in instrument flying is carburetor ice, which is just as prevalent in summer as in winter. It is much more likely to occur in instrument flying than in contact flying because when flying on instruments there is present an unlimited supply of moisture in finely divided form which is particularly available and susceptible to ice formation. Venturi-type carburetors are almost perfect mechanical refrigerators. The temperature difference . . . for modern, high powered, highly supercharged engines is close to 40 degrees F." He then goes on to point out that carburetor heat reduces engine power, so it must be used only when it is about to be necessary—after it becomes necessary it is too late, the engine has stopped, there is no heat to melt the ice, and the pilot is looking for a place to land.

NOTES TO CHAPTER V

1. Fuji was the wife of Captain Jimmy Walker based in Rio then, later to be chief pilot, then operations manager and my boss.

2. These are the stories we heard. They are not historically accurate.

3. Anne and Sally McAdoo were bridesmaids of mine and granddaughters of U.S. Senator William Gibbs McAdoo.

4. They went on to further posts including Washington, Paris and then Guatemala as ambassador, and finally to Switzerland where they spent Easter with us at Zermatt in 1966. Bobby was knighted and they retired to the English countryside where he unfortunately died much too young. They were our first non-American friends and luckily we were able to see each other through the years. Bobby had an extremely good mind and did an outstanding job. Margie, his wife, is one of the loveliest women I know, always handling herself with charm and courage.

5. My cousin, Tony Biddle, was then U.S. Ambassador to all the Axis occupied countries, based in London. Later he was on General Eisenhower's staff at Roquencourt outside Paris as General Anthony Drexel Biddle.

6. Prince Yurievich, a Pole, escaped when the Russians took over, crossing enemy Europe on foot, got an RAF ride to London, flew in the RAF Polish Squadron. His father and mother refused to leave Poland and remained through the war receiving occasional news of their son and some tea, all they asked for, through Lisbon and the Red Cross. One day an RAF pilot named Yurevich was killed and the Red Cross reported it adding the first "i". When the war ended and Skippy hastened to his family's place, the neighbors told him that both of his parents were dead. When they got the news of his death, they just sat and died, both of broken hearts.

NOTE TO CHAPTER VI

1. Much of the story of Pan Africa came to me first hand from Gledhill who set it up, Kraigher who was the operations manager, Kristofferson who was the chief pilot and from Goyette who was my assistant when I was chief pilot in Miami. I knew all of them well. Also, Jimmy Smith, later my boss in the Atlantic, had been sent to Pan Africa by Trippe. All these persons are fully identified elsewhere in this book. The story is extremely well told in the doctoral dissertation of Mrs. Ray noted in the Bibliography.

NOTE TO CHAPTER VII

1. Cocorite was the Pan Am seaplane base at Trinidad. Piarco was the landplane airport.

NOTES TO CHAPTER VIII

1. A more accurate story of what happened to the PAA/CNAC pilots after the war was given me by Bond and McDonald. Bond says: "When the war between China and Japan started in 1937, Pan Am advised Bixby who was then in China that Pan Am could not continue to participate in CNAC operations. I was at that time on the Pan Am payroll and to remain in China and take part I had to send Trippe a written resignation and I got a written acceptance. I was given no assurance of reemployment. CNAC was never mentioned in *New Horizons* at first, but soon CNAC began to get a lot of publicity from newspapers and magazines such as the DC2$\frac{1}{2}$ story, coined by *Time* and quickly adopted by others. Pan Am began bragging about the wonderful job Pan Am pilots were doing in China. . . . After Pearl Harbor, I never requested nor did Pan Am ever offer any special consideration to anyone employed by CNAC. No one with authority to speak for Pan Am ever indicated or implied that anyone in CNAC would become 'members of the family.'"

Veterans of flying in China or over the Hump have formed several associations. The publisher of *Wings Over Asia* is the China National Aviation Association Foundation set up by ex-CNAC pilots; and there is a Hump Pilots Association which includes pilots who flew elsewhere in the China-Burma-India theater to places with such exotic names as Tezgaon and Kurmitola.

2. "21" is a famous New York restaurant, once Jack and Charlie's, at 21 West 52nd Street.

Piping Rock Club in Locust Valley, Long Island is one of the best and best-known golf and country clubs in the country.

NOTES TO CHAPTER IX

1. To achieve radiophone communication across the Atlantic, diversity reception was used with stations at Gander, Santa Maria and Shannon. Usually families of five frequencies were used to cover day and night conditions. It was necessary to get maximum power into the ground wave or vertically polarized component of the transmitted signal. This was accomplished by putting the ground station antennas at the water's edge, almost in the water facing the open sea.

On the Gander to Shannon route, there was much interference from the close proximity to the North Magnetic Pole and almost all signals were blocked when there was intense Aurora Borealis activity. This difficulty did not occur on the Pacific due to the much greater distance from the North Magnetic Pole so that the San Francisco to Honolulu route did not require diversity operation.

A major problem was designing the aircraft antenna so as best to receive the vertically polarized component of the signal. The normal antenna, a short wire run from a mast forward to the top of the tail, picked up mostly the horizontally polarized component. McLeod solved the problem by removing the aft insulator of the antenna, using the tall vertical fin of the plane, the rudder and the fuselage as an incomplete loop which both greatly improved reception and acted as lightning protection.

Eventually, after McLeod had created reliable radiotelephone communication between the cockpit and the ground all the way across the Atlantic, a station was put up under the auspices of ICAO at Prince Christian on the southernmost tip of Greenland, and cables were laid to connect it to Gander and to Shannon.

Lynch was successful in obtaining full cooperation of the Irish, Canadians, and Portuguese in setting up transatlantic radiotelephone—quite an achievement—but it was opposed by the Pan Am Radio Operators' Union who saw their jobs being eliminated (as they were). On some of the CAA proving flights, the radio operators would sabotage the radiophone equipment in flight. Feelings ran high. I was on some of these flights and was able to fix the equipment, with the help of the radio operators if necessary for they knew and liked me, but it was unpleasant. At least we never had to turn back.

2. The Caterpillar Club was an organization of pilots who had made a successful emergency parachute jump. It was formed by the Irving Parachute Company who made parachutes only of pure silk in those times.

3. Norman Blake had started with Pan Am in U.S. Sales. With a reserve commission he was called to active duty in the War and assigned to ATC where C. R. Smith put him on his staff and Harold Harris, also in ATC, found him.

4. From *New York* magazine, Aug. 16, 1976, quoting the CIA and the Cult of Intelligence: "The CIA is currently the owner of one of the biggest—if not the biggest—fleets of 'commercial' airplanes in the world. Agency proprietaries include Air American, Air Asia, Civil Air Transport, Intermountain Aviation, Southern Air Transport, and several other air charter companies around the world. . . . For years this vast activity was dominated and controlled by one contract agent, George Doole, who was later elevated to the rank of a career officer".

NOTES TO CHAPTER X

1. *Julius Caesar*, Act III, Scene 2.

2. Pan Am in 1975 had revenues of $1,605,700,000. Union Pacific Railroad had $992,029,000 and P & O had £39,666,000 in 1972 before acquisition of U.S. oil and gas properties.

3. These stories are all heresay but were told throughout the Company at the time.

4. Mrs. Archibald was asst. vice-president in charge of the Washington office.

5. From *Pan American-Africa* by D. W. Ray.

6. See *Dean Acheson* by David S. McClellan, 1976.

7. The German zeppelin *Hindenburg*, filled with hydrogen because they couldn't get helium from the U.S.A., exploded over Lakehurst, N.J. in May 1937.

8. Furthermore, after the War, the 17 domestic U.S. airlines excluding only United, formed an organization of 17 to combat Trippe and even hired top public relations men to publicly denigrate Pan Am.

9. George Duff who was co-captain with Lodeesen on the Léopoldville uranium trip tells me: "The episode I remember most vividly was one which involved Mr. Dean and a green mamba on a fishing trip. We were on board the Pan Am launch at Fisherman's Lake where we were delayed 3 or 4 days with an engine failure. Mr. Dean whacked the snake with a boat hook. The snake took off up the boat hook after Mr. Dean. The native launch-boy and I took off for the bow of the boat. Mr. Dean smartly pitched the snake over his head towards the bow of the boat. Snake, launch-boy and I all arrived at the same time on the foredeck. The native turned a nasty sort of gray and I too. The snake looked very cross. The native prepared to abandon ship and I followed suit. At this point the only cool head aboard ship was the launch operator who drew the machete and neatly severed the head of the snake. The snake weighed in at 15 pounds and measured almost 9 feet."

NOTE TO PERSONNEL SECTION

1. There is a long, long list of firsts for Pan Am communications. At first all aircraft receivers had to be tuned manually. It just wouldn't do, especially in Pan Am's international operations involving hundreds of frequencies. McLeod in the shop at LaGuardia, modified an Army high frequency set with 10 channels to a crystal controlled one with 20 channels. When VHF (Very High Frequency) sets came along, McLeod modified 20 channel sets into 50 channel ones. (Today Collins equipment in Pan Am planes are capable of switching to any of 720 VHF frequencies.)

McLeod's developments aroused world-wide interest and, even though not patented by Pan Am, rights were sold to so many parties that it brought in about $100,000 in royalties the first year.

Every year Trippe held a directors' meeting in a foreign city served by Pan Am. Around 1955, Rio was selected. Morrison, V.P. of LAD, was responsible for arrangements. One day in a Miami bar, Lynch suggested an airborne radar. There were none then although Eastern had been experimenting with one in a DC-3 which had crashed. United also was experimenting. Morrison said "Go ahead". Lynch called McLeod from the bar and said "Get a radar on the DC-6. You have two weeks". McLeod called DelValle, the Pan Am resident engineer at Douglas in Santa Monica, who said: "Douglas has a DC-6 radome but I cannot borrow it for a year". McLeod then called Nat Paschall, V.P. Sales at Douglas. A request from Pan Am is not taken lightly, and shortly the DC-6 radome was on its way to Miami. The directors' flight went out on schedule with the first radar on a scheduled passenger flight. It worked. It was impressive. Soon the entire Pan Am fleet was equipped with airborne radars.

ACKNOWLEDGMENTS

My old friends were very helpful in refreshing my memories and correcting my recollections. I am greatly indebted to John Leslie, official archivist and historian of Pan Am; to Chilie Vaughn who read and helped me with each chapter as I wrote it; and also to Lodi Lodeesen, Doug Moody, Kim Scribner, Harry Beyer, Richard L. Kruse, Harry Canaday, Carl Gregg, Waldo Lynch, Ben McLeod, Pat Reynolds, Haak Gulbransen and many others who appear in these pages. Lastly, I am particularly grateful to Grant Winthrop, my son-in-law, who devoted much time to editing; and especially to Edward Weeks for his patience and professional editing, and always to Mary Jane Burnham who typed and retyped, again and again, always with pertinent comments.

Material on flying over the Hump is taken from *The Dragon's Wings* by William M. Leary, Jr. with the permission of Mr. Leary and of Mr. Bond. Material about Fred Noonan and Amelia Earhart is taken from *The Search for Amelia Earhart* by Fred Goerner, copyright 1966, with permission of Doubleday and Co.

BIBLIOGRAPHY

Books about Pan Am and about World Airlines

Empire of the Air, by Matthew Josephson, 1943
Skyway to Asia, by W. S. Grooch, 1936 (Very good. Pacific bases)
Winged Highway, by W. S. Grooch, 1938 (NYRBA)
Pictorial History of Pan American World Airways, by P. St. John Turner, 1973
Top Side Ricksha, Coolie No Got, by Harold Bixby, 1938 (*Very good*)
The Dragon's Wings, by Wm. M. Leary Jr., 1976 (Very good)
Airways Abroad–Story of American World Air Routes,
   by Henry Ladd Smith, 1950
Airport Development Program of World War II, by Deborah W. Ray,
   M.A. thesis, NYU 1964
Pan Am Africa, by Deborah W. Ray, PH.D. dissertation, NYU 1973
A History of the World's Airlines, by R. E. G. Davies, 1964
Airways, by Henry Ladd Smith, 1942
A Dream of Eagles, by Ralph A. O'Neil, 1943 (NYRBA)
The Eagle and the Egg, by Oliver LaFarge, 1949
Viceroyalties of the West, by R. Cameron, 1968
The Struggle for Airways in Latin America, by W. A. M. Burden, 1943
The Air Future, by B. Hershey, 1943

Books by or about Pilots

I, Airline Pilot, by Marius Lodeesen, 1939
Under my Wings, by Basil Rowe, 1956
Santos Dumont, by A. Brigole, 1943
Wind, Sand and Stars, by Antoine de St. Exupéry, 1939
Night Flight, by Antoine de St. Exupéry
We, by Charles A. Lindbergh, 1927
The Spirit of St. Louis, by Charles A. Lindbergh, 1953
From Crate to Clipper with Captain Musick, W. S. Grooch, 1939
Last Flight, by Amelia Earhart, 1937 (Diary pub. by Geo. Putnam)
The Search for Amelia Earhart, by Fred Goerner, 1966
Winged Legend: The Story of Amelia Earhart, by John Burke, 1970
The Way of the Eagle, by Chas. J. Biddle, 1929
The Lonely Sea and the Sky, by Francis Chas. Chichester, 1964
Antoine de St. Exupéry, by Curtis Cate, 1970
Red Ball in the Sky, by Charles F. Blair, 1952
Over the Hump, by Wm. H. Turner, 1964

The Lonely Sky, by Wm. Bridgeman, 1955 (Very good)
Always Another Dawn, by A. Scott Crossfield, 1960
Carrying the Fire, by Michael Collins, 1974 (Very good)
Wings Over Asia, 4 vols., by the China National Aviation Foundation, 1972
Up in the Air, by Mary M. Worthylake, 1977

About Flight and Air Navigation

Blind Flight, by Maj. Ocker and Lt. Crane, 1932
Instrument and Radio Flying, by Carl S. Day, 1938
Your Future as a Pilot, by Capt. Kimball J. Scribner, 1968
Equilibrium and Vertigo, by Isaac H. Jones, 1918
The Wind and Beyond, by Theodore von Karmán, 1967
The Book of the Sky, by A. C. Spectorsky, 1956
Aerobatics, by H. Barber, 1918 (Elementary)
The Raft Book, by Harold Gatty, 1943 (Very good)

Miscellaneous

Gabriela, Clove and Cinnamon, by Jorge Amaro, 1962 (Very good) (Ilhéus)
Twilight of the Tyrants, by Tad Szulc, 1959 (Vargas)
The Hurricane, by Nordhoff and Hall, 1936
The Murder of Admiral Darlan, by Peter Tompkins, 1965
Adventure in Diplomacy—Our French Dilemma, by Keneth Pendar, 1945

Pictures of Clippers

For 50 Years America's Airline to the World, by Capt. Richard L. Kruse, 1977
The Flying Clipper, pub. by Pan Am Educational Service, 1962,
   (Best pictures)
The Seaplanes, by Henry R. Palmer, Jr., 1965, pub. by Morgan
   Aviation Books, Dallas, Texas (Very good)

LIST OF ABBREVIATIONS

AD   Atlantic Division of Pan Am
ADP   Airport Development Program of Pan Am
AFB   Air Force Base
AID   Agency for International Development (State Dept.)
ALPA   Air Line Pilots' Association
AOA   American Overseas Airlines
ATC   Air Transport Command (U.S. Army)
CAA   Civil Aeronautics Administration
CAB   Civil Aeronautics Board
CAR   Civil Air Regulations
CAVU   Weather Clear And Visibility Unlimited
CB   Cumulonimbus or thunderstorm cloud
CG   Center of Gravity
CMA   Compania Mexicana de Aviacion
CNAC   China National Aviation Corporation
CPO   Chief Petty Officer
CQ   General radio call to any station listening
FCC   Federal Communications Commission
GCA   Ground Control Approach system (U.S. Army)
GCT   Greenwich Civil Time
ICC   Interstate Commerce Commission
ILS   Instrument Landing System
ICAO   International Civil Aviation Organization
LAD   Latin American Division of Pan Am
MATS   Military Air Transport Service
NACA   National Advisory Committee for Aeronautics
NATO   North Atlantic Treaty Organization
NATS   Navy Air Transport Service
NCO   Non-commissioned officer
NYRBA New York, Rio and Buenos Aires Airline
PAD   Pacific Alaska Division of Pan Am
PICAO Provisional International Civil Aviation Organization
RADAR Radio Direction And Ranging system
SAM   Special Air Mission
SATR   Scheduled Air Transport Rating
SCADTA Sociedad Colombo Alemana de Transportes Aereos
UMCA   Uraba, Medellín and Central Airways
VARIG   Viacao Aerea Rio Grandense

317

INDEX

Capt. = commanding officer. Cdt. = cadet. FEO = flight engineer or engineering officer. FI = professional flight instructor. FNO = professional navigator. FO = pilot not in command, first officer or copilot. FRO = radio operator. Amb. = ambassador. Gen. = general. Sen. = Senator. Insp. = Inspector. Pres. = President.

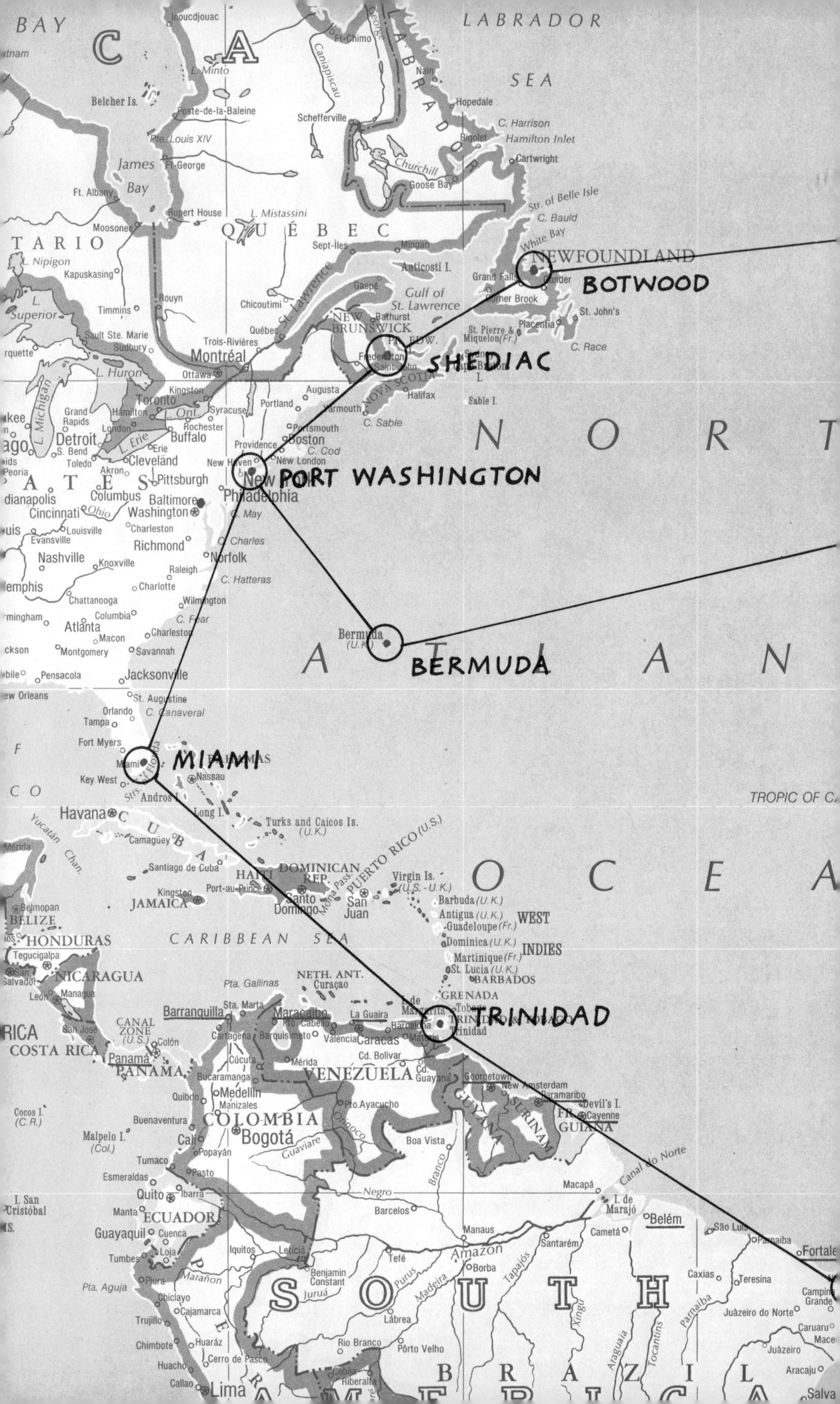

BOTWOOD
SHEDIAC
PORT WASHINGTON
BERMUDA
MIAMI
TRINIDAD
LABRADOR SEA
QUÉBEC
NEWFOUNDLAND
Gulf of St. Lawrence
NEW BRUNSWICK
NOVA SCOTIA
NORTH ATLANTIC OCEAN
TROPIC OF C
CUBA
JAMAICA
HAITI
DOMINICAN REP.
PUERTO RICO (U.S.)
CARIBBEAN SEA
WEST INDIES
BELIZE
HONDURAS
NICARAGUA
COSTA RICA
PANAMA
VENEZUELA
GUYANA
SURINAM
FR. GUIANA
COLOMBIA
ECUADOR
PERU
SOUTH AMERICA
BRAZIL
Amazon